HOW TO OPEN AND RUN A SUCCESSFUL RESTAURANT

Christopher Egerton-Thomas

WILEY

John Wiley & Sons, Inc.

New York • Chichester • Brisbane • Toronto • Singapore

Publisher: Stephen Kippur
Editor: Katherine Schowalter
Managing Editor: Corinne McCormick
Editing, Design, and Production: Publication Services, Inc.

Library of Congress Cataloging-in-Publication Data

Egerton-Thomas, Christopher.
   How to open and run a successful restaurant / Christopher Egerton
   -Thomas.
   ISBN 0-471-61681-8
     p. cm.
   1. Restaurant management. I. Title.
TX911.3.M27E34 1989
691'.95'068–dc19   88-8022
                               CIP

Printed in the United States of America

89 90 10 9 8 7 6 5 4 3 2

To Alison and Fred Conradie in the hope
that they will find this book useful

CONTENTS

INTRODUCTION

The U.S. Department of Labor, Bureau of Labor Statistics, *Monthly Labor Review* (Sept. 1987) forecasts that the industry generating the largest number of wage and salary jobs between 1986 and 2000 will be that of "Eating and Drinking Places."

In other words, in spite of the fact that it sometimes seems as though there isn't a square acre of the United States left without a restaurant, it's still a growth industry—in fact, the biggest growth industry.

This news may bring some comfort to restaurateurs in the still, small hours of the night. So may the encouraging news that McDonald's now employs more people than U.S. Steel.

It's estimated that there are four or five job openings for anyone qualified in the various skills required in the food industry—which almost compares with the booming computer field. At this stage in the history of the industry, while the "show biz" elements can't be ruled out, the rules for success can be discerned quite clearly.

They are all discussed in this book.

This is a book for doers and dreamers, for people who enjoy going to restaurants as well as those who seriously contemplate going into the business.

Potential restaurateurs will find the book extremely helpful because it focuses on the separate areas of the restaurant business, while never losing sight of the fact that all the factors—the service, the location, the decor, the food, the drinks, the atmosphere, and so on— must all be brought together in harmony if the restaurant is to work successfully. Details are not shirked, because detail is immensely important in this business, as in any other.

It's possible that those who love to dine out, or who do so because they have to, will get more out of their dining experiences as a result of glimpses behind the scenes. Some may find their dreams shattered, but it's unlikely they'll give up going to restaurants.

The restaurant business has much in common with the entertainment industry. This is a theme to which constant reference is made. Those who are tempted to think this a frivolous diversion will be forced to admit that they're wrong about five minutes after they get into business.

Many restaurant consumers are immensely critical. Few people will leave a restaurant without some critical reaction. This is hardly surprising when one considers the expense of dining out. Often they'll talk about it ("What did you think of that place?" "The food was OK, but the service was pretty gruesome.").

Even lovers and business diners intensely preoccupied with their affairs will register a subconscious reaction, though they may not voice it. Was their conversation spoiled by having to give too much attention to making sure they got what they wanted to eat? Did they get a bit irritated trying to catch the waiter's eye to order? Were they dying of thirst by the time the drinks arrived? Were they too hot or too cold? If their reactions are positive, they're more likely to come back.

This may be obvious, but do you consciously assess a taxi ride? Only if the cab is old and dirty, you believe you've been overcharged, or the driver is either nice or nasty. In most cases, you take prompt delivery to your destination for granted, and you don't store the memory—a fact of life that can be a nuisance when you suddenly realize you left your glasses in the cab. How about the other things we all consume, from soap and shirts to dental treatment and ballpoint pens?

As we get older, we all form tastes, preferences, and brand loyalties. But it's in areas such as movies, theater, books, vacations, and restaurant visits that we find ourselves instantly thrust into the role of critic. It's no coincidence that these products fall within the leisure industry. Maybe that's because when these products are consumed, we have time to digest and consider. Indeed, relishing the inquest after the event may be part of the total experience.

It's amusing to contemplate the ease and readiness with which the "closed mind" generation delivers verdicts on restaurants, films, and plays. In other contexts the passing of value judgments would be considered outrageous, in spite of the fact that all life is a continuous series of preferences expressed through choice. No restaurateur can hope to be all things to all customers, although many try and are upset when it doesn't work. Deciding who you want to appeal to can be tough, and many wallow in indecision. The urge to answer Yes! to all requests in any service industry is overwhelming, but those who know when to say No will stay saner longer.

It's important to understand that all restaurateurs live under the glare of the spotlight and the endless scrutiny of customers. The law keeps a beady eye on their activities, too. Everybody gets used to it in the end. To survive, they must.

Few of these considerations apply to the operator of a hot dog stand or a fast food establishment. Nor do they apply to the brilliant and famous chef who decides to open the kind of restaurant that is given unlimited funds by a wealthy corporation or personal backer and where the price of dinner for one approaches the national weekly average wage. But they are all of prime importance to the potential owner of a 50 to 150 seat middle-class restaurant, which is the kind of place most potential restaurateurs would like to own and which is the focus of this book.

It would be both redundant and impertinent to suggest that this book will help you to make up your mind whether you want to go into the restaurant business or not. Few need to be told that restaurant working hours are often antisocial and unnatural to a degree that can be health-threatening. And, although many delude themselves that the business is simple, few will be amazed at the revelation that there's just a little bit more to it than buying steaks for a dollar, cooking them, and selling them for $10.

Besides, as the old movie cliché has it, "Sometimes you have to do what you have to do." If the restaurant business is the business you want to pursue, then nothing will dissuade you. Telling a would-be restaurateur that the industry has a high divorce rate is a bit like telling Napoleon that his dreams of world conquest may get a lot of people killed.

But after reading this book, budding restaurateurs will certainly have a very good idea of what they're letting themselves in for. They'll be able to assess the hopes and fears, the triumphs and the woes of the business, and this may stimulate useful thought. In passing, it must be observed that the restaurant industry does seem to attract misfits and people who are working out some peculiar psychological problems. The indefinable, show business aspects of the business also allow the undeserving and untalented to succeed while the capable and decent fail.

This uncertainty, the entrepreneurial risk, is what makes it all so exciting. But the restaurant business isn't a crapshoot. The better qualified, more experienced, and intelligent you are, the more likely you are to succeed.

In fact, as in so many aspects of life, the life quality achieved by any career pursuit is largely a matter of individual response. There really are restaurateurs who are happily married, take regular vacations, live a full and varied existence, and make a good buck, too. Obviously, the casualties are more eye-catching than the survivors.

The hard information given in the book is based on practical experience. The author is no armchair warrior.

However, many of the anecdotes have their roots in New York and London experience. Some might think it absurd to suggest that the neurotic reactions of overcrowded cities, where every human being is shrouded in a cloak of anonymity and thus permitted to behave abominably without fear of recrimination, have any relevance to opening a mom'n'pop restaurant in Smalltown, Middle West. Since New York is the world's epicenter of the restaurant business, anything that happens there is bound to have an effect elsewhere.

To some consumers, the sight of a restaurant sign is an invitation to enter and behave like an imbecile. Who ever heard of anyone going into a hardware store, picking up a frying pan and saying to the clerk "Mmmm . . . stainless steel . . . is that made by the Bechamel method or the Doodleburger system?" Whereas, in restaurants, it's not uncommon for consumers to ask inane questions in a manner that tempts one to believe that that's exactly what they've come for. ("Which pressing of olive oil do you use? Could that be grilled instead of broiled? Is that on the bone or off the bone? Does your chewing gum lose its flavor on the bedpost overnight?")

It's sometimes the artificiality of the basic situation that creates the problems in restaurants. Try handing your steak back to your husband or mother sometime with the complaint that it's overdone. If you should ever convince yourself that people have come to your restaurant with the sole purpose of eating, then beware. The intake of sustenance in order to ensure earthly survival is only one of many motives.

The author even makes so bold as to suggest that quality of food may have little to do with restaurant success. The reader may react fiercely to such an apparently inane suggestion. When you see restaurants doing incredible business in spite of indifferent food, you'll begin to see what the business is all about. Restaurants owned by restaurateurs who've become media celebrities are notorious for the poor quality of the food. One could be forgiven, in some cases, for thinking it's part of the act.

But if you sincerely want to be a restaurateur, nothing should stop you. You can make a good living. Staying sane and enjoying a commensurate life quality is entirely up to you. This book may not answer all of your questions, but it will hopefully start you off thinking in the correct direction. The key to any new business venture is having accurate information so that you can make intelligent decisions. Making intelligent decisions is what will make you a sane and successful restaurateur.

HOW
IT
ALL
BEGAN

A BRIEF HISTORY OF
THE RESTAURANT INDUSTRY

Chaucer's fourteenth-century pilgrims were lucky to get a bite to eat at the Tabard Inn. Food was not always provided for travelers in those days. They often had to carry their own or buy from farmers and stores along the way. Salted pork was the most common meat and, even if April's showers had been unusually sweet that year, the choice of vegetables would have been small. Neither tea, coffee, chocolate, nor peanuts had yet arrived in Europe, and it would be nearly 300 years before Louis XIV examined his first potato (of which only the sparse foliage was eaten at that time) and sighed, "Always something new from America!"

Fortunately, Chaucer's crew was on a pilgrimage to Canterbury, which, like Santiago de Compostela and a score of other places on the continent, drew thousands of religious visitors every year, just as Lourdes and Mecca do today. They were in effect early tourists, and their routes were as well marked as those from New York to Miami or London to Paris now. Naturally, the locals along the way soon cottoned to the fact that there was money to be made from feeding them.

At Chaucer's Tabard Inn, the pilgrims were doubly lucky. Their host offered a free meal to the traveler who told the most entertaining story. Is this the first recorded instance of what might be called the "theatre of the restaurant experience," using a gimmick to drum up business?

Travel was dangerous then. Finding a meal and a bed before nightfall so as not to be "benighted" were real problems. Highway robbery was common. Jaded modern tourists may opine that, in some respects, little has changed.

There are scarcely any references to any aspect of "dining out" in European or English literature up to the middle of the eighteenth century. There were always taverns, at which Falstaff and his cohorts could quaff vast quantities of sack—cheap, and probably rough, Spanish red wine. At the Globe Theatre you could buy oranges from the baskets of budding Nell Gwynnes. For the small middle class there were clubs and coffee houses in the major cities.

The rich usually ate well at home, judging by household records and menus. Even Roman villas well inland have been found to contain large quantities of oyster shells, presumably brought from the shore along those long, straight roads in carts with regular changes of horses. But there weren't any places where, for a few denarii, you could pop in, check your toga, order a medium rare dormouse with lark's tongues in aspic on the side, and inquire the way to the "vomitorium."

Even for the affluent, foods were largely seasonal. Medical historians believe that the bleeding gums and other symptoms observed in late winter in medieval times were probably early signs of scurvy. There were no vitamin C–bearing fruits or vegetables until spring broke through.

The problem of food storage was acute throughout the ages. The fact that food had to be transported fresh, and was subject to swift wastage, inevitably made the notion of restaurants as we know them today a highly risky and expensive business.

In 1795 Francois Appert invented heat sterilization of food, which led to canning. Although used by armies as early as the Napoleonic Wars, canned foods were expensive and not a common consumer item until the middle of the nineteenth century.

Ice was used at the ancient Roman and Chinese courts, and was brought at great expense from the Arctic to Europe and America. It was often stored underground during winter, but was generally a luxury until the end of the nineteenth century when steam-driven refrigeration was invented. This created the massive meat industries of New Zealand and Australia.

In 1913 the Domelre electric refrigerator was invented in Chicago, followed by the English Electrolux silent electric refrigerator in 1927. In 1929 Clarence Birdseye invented deep-freeze food, and by the early thirties frozen foods were a fixture in many grocery stores.

The repertoire of recipes was expanding continuously throughout history. Ancient corpses preserved in mud usually reveal a depressing diet of porridge. Someday, someone may write a paper relating the effect of increased protein in the diet to technological improvement. But useful accidents were happening, starting with the realization that meat tasted better and was easier to chew when burned a bit, and grain was more easily digested when cooked in hot water, progressing through famous incidents which produced such dishes as Peach Melba and Chicken Marengo. Strasbourg geese were stuffed to enlarge their livers for paté in the sixteenth century, the trade in spices from the East was always a lucrative one, and the court of Louis XIV went wild when peas were imported from Italy.

Towards the end of the eighteenth century, the Industrial Revolution increased travel and created commuters and—that indispensable element to the restaurateur—an affluent middle class. Gradually, supply and demand created the modern restaurant industry.

By 1776 a few restaurants did a roaring trade in the major cities of the United States. The Bull's Head, Fraunces Tavern, and Mr Little's were landmarks in New York. They laid on banquets with extensive menus, but the ordinary bill of fare was usually limited to beef, ham, and vegetables.

Restaurants had become commonplace in Paris by the time of the French Revolution. In 1814 an allied army of English, Dutch, Belgian, Prussian, Spanish, Russian, and Austrian troops occupied the city, having defeated Napoleon at the Battle of the Nations. The World War I song, "How ya gonna keep 'em, down on the farm, after they've seen Paree?" might equally well have been composed at this time. All ranks had a high old time in Paris. Those lucky enough to have received wages could spend their money at last. Officers' families paid long visits.

The troops took home the memory of the fun they'd had and they spread the word. As society changed from agricultural to industrial, the demand for restaurants grew naturally. An increasing number of people needed to eat away from home. But growth was slow. Then as now, the rituals of courtship and adultery provided restaurants with regular customers, mainly from the ranks of the rich and the newly rich. By the 1820s strangers entering Stephen's Hotel in London would be stared down by the waiters and served with reluctance—an early example of what's now called the *in crowd*! At Crockfords, a gambling club where fortunes were lost, dinner was served from midnight to 5 in the morning by a named chef, Ude. There was no charge for the expensive delicacies and excellent wines. But the gamblers were encouraged to leave a £10 note on the green baize, if they chose.

Socializing, the privilege of the rich, took place mainly in private houses. In London in 1821, Lord Alvanley, a Regency character, had an apricot tart on his sideboard every day of the year, at a time when eight months' wages for a domestic servant would buy one bottle of champagne. The menus for the Prince Regent's feasts at his Brighton Pavilion by super chef Antonin Careme indicate the vast array of foods available for those who could afford them. The Prince Regent *couldn't*, as it happened, but he enjoyed them anyway.

As the century went on, restaurants boomed. Railway travel all over Europe increased. By 1880 Dickens was complaining about the sandwiches at the railway buffet. In 1908 Edith Wharton mentioned four restaurant experiences in the same love letter: "The last course of luncheon was being served with due solemnity . . . our first luncheon at Duval's . . . our waiter at Montmorency . . . you . . . caring about the waitress's losing her tip if we moved our table. . . . "

France, where gastronomy is a national passion, remained the fountainhead of the trade, and many elements of restaurant routine originated there, although Italophiles will insist that the French only stole ideas from the Italians! It is at this time that restaurants became common in America, but only in the major cities. Maxim's system of chefs, souschefs, sommeliers, and brigades was widely imitated in the grander restaurants, and still is.

MODERN INDUSTRY

Today, in the United States, there are thousands of eating places. They range from coffee shops where an early bird special—orange juice (sometimes freshly squeezed), two eggs any style with bacon and toast, and coffee—costs $2.95, through every type of ethnic cuisine from Tibetan to Thai, to the kind of restaurant where the white truffles are whisked in from the airport by special messenger (or so the restaurateur's public relations firm would have you believe!) and the set menu, without wine or tips, costs $80 and up. At these prices, of course, the set menu becomes the *table d'hôte*—literally, the "host's table." There are about 100 restaurants in America where dinner for two can cost $250 with very little effort, and about 200 more where the same punishment can be exacted by insisting on outlandishly priced rare wines.

All restaurateurs are in the same business and are bound by the same dynamics: supply, demand, competition, fashion, rent, the state of the economy, and the weather. Some restaurant chains include hot dog stands and luxury joints, taking the profit from each with equal pleasure. Whether it's preferable to sell 100 hamburgers at $10 each or 20 roast pheasants at $50 each is not merely a matter of taste, however. Different circumstances require different operations.

EDUCATION

An old military cliché states that "Time spent in reconnaissance is seldom wasted." The more you know about the restaurant business, the better. You must start observing when you go to restaurants. And thinking. Why is this place a success? What's it got? Why isn't this joint jumping in such a nice location with such great décor and marvelous food? What an unimaginative way to position the tables! Is there some structural reason why the restrooms are in that awkward spot, killing three tables stone dead? Why don't they partition off the entrance? Couldn't someone tell that busboy *not* to crash a load of dirty plates into the tray so noisily every two minutes? The maître d' is handsome, but why does he look so sad? Why did that waitress suddenly burst into tears and rush off the floor? What a boring menu! Ah, but here's a good idea! And so on. Discussion will help, though there will come a time when the requirement is not for conjecture but for *action*.

Most restaurateurs work in the business and graduate to open their own places. They learn on the job and rarely undertake any formal study, confining themselves to occasionally checking out the competition. They start young and gradually absorb information. A long line of successful restaurateurs started as chefs, but they often employ "front men" as managers and maître d's to cope with the fine art of handling the public and staff.

Reading is important. Advertisements, food critics' reports, and an enormous number of publications covering aspects of the industry will all yield useful information and ideas. The public library should have a copy of the *Small Business Source Book*, which lists publications pertinent to your business.

You should be aware of the ways in which you can learn about the business. Most major cities, but not all, have places where you can study. Since tuition is expensive, the cost of travel and board should be considered. If you live in, and plan to open your business in an "under-restauranted" part of the country—a very smart idea—you'll have to travel to a city to study and get your first jobs.

Cooking Schools

There are cooking schools everywhere, but they don't all teach chefs how to prepare for 300 dinners a night. The CIA (Culinary Institute of America) at New Hyde Park, New York, has a good reputation and offers a full training course.

A comprehensive course in cooking and restaurant management is offered by the New York Restaurant School, 27 West 34th Street, New York, NY 10001. Their 16- or 34-week courses cost $7,400.

An impressive aspect of their training, as of other establishments, is that they do get you out into functioning hotels and restaurants so that you can undergo your baptism by fire. Their list of alumni who've opened their own restaurants is impressive.

Many colleges also have courses, most notably Cornell, which has a Hotel and Restaurant Management School. In addition, there are wine courses at various colleges in New York and California as part of their agriculture curriculum. (For a further list of schools, see the appendix.)

Most major cities now have bartender and waiter schools, which are not terribly expensive and offer short courses, sometimes lasting only two weeks. Most of them are no better than adequate, but they do orient a complete beginner in the basics. They'll teach you how to make a Bronx cocktail, which nobody orders anymore, and how to separate a locked shaker and mixing glass with a sharp blow to the heel of the hand instead of a bang, bang, bang against the bar, and with a bit of luck, they'll teach their pupils not to slam cheap glassware into icecubes so that it breaks, necessitating replacement of the ice and possibly a trip to the emergency room. They'll show waitresses how to organize their orders and marry up half-empty ketchup bottles. They don't teach charm, deportment, or the way to a customer's heart, however.

Although some have a job placement service, most of them can't offer any public exposure. Only the better established college schools can do that, and their training restaurants, which are open to the public, are a good bargain. (Because the students are willing and positive in their approach, the service and food are often better than you'll find in many a "real" restaurant. They offer a good bargain and are well worth checking out.)

All these establishments are good sources for staff as well as places where you can learn the business. Students have to make the transition from the ideals of the classroom to the reality of business. Only real experience can teach you how to feed everyone at 8, how to lie convincingly, or how to compromise when you can't reach the standards you've set for yourself.

It's worth repeating that many—possibly a majority—of restaurateurs have no formal education at all. Many hardly speak English. They work in all the disciplines of the business until they have enough confidence, money, and initiative to go it alone. On the whole, they don't seem to do any worse than those who have expensive training, but this is a matter of some controversy.

One head waiter decided it was time to teach his young son the ropes. He had him work as a busboy and general lackey for a while. Then one night he threw him in the deep end. A regular, friendly couple came in. He thrust a pencil and a pad into the boy's hand and said, "Go over to that table and say 'Good evening, sir'—and we'll take it from there." Despite some trembling, there were no disasters. The young man knew he could do it, and he soon became an expert.

It doesn't much matter how you learn, as long as you do learn.

There is no proof that greater profits accrue to those who are expert chefs, scour the vineyards of the world, and know every fine restaurant in civilization. They probably enjoy life more because knowing one's job and liking it usually means less stress and worry. But there appears to be no correlation between worth, merit, talent, and success.

In the process of learning the restaurant business, many people learn a lot about themselves. Occasionally, they may regret that greater self-knowledge. So may their friends and loved ones. For better or for worse, it's a business that can change people.

It's a tough business, arguably a bit tougher than many, because of the hidden stresses. But it doesn't have to be depressing.

The grim millionaire restaurateur who was heard to snarl, "There's two kinds of people. Those who pay plastic, and those who pay cash," is a classic figure. But there *are* happy restaurateurs! Some of them still find the human race quite tolerable.

How often one hears it said, sadly, of some twitching, morose, recently divorced fellow: "He should never have gone into the restaurant business!" This isn't said only of people who went in and got hurt. It's also true of people who were enormously successful. It takes a lot out of you. Only the very strongest characters—some might say the least sensitive—will not be affected by the constant contact with people and the need to wear a dozen hats a day in order to survive. The power of detachment is an elusive one.

THE RISKS

Many people will tell you that the restaurant business is *the* highest risk business in the retail spectrum. This simply isn't true. That dubious accolade belongs to apparel stores, with furniture and camera stores in close pursuit.

Nevertheless, the restaurant business lies comfortably in third or fourth place in the list of failures, according to Dun & Bradstreet's *Business Failure Record,* which is mandatory, if harrowing, reading for people in business. The failure rate for "eating places" in general is above average nationwide. There were 142 closures per 10,000 in 1986, compared with 172 apparel store and 157 camera store failures, and 91 closures in 1987 compared with 138 apparel store closures.

Some may doubt the relevance of comparing apparel stores to restaurants. It may not be realistic. Apparel stores just sell clothes. Shirts don't rot, but lettuces do. Many restaurants don't just sell food. They sell service, convenience, atmosphere, escape, ambiance, theater, romance, adventure, excitement, love, therapy, and dreams. They offer their customers a unique playground. And they require a large capital investment—the single biggest roadblock to entering the business.

Perhaps a better comparison would be between Broadway musicals and restaurants, but market research hasn't gotten that far yet.

Unfortunately, no one has found a method of refining the figures to the point where the failure rate for licensed restaurants seating 50 to 200 can be calculated. The Liquor Authority can give no clue either, since the failure of a restaurant doesn't mean the cancellation of a license.

Ten percent of the 5,000 (approximately) full liquor licenses in the five boroughs of New York City turnover every year, and the figure is just about constant. Turnover doesn't necessarily indicate failure; it indicates change—which might be due to failure, sale, retirement, death, or expiration of lease.

Reasons for Failure

The stark reasons for business failure are worthy of study. According to Dun & Bradstreet, most retail businesses (68%) fail as a result of economic factors, some of which may be beyond their control. These include loss of market and no consumer spending. A more significant figure, perhaps, is the next most common reason for failures (22%), grouped under "experience causes." These include incompetence, lack of line experience, lack of managerial experience and, quite important, unbalanced experience. Kitchen experts with no flair for the handling of the public, beware!

Most experienced restaurateurs agree that the two most common reasons for failure are:

1. Inadequate funds. You run out of money before the restaurant attracts enough custom to go into profit.
2. Poor management. This is a catchall phrase, but should not be dismissed on those grounds.

Sometimes it becomes apparent soon after you open that a restaurant just isn't going to work. The chef, whose credentials were so impeccable, turns out to be a drunkard or incompetent, or both, when you actually commence operations. A replacement takes time to find, because the next two you try out are no better.

Poor security may mean that your takings are stolen. Food and alcohol may disappear, too. An unattractive crowd may monopolize the place, driving other customers away. A know-all manager may insist on loud rock music when the average age of the potential clientele is 50.

Then there are the ordinary accidents of life. Key personnel may drop dead on opening day or—as is common—just not show up. Remember, everyone dreads working in a new restaurant, and if a prospective employee finds a job in an established place before you put her on the payroll, you've lost her in a majority of cases. This is why you should always compile a list of prospective employees that is larger than your basic need.

Remember also that employees are likely to quit on the spot, Day One, if their worst fears are confirmed. They will be particularly irked by managerial eccentricities that are not immediately matched by good earnings. Suddenly remembering a heavy, time-consuming task that absolutely must be done just as people are thinking of going home is a real morale killer. One owner insisted that every single movable item on the bar had to be sent down to a long flight of steps and locked in a cellar, only to be brought up again at the commencement of the next day's business. It's simply no good saying "They're there to work." "They" don't necessarily share your mystical conviction. Another owner insisted upon examining the contents of employee's bags before they left—a common and highly degrading house rule in many places.

In time, everything can be perfected. But if the money runs out, you fail.

A sudden rerouting of traffic or the disappearance of a local parking facility can ruin a restaurant. And kitchen fires are extremely common.

Sabotage by rival restaurateurs is fairly common, too. They'll burn you down, report violations real or imaginary, or stage incidents in the restaurant.

In spite of the endless discussion of the subject, you rarely hear of a restaurant failing because of its lousy food. That's because, although finding the chef of your dreams isn't easy, it is feasible.

Some restaurants fail because they were never intended to succeed but only to launder money or provide some big-shot with a private supper club. No one can estimate the number of restaurants that are simply not intended to be anything but a money laundry or tax-evading device of some kind. One bartender tells of an excellent job he once had where there was no tape in the cash register, and only a trickle of customers, invariably bedecked in diamond rings and yellow leather jackets, accompanied by beautiful women. They tipped lavishly, but laughed when they were presented with bills. "Don't gimme no tab, pal!" Excellent food and wine were served, but ordinary customers were positively discouraged from entering. After six months, the bartender went to work one day to find the place burned to the ground.

The bartender was understandably sad, but felt it'd been a good run for the money. Interestingly enough, he felt that, had the restaurant been operated with serious intentions, it would have been a roaring success.

There's a big "fools rush in" factor in the restaurant business, meaning that like any other business, efficient management is essential. It isn't a difficult business, but it isn't quite as simple as it looks to the casual eye. Many people are overwhelmed by it and can't get out fast enough.

The purpose of this book is to steer budding restaurateurs in intelligent directions and to reduce that inevitable X-factor—luck—to the smallest significance possible.

Fools often prosper where the wise fail in the restaurant business. There are also accidents. Many failures remain unrevealed, except to those who lost money in the process. No successful restaurateur is likely to bend the ears of her admirers with the story of her failures or of the businesses she owns that are losers and that she's dying to unload. Loathsome establishments offering indifferent food and offhand service often make fortunes, even if nobody visits them twice. It is not too fanciful to suspect a "masochism factor" at work somewhere in the consumer psyche! In the 1970s a restaurant in New York was called Coup de Fusil. That means "gun-shot," literally. But it's also French slang for *rip-off*! Nice places close, much to the chagrin of their founders. It would be nice to be able to say there are a few basic rules that can guarantee success, but it wouldn't be realistic to do so. In the end you'll be on your own.

There's another business where fools often prosper and the wise fail. It's the business that has 82% of its union members out of work at all times. You guessed right—show business!

THE THEATER
OF RESTAURANTS

Even if you don't have a proper kitchen you can easily fix dinner at home for one for $3 or less, without alcohol. A middle-class saloon, bar-and-grill, bistro type of restaurant (which is the main target area of this book) will not feed you for that amount. If you feature a bowl of soup for $2.95, you'll occasionally get thrifty customers who'll order just that and no more, and eat all the bread in sight. If the place is busy enough, you'll hardly notice. If it isn't, you'll find that waiters and waitresses have a way of freezing out such people—or, if it becomes a standing routine, pocketing the money without making a check! In the words of the old song, "Ya git no bread with One Meat Ball!"

Since it's clearly possible to satisfy the basic human urge to eat for quite little, why are so many people prepared to pay the truly astronomical prices to be found at some restaurants? Note the precision of the question. The question is not, Why do restaurants charge such high prices? There are plenty of reasons for that, which will be discussed. The question is, Why are people prepared to pay them?

Clearly, the desire to eat is only one of the reasons why people go to restaurants, because you don't have to go to a restaurant just because you're hungry. The worker too far from home to return for sustenance or the traveler obviously need to eat somewhere, although it's amazing how many people either take a sandwich to work or buy a sandwich and eat it on a park bench during the lunch hour.

Most people go to restaurants in order to socialize, talk about business, or a happy mixture of both. The enormous affluent middle class, with 128 hours a week to spare after its 40 hours of labor, has both time and money on its hands. Restaurants could be said to form part of the leisure industry.

In the television age, some argue, conversation is a lost art. Cute one-liners are what most people give and seek. The alternative is the long, often repeated speech from the soapbox.

Since entertaining at home *always* poses the threat of conversation, it's not surprising that so many people, who could easily afford it, avoid it like the plague. Even when people entertain at home, in cities it's quite common for them to take their guests out for dessert and espresso. Also, with spare money available, why shouldn't people avoid the labor of preparation and planning, especially if they have jobs?

Thus, the restaurant takes its place alongside the cinema, the theater, and the ballgame on the list of Things To Do. It has become a modern ritual. The fact that business entertainment is tax-deductible assures many a restaurateur of a good night's sleep. Some put the percentage of city restaurants that would close if all bills were paid from personal disposable income as high as 60%.

Restaurants offer a useful service and solve a lot of problems, including what to eat and where to meet, for people who live at a distance from each other. The restaurant is also a heaven-sent compromise for the affluent but inarticulate person who nevertheless wishes to "relate" to someone, whether for business, sexual, family, or social reasons. It provides unthreatening neutral ground, as well as an arena offering opportunities to flatter and impress for any number of purposes. If conversation suggests itself, you can have conversation. It if doesn't, you can discuss the other customers, the food, the view, other joints you've been in, or the way mother used to make whatever it is you're having. "Whatever happened to mashed potatoes/chicken à la king/garlic bread?" you can wittily demand, often prompting a flood of responses. Many people visit restaurants as an exercise in itself, in search of escape, in the same spirit that they would go to the movies.

Other customers can be very important, as people-watchers watch *other* people-watchers in a sort of built-in cabaret that doesn't have to be listed in the owner's overheads. Experienced maître d's soon learn the art of "dressing the room" by putting the most beautiful and affluent people at the most prominent table. Regular customers sometimes reciprocate by always wanting the same table, and that is just one typical restaurant situation you have to learn to handle. Nine out of ten times customers accept alternatives with good grace. Sometimes they'll sit at the bar for a while, and sometimes they'll take another table on a temporary basis, which can cause some gnashing of teeth if, while two tables are occupied, only one of them is consuming. Customers who don't conform to the happy, beautiful, glossy ideal and who look as if they might drink beer straight from the bottle and swear loudly are usually consigned safely to an out-of-the-way spot.

For some people, being greeted by name by a hostess is the very stuff of heaven. Magazines regularly show restaurant floor plans, indicating the "power tables," where famous regular customers sit. At many restaurants, such as Smith and Wollensky's in New York, there are brass nameplates over some tables, indicating the names of their favorite occupiers. "Abe Weinstein sat here." "The Irving Schwartz chair." Glory indeed!

How long will it take before a diner commits suicide after being forced to occupy a table of less "power" than usual or after being consigned to "Lower Slobovia" instead of "Banquette Number Two" (the hot table at the old El Morocco)?

It's a form of theater and a form of escape. Often, newspapers accord more pages to the subjects of food and restaurants than they do to theater and cinema combined. Restaurant scenes are hard to do on stage, but it's unusual to see a movie without one, and at least one restaurant scene is de rigueur in the modern novel. Dramatic events occur in restaurants. People decide to get married, occasionally die, are murdered, or give birth. Both sexes have been known to remove their clothes. Customers walk in with lions or ocelots on leads, parrots on their shoulders, and boa constrictors round their necks.

Fights are not uncommon. Tablecloths offer an irresistible target—usually for jealous lovers. One vicious tug and there's chaos! At the Hotel Lexington in New York, a plaque on the wall in the bar commemorates the occasion when a woman blew her brains out, though whether this was meant as a comment about either the service or the prices isn't indicated.

Incidentally, what happens in restaurants when murders or suicides or fights occur is quite simple. Everybody leaves. They very sensibly don't want to get involved. And they often never return. For a version of what happens in a restaurant when a diner simply drops dead, Tom Wolfe's *Bonfire of the Vanities* makes highly entertaining reading.

Thankfully, few customers are as eccentric as William Astor Chandler, who became impatient while lunching at Maxim's one day in the 1920s because he had a horse running that afternoon. He threw his artificial leg plus sock, shoe, and garter at the waiter's back and shouted, "Now may I have your attention?"

Budding restaurateurs will breathe a sigh of relief at the assertion that 90% of customers enter, sit, drink, eat, pay, and leave without any noticeable contretemps. Smiles are part of the ritual.

It's vitally important that restaurateurs be able to put themselves in the customer's chair and sense what they're thinking. Here are two examples of people who had strong views on restaurants. What they have to say should be taken with a pinch of salt, and it's unlikely that you'll recognize any of your friends. But what they say may be illuminating and interesting.

Here's what a woman who loves to lunch, and dine, and take afternoon tea—in other words, a woman who just lives to go to restaurants—had to say:

I simply love going out to restaurants. It's such a wonderful escape from the cares and woes of everyday life. I have my favorite places, but I like to explore new restaurants, too. One of the things that makes being a woman such fun is that I often get taken to quite expensive restaurants free, because my charming male escort pays. If I'm with a woman friend, or a guy who really can't afford it, I pay my share. I think you can learn a lot about people from watching the way they behave in restaurants. I don't just mean their table manners. I mean the way they handle waiters and the various little situations that occur. Some people are gracious, kind, understanding, and forgiving, even when things aren't quite perfect. Others are quick to complain. I always notice how much men tip, because that's a good indication of what they're really like. Under-tipping indicates a mean streak. Over-tipping indicates insecurity and a desire to impress, and that always leaves me cold. I always take an interest in the decor, and what people around me are wearing. I think fresh flowers can turn a restaurant into a fairyland.

If I have new clothes I like to wear them to a restaurant and gauge the effect they have on people. Above all, I love the moment of entrance, when everyone looks up at you. Sometimes it can be a little intimidating, but it's exciting, too. You feel like a great actor stepping on stage and about to deliver a thrilling line. Of course, this sensation is heightened when there are *real* actors of celebrities in the restaurant! I do like good service, when the waiters really convince you that they want you to enjoy the whole experience, and try to satisfy your faintest whim. Good waiters know exactly when to take away your plate and when to serve the next course. They anticipate your needs. It's nice to be treated like a star. I especially like it when the help can answer your questions properly, like "Do you use first pressing olive oil in the salad dressing?" or when they fall over themselves to get you something that isn't on the menu. I simply hate it when they get the orders mixed up and you suddenly find yourself looking at a *canard roti* when you were expecting a veal chop. It's even worse when they interrupt important business conversation or intimate confessions by asking, "Who gets the steak?" In my favorite restaurant, the maître d' always presents me with a carnation the minute I walk in, which makes me feel so wanted and cherished, and the waiters are so kind and sweet, they actually run when you ask for something, which shows they really care . . .

At the other end of the spectrum, which one might describe as the extreme right-wing of restaurant customers, a restaurant-hater—by no means an uncommon species—says:

I loathe restaurants, and have done so since I was a child, when I could never believe the enormous amounts of money my father was paying for food which tasted funny and not at all like we ate at home. Although the people smiled at him a lot, I could tell they didn't really like us. Nowadays I notice the awful pain in the eyes of some of the restaurant help, particularly the hostesses. It can be quite heartrending, and is hardly conducive to a good time. That servile whipped-cur look. Am I their temporary jailer? The other customers were a real turn-off, too. All those phony voices and smiles. Restaurant customers always look faintly embarrassed, like children on strict orders to mind their manners. All that intense buttering of bread and dainty chewing!

One of the reasons I hate restaurants now is that I can't escape the ritual. I *have* to go to lunch and dinner as part of my business, and I resent it, even though it costs me nothing, because important discussion of business gets lost in discussion of restaurant trivia. I hate having to listen to long descriptions of the Daily Specials delivered with the solemnity of medieval High Mass, and loud-mouthed conversations from other diners, often sprinkled with four-letter words I can do without.

Nor do I like the sound of my own voice as I desperately try to get something to eat and drink that approximates to the way I'd have it if I were at home. "Rare, but not too rare" and all that sort of thing sounds so inane. No wonder the waiters sometimes look at me in an indulgent, pitying way, as though they knew I was just recovering from serious brain damage! At home I just cook things my way, and shrug it off if I get things a bit wrong. I sound so cantankerous insisting on a fresh bottle of soda for my drink, with just so much ice and extra lime. I often suspect the server thinks I'm a jerk, and who's to say he's not right, temporarily, at least? But at home I make my drink like that automatically, with a huge piece of lime, and top it up with a little extra vodka or soda the split second I feel like it—not when I at last manage to catch the waiter or the bartender's eye! The fact that the drink is costing me $3.50 plus tip, when I can buy a whole bottle of vodka for less than twice that amount, doesn't help. Sometimes I feel I'm locked with the waiters by mutual consent in a form of ritual imbecility! Banging kitchen doors, dishes crashing into bustrays. Nor do I like to be sneered at by a waiter or waitress who's obviously just doing a little social research while awaiting the release of the hit movie in which he or she has a starring role. I don't like seeing people grubbing for tips—it doesn't seem very American to me. And, although I tip a straight 15% or more in order to make sure I get out alive, I really don't see why I should pay the restaurateur's payroll as well as his entrepreneurial mark-up, not forgetting a dollar to hang up my coat! Mind you, I was in Russia once, where you're not allowed to tip, and the service was so bad I thought I was going to starve to death!

As to the food, it's not what I'm in a restaurant for, so it hardly matters. If I'm paying, I just have the smallest, cheapest thing on the menu, having fixed myself a sandwich at home before I go out. But I do notice that, unless you're in an expensive gourmet joint, there isn't a damn thing on the average menu that I couldn't fix myself at home in five minutes flat for $2. Bah! Humbug! There's no escape. I shall just have to grin and bear it. However, there's a bistro place not far from where I live that isn't too expensive and the food's okay. They have good value wine specials. The owner's a nice guy, and the waitresses are efficient and friendly. I go there pretty often.

Experienced restaurateurs would not be impressed by these comments. They know there's resentment out there, and they know how to beat it and turn the most reluctant cynic into a paying customer. They also know that business people are, in fact, the best customers and the easiest to deal with. Prompt service, decent food, and good drinks in a pleasant atmosphere will send people home having had an agreeable experience. That's the way to make them come back.

WHO OPENS RESTAURANTS, AND WHY?

If your objective is to be in business for yourself, there are lots of things you can do besides open a restaurant. To some budding entrepreneurs, the prospect is unattractive. For one thing, you need a large amount of start-up money. You might just get off the ground with a 50-seat bar and grill in the country with $100,000. In a major city, $400,000 would be a more realistic figure, given current rents.

There's a lot to be said for sticking with the business you know, and a lot of restaurateurs are people who entered the industry young and can envision no other way of life. They're usually the ones who succeed, but good privates don't always make sergeants.

Many restaurants are inherited. For instance, many immigrants into the United States have received the call from an ailing relative to begin learning how to hustle their way into the restaurant world. It's amazing how swiftly and easily most of them take to their new role in life.

Opening a restaurant is sometimes the only way of making an old much-loved home viable. Many European aristocrats, notably Lord MacDonald and Sir Fitzroy MacLean in Scotland, have done this, and the syndrome exists in the United States. The success rate in such operations seems to be high, but the aristos invariably complain, both in public and private, about the hard work involved. They look forward to their vacations.

Personality

A dangerous illusion persists that the restaurant business is one in which personality counts for a lot. There's some truth in this. After all, you're selling goods at the retail level to people who may be seeking entertainment and relaxation as well as simple sustenance. The ability to make easy small talk with customers is obviously no bad thing, and restaurateurs do exist where the owner is established as a figurehead, sometimes a charmer, sometimes a rogue, but always wise, warm and welcoming. Such owners build a following that is great for business but sometimes a bit of a problem for the new incumbent if the restaurant changes hands. ("Joe here? No? He retired? Oh, well, give him my best if you see him. Er . . . no, we don't have time for dinner, we just thought we'd look in.")

Sacred Monsters

Some of the most successful restaurants in the country are owned and run, often with an iron fist and a beady eye on the cash register 14 hours a day, seven days a week, by highly unattractive people with no personality whatsoever, who are delighted to proclaim their contempt for mankind in general and their customers in particular. The total absence of any kind of sense of humor—the factor that made the Bible unique in literature, according to Northcote—in some owners is quite striking. Those in the "people business" often rely upon their sense of humor to keep themselves sane. Even airline attendants with their chilling plastic smiles will sometimes unbend if they're not too tired and don't feel themselves threatened. But many restaurateurs reflect, in their unswerving cold seriousness and dedication to the dollar, the pomposity of some of their bullying and demanding customers, who know what they want and intend to get it by hook or by crook, the irrefutable punchline excuse for their hideosity being, always, "I'm *paying* for it, aren't I?"

Many restaurateurs develop absurdly inflated egos, perhaps as a reaction against the essentially menial nature of the work. Small wonder that a magazine reviewing restaurants recently referred to "Restaurant Gods"!

The late Henri Soulé made a great ceremony of tearing up the checks of customers who dared to query them, informing his foolishly impetuous ex-clients with a sneer that they had "dined as his guest, but that they needn't expect ever to be served again." When anyone offered the slightest comment he would bow sarcastically and say, "Je suis Simonizé, m'sieur!" (It's a labored joke in translation: "I'm Simonized"—in other words, "I'm waxed, impervious to your remarks.") It's difficult to imagine him ever smiling or even being remotely polite to anyone. Yet Le Pavillon is often invoked with nostalgia by elderly gourmets who remembered the food as being outstanding. The place always had the air of a funeral parlor, such was the profusion of flowers. The bill for flowers was supposed to be enormous. (One restaurant in New York today claims an annual flower bill of $60,000. Skeptics may reflect that every petal and every stalk must be paid for by the customer.) Bing Crosby was turned away after daring to enter without a tie. "An insult to my restaurant!" the owner cried, lacking the gumption to lend the crooner a tie for an hour.

Italian war hero and socialite Gianni Agnelli's proudest moment was when he was allowed into "21" wearing blue jeans!

Another "sacred monster" is the woman who spends all night at the end of the bar and makes out all the checks herself, using a selection of very sharp pencils. She pads the checks shamelessly, and when, as regularly happens, her unseen, undelivered, and certainly unconsumed additional "2 Stuffed Mushrooms, $28.00" is discovered by an alert diner, and she is forced to erase the line from the check, her language would make a stevedore blush! The hapless waiter makes the necessary apologies. She never explains, often complains, and never apologizes. Quixotically enough, apart from occasionally foaming at the mouth, she doesn't bother her employees much, and they speak of her with wry smiles rather than contempt. They make good money working for her. Her employees are queasy allies. They are not the enemy! She has been known to physically attack customers who displease her. On one occasion she insisted on levying a cover charge on an ambassador's bodyguards, who'd hoped to sit discreetly at an adjoining table while their master dined. And when the ambassador declined to pay the sales tax on the bill, pleading diplomatic immunity, she socked him in the nose with the cry, "I pay sales tax in *your* country."

Nevertheless, restaurants like this attract celebrities, and their public relations firms keep them appearing in the gossip columns even though food and service are mercifully forgotten.

The probable reason for this joint's undoubted success is that it's always full, and there's always a buzz of noise from the crowded diners, which helps to dampen the loneliness of the many lost souls who go to the restaurant, not only to eat and socialize, but for some reassurance that there's life out there. Whether you like it or not, busy restaurants are generally more attractive than empty ones.

Then there's the ex-haberdasher restaurateur whose normal battlestation is beside the cash register. He manages a thin smile as he regales his admiring customers with stories about the time he bought a large quantity of white wine of such poor quality that the customers actually noticed and kept sending it back. He had the bright idea of using it only to make spritzers (white wine with seltzer and a twist of lemon—what the Victorians called hock and seltzer). Lo and behold, he got away with it and turned less than $1,000 into about $20,000.

Often, people are turned away even when there are tables available. Since reservations for "deuces" or couples are not taken, it's assumed that he's hoping someone a little more interesting or glamorous will come in. If they don't, that's okay, too, because he's a multimillionaire.

One might suspect a variation of the old joke about the masochist and the sadist. "Hit me!" begs the masochist. "No," snarls the sadist. "Please let me come in and be ripped off," implores the would-be diner. "No!" says the restaurateur.

Lots of society functions are held at his restaurant for grand-mothers hoping to be mistaken for debutantes, their incredibly distinguished, sensitive "walkers," and rich foreigners desperately trying to be Americans. The Monster is easily distinguished at these black tie gatherings: he's the one in the crumpled polyester business suit and the crimplene tie. The list of guests, which is always the same, is faithfully recorded in the widely syndicated "Suzy Knickerbocker" gossip column. If you call him and ask for the number of his public relations people, he'll snap, "I don't do public relations," and hang up.

But the truth is his public relations is relentless and expensive. Again, every celebrity you could name has been to his restaurant, including Claus von Bulow, Jackie Collins, Joan Collins, Tom Collins, Elizabeth Taylor, Princess Margaret, the Dukes and Duchesses of Roxburghe and Westminster, the Earls of Erroll and Westmoreland, the Aga Khan (who employs at least three gourmet chefs of his own at home), the kings of Spain, Greece, Bulgaria, and Albania, and the wife of a president of the United States with her sandalwood scented "walker." Unlike our lady monster, this owner is not looked upon by his staff with wry fondness. On the contrary, one of them tried to "put a contract" on him!

This is an excellent example of snob appeal. People will go to a restaurant because it's the place their crowd—or the crowd they aspire to join—goes. Such restaurants work very well when they work. But groups are fickle, and it doesn't take much to make the flock suddenly switch its allegiance. Should its leaders start going elsewhere, if the food is *too* awful or overpriced, or if the staff become rude in a way that is merely offensive and tiresome, affords no grotesque, pseudobaroque amusement and no masochistic delight, then death will come quickly. No restaurateur should assume that today's recipe for success will last forever.

The Masochism Factor

In the face of such success, it may not be too fanciful to suspect that a masochism factor exists and that some people really do like a little punishment. We all know the "fashion victim" syndrome, where people squeeze themselves into uncomfortable clothes that really don't flatter them at all, for the sake of being up to date and state of the art. Some people want to go where they're told they can't, in the same way that some cannot resist touching what is clearly marked as wet paint. Establishing *exclusivity*, or the illusion thereof, can pay. Some people don't care how they're insulted or ripped off as long as they can enjoy the warm conviction that they're in the right place, the hot spot where the action is and the movers and shakers congregate. But most experienced restaurateurs feel it's a dangerous game. There's too much competition in most cities.

But are people really that much into pain? It's more likely a slavish following of fashion, relentless PR, and the attraction of cell activity. Precisely, it is the pleasant prospect of either seeing someone you know, or someone you'd very much *like* to know, which brings affluent socialites, or would-be socialites, to a restaurant like moths to the flame and, credit where credit's due, these ghastly ogres deliver! Your hamburger might be like minced shoe leather, your wine reminiscent of a herbal concoction, and your cognac of dubious provenance and measured with a thimble at an exhorbitant price. But the modest, unassuming fellow at the next table, should you be so lucky, really *is* Mick Jagger. You are temporarily part of his world. If you catch his eye, he might even give you the Famous Grin. With a little effort, you might almost arrange to surreptitiously touch the hem of his garment.

Thinking Positive—the Fun Side

There's no doubt that a successful restaurant is a wonderful thing to own. There are many restaurants that turn over several million dollars a year. Cash flow is immediate. The sight of new restaurateurs queuing at the local American Express office to get the cash for the day's slips is quite common! It's mostly cash on the barrelhead, and the restaurateur suffers less than other businesspeople from the curse of credit and unpaid bills. Also, there are many attractive, perfectly legal tax and expense perks. A little bit of flair and personality can go a long way. And, although the initial work effort is enormous, once the thing is flying, you can put it on automatic to a certain extent and work on a normal healthy schedule. Ideally, you should be able to say, like the owner of Le Cirque, "Our foundation is so strong that the restaurant could function for quite a while without any given chef, or maître d'hôtel, or me."

An awful lot of people open restaurants for reasons that are not purely businesslike. There's a certain mystique about owning a restaurant which makes it a dream for some people. You create a world which others enter. Sometimes there's reciprocity and you're invited into their worlds, too! One might call this approach the Casablanca factor.

The Casablanca Factor

Few cult movies enjoy a greater following than *Casablanca*. Most would agree that it's a good flick—Claude Raines and Ingrid Bergman help it along. It's set at a crossroads of time and circumstance, in the subtropical Moroccan city of Casablanca, just before America entered World War II. Vichy French view Nazis with suspicion. Rick is played by Humphrey Bogart, that ingratiating bassethound with the sybilant, distinctive voice. The owner of Rick's Cafe oversees his own microcosm of mankind through a sad but compassionate eye. Rick's Cafe is a white tablecloth restaurant with a black singer pianist and is, very conveniently, the general rendezvous for the cast.

The truth is, Rick lives! While making a better than average living and calling his own shots, he is the catalyst and sometimes supreme arbiter of people's lives. We never know quite where he comes from, whether he has brothers or sisters, or prefers fishing to football, or whether he's 30 or 60, but one thing's for sure: in Casablanca he has stature, authority, and identity. He's a reference point of local life, and he knows all the "usual suspects," or regular customers, intimately. When people want to sing their national anthems, they do it in his place. No arena could be more appropriate. And Rick? Well, he's lonely and sad, but chances are he would be no matter what he was doing. His white tuxedo never has sweat patches, it's unlikely that he pays for his cigarettes, and he eats three squares a day.

Many budding restaurateurs want to be Rick. All successful restaurateurs become Ricks, whether they like it or not. (Some don't!) Their restaurants become the center of many people's lives, a reference point and arena for their employees and customers alike.

But in the movie, we only see Rick enjoying glamorous dramatic moments. True, the police close him down at one point, but we don't see him trying to find two waiters or waitresses, a bartender, and a dishwasher who failed to show for work 20 minutes before 40 customers arrived to take up their reservations, with two sinks blocked, a toilet out of order, the air conditioning on the blink, and not a loaf of bread to be found because of the bakers' strike. The languages of Casablanca are French and Arabic. So why does everyone so conveniently speak English?

The escapist function of the movies wouldn't work if, instead of looking at the interesting bits of people's lives, we wallowed in their plumbing problems. But to enjoy the ephemeral delights of glamorous Rickdom, one must first suffer a little. As the old English motto has it, "Through mud and blood to the green fields beyond!"

TWO

LOCATION

IMPORTANCE OF LOCATION

The question of where your restaurant is located is of such obvious and critical importance, some might think it hardly worthy of discussion. But there's a lot to consider. Many restaurateurs believe location to be *the* most critical factor in the restaurant success formula. Those who don't agree with that will cite the example of restaurants in situations which are clearly less than ideal, but which are successful anyway. There are ways and means of making some mediocre locations successful. But a bad location can be a heartbreaker. Some restaurateurs, who can afford to wait, will spot a changing residential trend and move in in order to be in place when the unattractive neighborhood becomes fashionable. That takes shrewd judgment, patience, guts, and more money than the tyro restaurateur can usually raise.

Would-be restaurateurs are sometimes put off by the presence of other restaurants near a premises they like. If you plan a steakhouse, and there are already two others on the block, you may be unwise to join the throng. But if *your* operation is only in general competition, and not in specific competition with the neighbors, there may be no reason to be put off. On the contrary, a conglomeration of restaurants is often a business booster. Restaurant Row in New York consists entirely of restaurants, all of different style and quality. The suburb of Highgate, near London, supports a coffee shop, a Chinese restaurant, an Italian restaurant, and a steakhouse. All do well. If you look around you'll see that restaurant grouping is quite common, as it is in other businesses. London's tailors crowd into Savile Row, New York's diamond merchants all seem to be on 48th Street, and so on.

Many, but by no means all, new restaurants simply replace ones that have failed, or whose owners want to retire or move on for some other reason. Sometimes a renewal of a lease with consequent rent hike may make the operation nonviable. To pay, the restaurant is going to have to take in more money, and the owners don't see how it can be done. Maybe those spaghetti and meatballs have to be replaced by Chateaubriands. In contemplating the failure of predecessors, clues to future success may often be discerned. Frequently you can get it right by carefully noting how someone else got it hopelessly wrong.

Clearly, an ideal situation for a soda, coffee, and doughnut shop is across the street from the local high school or in the middle of a busy business or shopping district. A licensed, middle-priced bistro will do well either in a city residential area or, again, a business or shopping area. For a successful restaurant you simply must have customers!

A really high-class "gourmet" restaurant may do better in a high-class city or suburban area. If you check the addresses of those restaurants listed in guides as "Expensive" you'll notice that the majority reside in high rent areas. It is often the case that a restaurateur, for one reason or another in possession of a property in such a neighborhood, will opt for the top end of the market, for all its extra problems and the well-known fickle nature of such clientele. In the same way, if you inherit the premises opposite the high school, your ambitious escargots and white truffles may be cast like pearls before swine!

Such exceptions will usually prove the rule, but square pegs just don't go in round holes. The location and the type of restaurant should complement each other.

Some locations are obvious winners. Top floors of skyscrapers will place as much emphasis on the view in their advertising as they do on the food, service, reasonable prices, and general joy of it all. P.J. Clarke's in New York became famous after being used as a location in the movie *Lost Weekend* and now enjoys a quaint solitude on a corner, surrounded by towering skyscrapers. The Russian Tea Room is in a similar situation, and people hazard guesses in hushed tones as to how much the owners have turned down in order to continue in business.

Mystical Factors

But some locations just don't make it—ever. One owner of a corner restaurant which had changed owners frequently called in an exorcist to try and drum up business. It was a dead corner, and such apparently cursed locations do exist. They're the first ones you'll come across once you start looking for premises!

But how come the restaurant at the diagonally opposite corner was such a roaring success? It offered nothing that the haunted house didn't have, but it was always full. The simple truth must be that some corners are more inviting than others. There are exposed corners and there are inviting corners, warm ones and cold ones. If this sounds illogical, welcome to the wonderful world of restaurants! The reasons for it may be buried deep in the subconscious, but people do seem to make instinctive choices in these matters. Nine out of ten people, walking into a room where the reasons for going to the left are absolutely as good as those for moving to the right, will move to the left. Lost in the desert, the legionnaire who doesn't know how to navigate by the stars will walk in a wide counterclockwise circle. So there *are* mysterious forces at work!

"I do business charts for someone opening a business" astrologist Lynne Palmer told *The New York Times*. "If a person is starting a restaurant, I determine the best time to open it. Years ago . . . there was a restaurant down the block from me. Good food, reasonable prices. And yet there was never anyone there. The owner gave me the date he opened. I looked it up in my book of planets. Sure enough, he opened at the wrong time. Within a few months he closed" (May 15, 1988).

At the risk of appearing unromantic, sticking to the normal disciplines of business is more likely to achieve desired ends than stargazing. However, any experienced bartender will tell you that the public's behavior often becomes very strange at the time of the full moon!

A keen eye will be able to tell whether or not a location can be developed and improved. When Michael Wharton opened Oliver's in New York, he took a chance on a bar that formerly housed illegal gambling in the back room on a rather bleak block. Neighbors assured him that bodies had been carried out of the place on more than one occasion! But he sensed that, though it wasn't ideal, there was nothing basically wrong with the location, and he opened a moderately priced American restaurant which, after a few nail-biting months, soon became a great success. On acquiring the lease to the upstairs space, he even managed to make The Upstairs Room profitable, in spite of the dour restaurateur's maxim, "They won't go upstairs." The simple truth is that "They" *will* go upstairs if it's made inviting enough! If they see a nice room with a bar and an attentive crew who give every promise of prompt service, there'll be no resistance. But The Upstairs Room is empty, cold, and forbidding so often that you suspect the visits from the waiters are going to be intermittent at best.

Country and Suburban Locations

The oft-quoted statistic that 70% of Americans live in cities can be a bit misleading. Some American cities—Los Angeles, New York, Fort Worth–Dallas, Boston, Chicago—are enormous and include large areas of rambling suburbs that are not quite country. Nor should one forget "the country" itself, although usually a restaurant will not do well in distant, wild country unless it's a landmark or cult kind of place. Few people in California or Connecticut live more than 20 minutes from a gas station, police station, general store, or village center.

Rents and property prices are, inevitably, much lower outside cities. Getting help can sometimes be a problem, but most manage. Some restaurants get around this by offering accommodation "over the shop" to their employees. Then comes the happy day when the owner needs their accommodation for his expanding business and the ball starts to roll.

The automobile is what makes the country liveable. Americans will commonly drive 50 miles to a restaurant on weekends or during the week if they're retired or on vacation. At the Hilltop Restaurant in Saugus, Massachusetts, two of the restaurant's 625 employees direct traffic to the parking lot, which is soon to get a second level. Opened in 1961 with a seating capacity of 125, the restaurant now seats 1,400 souls, summoned to their tables by public address system at the appointed hour. A visit is a *must* for any budding restaurateur who happens to find himself in the neighborhood. They've done more business than any other restaurant in the country for five straight years, according to the magazine *Restaurants and Institutions*, and it's just possible they may be doing something right. The location hasn't hurt! It's easily reached by car, and there's a huge landmark cactus sign outside to reduce a driver's chance of overshooting the target.

Fortunes await restaurateurs who correctly gauge the point on the map that will serve as a cachement area for local residents living within a 50-mile radius. The country is full of such unexploited sites. When thinking in this area it's important to determine whether there's a heavy weekend factor or not. You'll be lucky to get a table at Nando's Miramar in Quogue, Long Island on a Saturday night in July. You might have to wait until midnight. But on Monday night you can probably walk in, and the maître d' will even have time to make zabaglione at your table and discuss the weather. The fact that so many country and suburban restaurants are closed on Mondays gives you the clue!

Rent

With commercial rents in New York now at $250 per square foot per annum, it's clear that in any major city, rent is going to be the restaurateur's main and inescapable overhead. Many restaurants are only viable as businesses because their owners also own the building. Thus, the restaurant business merges with the real estate business. A man who owns a large building will often find that the best thing to do with the ground floor space is to turn it into a restaurant, especially if he has difficulty in letting it for some other purpose. At least he won't be paying any rent! This emphasizes the attraction of finding an inexpensive location. But defining a cachement area and opening up in it takes judgment and courage.

HOW TO FIND PREMISES

Restaurants for sale are often advertised in newspapers. There are firms, called restaurant brokers, who specialize in the handling of restaurant properties. They will supply you with a list, usually free. You pay them a commission if a deal goes through. Some of these lists get pretty dog-eared with old dogs of restaurants sitting in the lists for months and years, waiting for a sucker!

The lists give you all the information you could desire except for the very information you need, such as the rent, the price of the lease, and the exact location. That's because they don't want you going behind their backs and doing a private deal that excludes their commission.

Up to a point, *all* restaurants are "for sale" if the price is right. Many in business specialize in "in-and-out" operations. They like to set up a restaurant, get it rolling, sell it quickly, and move on. There are few bargains to be had. Potential owners must decide what sort of operation they're going to have, and they must have at least a general idea how soon they'd like to recover their investment. The rule of thumb used to be five years. Many people now expect to cash in within one year.

Again, we're in the area of "the buck stops here," and you're on your own. But if you're totally immersed in the subject, as you should be when looking for a place, you should have a realistic view of local conditions. "Caveat Emptor"—let the buyer beware!

The Neighborhood

It's important to know what's going on in the neighborhood, especially if you suspect that most of your customers are going to be local residents or workers, as distinct from distant commuters or bold adventurers from the other side of the town or county. If the main source of your business is the local hospital across the street, and suddenly half the workforce is transferred to another location too far away to maintain customer loyalty, then you could have a problem. This is why you should never be complacent about your source of customers but should always try to expand into other areas—which, of course, must be acceptable to and compatible with your regulars. You don't want Hell's Angels forcing out your accountants and legal secretaries!

Equally, a sharp eye for future development may pay dividends. If you suspect that a street will not be the last ditch before the slums for long, but will soon be taken over by the beloved bourgeoisie (and this is fairly easy to assess), you may take a calculated risk and get a friendly price or rent. Similarly, if you have it on good authority that a nearby empty space will soon become a skyscraper housing 12,000 workers, and this is not generally known, you may be a winner.

Converting Premises

The easiest and most common method of finding premises is to take over an existing restaurant location and revamp it to your taste and plans. Frequently a grossly inflated "goodwill" factor is built into the price. But sometimes you can convert another kind of premises—a shoe store or whatever—into a restaurant. This involves zoning permission from the local authorities.

Laws and trends vary greatly from place to place, and need to be explored thoroughly. Bearing in mind "the law's delay," it's *never* too soon to explore these matters. There's no necessity to spend money on professional advice, but City Hall will want to see the plans for your proposed conversion, which may have to be prepared by a qualified architect. They'll tell you their legal requirements for conversion, should they decide that your character is sufficiently decent to deserve their permission.

Conversion Costs

These can vary enormously. If you want plush carpets, spacious restrooms, and a modern, fully-equipped kitchen, and if you have to install walk-in boxes and freezers, air conditioners, heaters, and so on, then the sky's the limit. You could easily spend $200,000 on assembling a 50-seater restaurant.

But there are ingenious means of getting around this. In France, the average restaurateur doesn't spend a penny more than necessary on furniture and decor. Plastic chairs and tables, paper tablecloths and napkins abound. If a local artist wants to exhibit landscapes on the walls, that's acceptable, and the commission exacted in the event of a sale will not be enormous!

In this respect, the more you look, the more you'll see. Once you "get your eye in," you'll be amazed at the number of restaurants that have only two or three attractive tables, all the others being equally unattractive. But—another contradiction in a quirky industry—some of the least charming oblong rooms, with rows of deuces along the walls and fours and sixes in the middle, serve the best food.

WHAT
KIND
OF
RESTAURANT?

WHAT IS THE TARGET MARKET?

Most new restaurateurs have a good idea of the kind of food they want to serve. The most common notion is to offer middle-of-the-road American cuisine, with perhaps some European overtones and gestures. In this area, menu inspiration can vary from moderately expensive steaks, chops, fish, and chicken dishes, through the exciting "Russian Burger" (a hamburger topped with caviar) to the bleak "Individual can of tuna" and "No substitutes." It is rare for an owner not to make a gesture in the direction of his ethnic origins, which usually adds a welcome, exotic touch such as lasagna, moussaka, fish and chips, or corned beef and cabbage to the menu.

Often the choice is limited by circumstances. An ideal premises may be found near a highly successful steakhouse, with a terrific seafood place nearby. It might be asking for trouble to seek head-on competition by opening the same kind of operation.

It's interesting to note that the steakhouse will almost certainly feature two or three fish dishes, including lobster, while the fish joint will probably offer a steak for those who either don't like or are allergic to fish. This is an example of the striving to please everyone all the time which can make the business such very hard work. A typical result of this is the overcrowded menu where everything's equally dull, usually because the only way a large menu can be maintained is by keeping many items deep-frozen. The microwave may be a godsend to the hungry and to the hard-pressed cook, but it has added little to the restaurateur or the gourmet's pleasures apart from swiftly heated pie and quiche.

A very happy compromise can be achieved by having a set menu with "Daily Specials." These can either genuinely be the chef's inspiration of the day—perhaps coinciding with an excess supply of, or special market prices on, some item or other—or a regular routine: pot roast every Tuesday, lobster every Friday. This is a useful way of attracting regular customers.

Given an experienced nation of consumers, an advantage of precise ethnic identification of a restaurant is that the customers know what to expect! Few would have foreseen the day when red-blooded Americans would eat raw fish, but Japanese restaurants are currently all the rage. Indeed, there are those who will tell you that America is a great place for sushi!

The broad classifications of restaurants are: American, English, Irish, German, Austrian, Greek, Turkish, French or Continental, Italian, Spanish, Chinese, Japanese, Thai, and Indian. In the larger cities the choice is even larger, extending to Afghan, Argentinian, Columbian, Tibetan, Indonesian, Ethiopian, Cajun, and Czech. An interesting, and often highly successful concept is Tex-Mex. Health food restaurants, catering to vegetarians and to diners who seek purer food, are now an established genre. Many restaurants simply fall into a certain category by limiting their range of food to fish, steak, chili, pizza, or kebabs.

Each of these types of cuisine poses its own problems and challenges. But cooks are an artful crowd and that which looks difficult is often quite easy when you know how.

Opening Hours

Some restaurants open only for lunch or dinner. French restaurants are commonly open for lunch and dinner six days, closing on Sunday and often for the whole month of August. If the amount of business missed by these closures is insignificant, then the free time enjoyed by owner and staff will be worthwhile. But the pressure to do business during the open period is naturally so much greater, since the rent has to be paid whether the restaurateur opens or not. Restaurants that are open daily for lunch and dinner save their regular clients from wondering whether they're open or not. Most of the few remaining 24-hour restaurants or coffee shops in the country are gold mines.

Which End of the Market?

Restaurateurs pay their money and take their choice. If they try to appeal to a wealthy gourmet crowd, they'll need a highly trained chef who will require a high salary. Sometimes, of course, the restaurateur *is* the chef, which helps enormously. A special problem of this genre of restaurant is the necessity of maintaining a high standard of cuisine and service that will stand up to the scrutiny of food critics, who can make or break such places. Restaurateurs with the ego, the confidence, the financial backing, and the courage to open a restaurant at this end of the market will need no instruction from anyone in the restaurant industry. As a rule, they don't ask for advice anyway.

The hotel restaurant at the Dorchester in London employs 85 people in the kitchen, from *apprenti* to *demi-chef, chef, saucier,* and so on. The Hilltop Steak House employs 625 people. The bills for flowers, publicity, and laundry at this end of the market can be daunting. Even a neighborhood 50-seater will employ at least ten people if it's open seven days a week. In the early days of a restaurant, however, the owners can cover several jobs and save on payroll.

But middle of the road is the safest path, as in so many businesses. There are some food items with which you can hardly go wrong. Every restaurant in America that serves hamburgers claims to serve the best hamburgers. Few hamburger oases are empty for long.

Italian restaurants are immensely popular, whether they serve cheap-and-cheerful spaghetti, meatballs, and pizza or more expensive osso bucco. The food is easy to prepare and leans heavily on safely familiar tastes, colors, and sensations. At one end of the market the keyword is *al dente*, which means the pasta should be faintly resistant to the teeth. Some gourmets may resist the association of Banquette Number One with the dentist's chair, but that's the style. At the other end of the market, it's "heavy on the tomayder sauce and can we git some more bread?"

Because of their popularity, the competition is fierce. In many cities it's not uncommon to find five or more Italian restaurants in the space of a block, all doing a roaring trade.

The more distinctively ethnic food operations are best conducted by their native sons and daughters, and will often appeal more to customers of that background than to adventurous diners. But most people enjoy a change, and even purists will do well to make some concessions to those of mundane tastes by having some safe and easily recognizable items available on their otherwise exotic menus. Personal tastes should be accommodated, too. If customers want ketchup on their filet mignon, there's really no good reason why they shouldn't have it. Let the waitresses snigger in the kitchen, but good manners dictate that *de gustibus non est disputandum*—there's no disputing taste.

In China they eat dogs and cats. In Belgium and France they eat horse. Goat is eaten throughout the Middle East. In areas plagued by locusts, children will pluck insects from the air when they swarm, tear off their legs and wings, and eat them raw. A Borneo tribesman, who disturbs a log in the rain forest to reveal a glowing green slimy slug, will beam with delight and either eat it himself or, if he's a gent, offer it to one of his wives.

THEME RESTAURANTS

Some successful restaurants rely for their attraction upon gimmicks that have nothing to do with food. This might include such theme decor as model car collections, bicycle wheels, or barnyard implements. The theme is often pursued to the *n*th degree, with varying degrees of success. Menus will rely upon puns or far-fetched adjectives to describe items, such as "dawn-gathered wild mushrooms," and so on.

Experienced diners' hearts sink when they read such guff, usually on menus that have been composed by a publicity writer rather than the chef. It practically guarantees that the food will be tasteless. Generally speaking, the more authentic the staff's costumes, the less likely they are to have a slice of lemon for your fish and the more likely it is that the whipped cream will come out of an aerosol can.

Other restaurants rely upon such things as a wonderful view or singing waiters. Some restaurants are done up like 1920s speakeasies or as cabarets with a running talent show.

ENTERTAINMENT

The piano bar is a great favorite, but some restaurateurs grumble that they could seat several parties in the space occupied by the pianist, who is naturally on the payroll and gets a staff meal on the house. The question of whether or not to have entertainment is an old and harrowing one, and it's never easy to please everyone. One pianist will play a potted version of a classical concerto to the delight of some but to the annoyance of those who would prefer to hear "Send in the Clowns." Another will delight with her own inspirations, such as a medley of popular jingles from current commercials. One pianist who knew the Finnish national anthem made a regular tip from a homesick old lady. In general, a pianist whose repertoire embraces "Happy Birthday to You," "Our Love is Here to Stay," and "As Time Goes By" will be perfectly adequate, and if the fingerings aren't quite right, few will notice.

Wandering guitarists and gypsy trios are not very much in vogue these days. Perhaps they could be revived?

Some budding stars are so fond of the sound of their own voices, and so eager to have an audience, that they'll perform free at your restaurant and bring in paying friends, too. It would be unrealistic to expect any big spenders on such occasions, however.

Established supper club singers can get shirty if diners—or "guests," as they are often called in the business, in spite of the fact that they get a bill when they leave—dare to talk while they're performing. The restaurant that features Woody Allen on clarinet undoubtedly pulls in a few curious customers who want to hear their multitalented hero. A restaurant that makes a feature of jazz groups can do well, as jazz lovers are a solid, gregarious crowd. But there's never room for many such establishments. Occasionally restaurants even flirt with chamber musical recitals and poetry readings.

Some restaurants revolve on top of skyscrapers so that the view changes constantly. Before the war there was a popular restaurant in Berlin with telephones at each table, so that people could ring each other up!

Neighborhood restaurants often profit by having a big TV over the bar. This enables diners and drinkers to watch ballgames as they consume. Sometimes consumption is inhibited by too much concentration on the silver screen, sometimes it's increased. Inevitably, some customers won't like the blaring TV and the occasional touchdown war whoops, but most will feel they're part of a living, warming experience. Restaurants that actually build themselves around huge TV screens showing ballgames and so on seem to do well, but there is almost certainly a limit to the number of such operations any given consumer population will bear. Again, if this formula doesn't work, it is but the work of a moment to remove the screen and revamp! Nothing is forever, least of all in the restaurant business.

Entrepreneurial decision is required. If that big stuffed bear delights the children, then its space is well used. If not, then perhaps it should be replaced by a cash-generating table.

Appealing to Different Age Groups

Corny as it may seem, there's no doubt that restaurants that aim to please an older clientele may do at least as well as those that solicit the custom of the young! The vast majority of customers in expensive restaurants are over 45. Many retired people have lots of time on their hands and lots of money to spend. There's a big hole where their jobs and children used to be, and regular trips to restaurants help pass the time. They'll prefer quiet "standards" to "Heavy Metal" and will be quick to complain about drafts. They are often bullies, determined to exact due deference to their age which the younger help may be reluctant to offer. Their loneliness can often make them garrulous, too. The restaurateur must be able to deal with people at all stages of the vale of tears and laughter!

The young have plenty of money to spend these days. They are unpopular as customers, however, until they become "Yuppies" because they tend to be rude, larcenous, highly demanding (because it sounds so clever to ask for something special), noisy, and poor tippers. Television and fashion magazines assure them that today's youth own the world, and many of them have accepted this doctrine with pleasure. Junk food and carbohydrates are what they crave, not haute cuisine, and blasting disco music will attract them in droves.

MIXED BUSINESSES

It's sometimes possible to combine two businesses in one. You can build a full-fledged boutique round an ice cream parlor so that, after finishing their meal, customers may be prevailed upon to part with a little more cash for an obscene T-shirt, a stuffed elephant, or a clever card.

These restaurants, on the whole, are best left to big restaurant groups who are in a better position to take risks and make mistakes. New restaurateurs would do well to consider such ventures carefully. Twenty years' work was wiped out in six months recently when, in a classic case of wildly speculative overextension, a 12-unit chain went bankrupt with an expensive new operation near New York's Times Square. For reasons much debated, but never established, the venture never showed a ghost of a chance of succeeding. A possible explanation, fanciful though it may seem, is that the chosen building was one of those "black holes" where nothing ever succeeds. Some locations just won't make it. But it's possible that the "Yuppie chic" ambiance, with beautiful young male models as waiters, was simply wrong for an area largely populated by tourists and pornographers! No one can really afford to make mistakes, but some can afford it better than others, and accidents will happen.

ALCOHOL AND LICENSING

An important basic decision to be made is whether or not you intend to serve beer, wines, and spirits. You almost certainly will. You don't have to, but if you don't, you'll relinquish enormous profits. If you do, you'll need a general liquor license, or a beer and wine license, from your State Liquor Authority.

Such licenses can take several months to obtain. The day you wonder whether you're ready to open a restaurant is the day you should check your local licensing situation and the required procedure for obtaining an alcohol license. While there are some safe generalities, there are also some extraordinary exceptions, and you'd better be aware of them Day One! Some states are either dry or extremely quirky. In liberal New York, getting a license is usually pretty easy. In neighboring New Jersey, the number of licenses is limited to a certain number per capita. New licenses have to be approved not only by the State Liquor Authority but by city officials.

Jurisdiction of the sale of alcohol is a matter for the State Liquor Authority, not the federal government. All states keep a close eye on liquor transactions, for obvious reasons, and any query or impediment to your application can cause a lengthy delay. In most states, liquor deliveries may *not* be paid for COD. An account must be rendered, and payment must be made by check or money order. Also, certain structural conditions have to be met where alcohol is served, of which the most common, important, and expensive is the requirement for restrooms.

There are lawyers who specialize in obtaining licenses, and since most restaurateurs will need such services from time to time, this can be part of their duty *ab initio*—from the beginning. These lawyers can speed things up, but as is well known, it is often in the interests of a lawyer to slow things down, so that he can submit a larger bill. A price for the service should be agreed upon in advance, whenever possible.

It should be emphasized that you don't have to have a lawyer to obtain a license, in the same way that you don't have to have a lawyer to handle probate when you buy a house. But life is short, and once the decision is made to get into business, there is an urgent need to get going. Money's going out or is tied up.

The cost of a three-year alcohol license for on-premises consumption of beer, wines, and spirits ranges from a national high of $5,100 plus $100 filing fee in Manhattan to $3,600 plus $100 filing fee in Staten Island, and all the way down to giveaway prices in some western states. The license must be prominently displayed. Look for it near the entrance of the next licensed restaurant you visit!

You'll also need a business license, again a state matter. This is simply a matter of getting the appropriate forms from your local City Hall, filling them out, getting them notarized, and handing them in. It's unlikely to cost you more than $40 anywhere in the country. But, as in all such matters, if you don't get it absolutely right the first time, you may find yourself wasting a lot of time on getting the correct forms, deciding what kind of business you have, and all the rest of it. Eventually you may wish to become a corporation. At that point, you really would do well to find a lawyer.

INSURANCE

By law, you are required to be insured against damage to your customers. A comprehensive agreement will cover this, as well as the risk of your being sued for damage caused by alcohol served on your premises. Employees are generally covered by workmen's compensation if you are correctly registered with the state authorities and have prominently displayed a notice to that effect. But occasional special suits from damaged employees are not uncommon, and you may wish to specially insure against them. A typical example was a waitress who decided to sue her boss because she broke a tooth on a pretzel (by no means uncommon!). The matter was settled when the restaurateur agreed to settle her dentist's bill.

In the age of the $600 raincoat and the $50,000 fur, you may wish to insure against loss of such items. But if you don't want to, you don't have to. If you don't, you should prominently display a notice to this effect (Not responsible for goods, clothes, or chattels left in this restaurant, etc.). If you sell your cloakroom concession to an outsider (a not uncommon practice), you may find that they will refuse to accept furs. This may suit proud owners, who are loath to check them anyway, but who can crowd the dining room terribly. Some restaurants simply don't have cloakrooms. This works well sometimes, except that on rainy days, the dining room can be a sorry sight with dripping coats and umbrellas everywhere. High class restaurants have spacious, properly insured cloakrooms. The cost of this useful luxury, of course, finds its echoes in the menu prices.

TAXES

All businesses are liable to tax, but the system of collection varies slightly from state to state. You are required by law to keep records, and you will be accorded an employer's number that validates the W2 forms you issue to your employees at the end of the tax year.

This is such a potential source of time-consuming work that almost every restaurateur in the world employs an accountant to take care of it. They know what it's all about, save you lots of ulcers, and— *mirabile dictu*—are not terribly expensive. The reason for this, quite simply, is that what looks to you like a solid weekend of ulcer-making grind is easy to them because they know what they're doing. Also, the tax authorities are happier talking to accountants. They have their jargon and their accepted rules of combat. They get their work done faster by talking to professionals.

PRICING

Deciding the price range of your menu, bar, and wine list is important. Initially, your prices will relate directly to the overheads and outgoings you anticipate. If your rent is $15,000 a month, and you only seat 50, you probably won't make it if your most expensive entree is a $5 chicken pot pie. Despite the attractiveness of the price, you just haven't got the capacity to feed enough customers to cover your expenses and overheads.

Fortunately, pricing is one factor that is easily changeable. Sometimes a restaurateur may feel that the only way to attract business is to undercut the local competition, and there's a lot to be said for this. In a busy neighborhood that has three restaurants and draws its customers from one or two central sources, word gets around. It's amazing how even a small reduction in price can improve business.

On the other hand, there are consumers who simply don't care what they spend if they get what they want. This small but happy band tends to congregate in the major cities, however, and many budding restaurateurs find themselves, willy-nilly, hoping to establish themselves in other areas, trimming their sails to the prevailing market wind.

Certainly, a close awareness of what other restaurants in the chosen category are charging and serving is essential to competitive operation. You will soon learn the true meaning of phrases like "what the traffic will bear" and "price resistance."

If the restaurateur is largely dependent upon neighborhood business, she will do well to establish a friendly atmosphere, maintain consistent standards, and offer good value. Some might think "good value" a contradiction in terms, or even an oxymoron, since a diner who wants a steak doesn't have to pay $12 for it! But in the consumer society, everyone is trained to consume and has an idea of what to expect for prices in the context of restaurants.

Regular diners-out, especially those who are spending their own money as opposed to the company's, often like to have a rough idea of how much they're going to have to spend. A restaurant will register in their minds as a place where, say, lunch for two with a couple of drinks and the tip will cost about $30. It's a good idea to have a quick selection from the menu as a price guide to offer over the telephone as an example of what customers are in for, should they ask—which they often do. A testy "We have a large menu with all sorts of different prices. It depends on what you have" is not positive selling. A common complaint in all areas of retail is the difficulty of getting a simple response to the question "How much?"

Some restaurants make things easier by having a wide range of prices, so that it's possible to have a light lunch for quite little or a slap-up dinner for rather more. A sad aspect of this civilized view of life is that waitresses can sometimes become disgruntled by customers who aren't spending enough as they take up valuable table space, especially during the busy two-hour lunch period, which suddenly ends, leaving an empty restaurant. It can be a bit daunting to see your best table, that cosy corner for four, occupied by three who are sharing a salad and a bowl of soup, and taking their time about it!

Since tips are figured on a percentage basis, one might see their point, but appearances are deceiving. As has been said, tips average out uncannily, rough with smooth. But often, waiters will administer a cold bum's rush to small spenders, and you certainly won't acquire a regular customer in this way.

There is something to be said, however, at the lower price range of the restaurant business for making it quite clear to customers that they can spend as much or as little as they want and still get the same cheerful service. The person who regularly spends $2 will occasionally come in and spend $20.

Naturally, there will always be a few customers who exploit such tolerance. From a waiter's point of view, $2 trips to the kitchen can be as arduous as $20 trips, with the irritating prospect of small reward. Perhaps this is a situation where restaurateurs can turn a blind eye, while their waitresses administer the bum's rush to a time and money waster!

One of the luxuries of writing about the restaurant business is that one need never fear appearing somewhat contradictory. It's a contradictory business! As in French grammar, there are almost as many exceptions to the rules as there are rules. Indeed, learning the "language" of the restaurant business is mainly what it's all about, as in banking, aviation, or anything else. And every language student knows that there comes a time when the books just don't help you anymore. You have to get out there and talk.

WHO ARE THE CUSTOMERS?

It doesn't take computers or Harvard MBA market researchers to work out who the customers are for a restaurant. The location and nature of the neighborhood usually define the clientele. A restaurant opposite a hospital will attract customers from it. The sheer presence of people, the coming and going of patients and visitors, provides a business opportunity. Average income will affect prices. The strange hours worked by some shifts may provide an opportunity for very early or very late business. Meat and fish market workers, for example, are famous for their inverted lives. Because they work by night, they often feel like a drink and dinner at six in the morning, and there are usually restaurants to accommodate them.

In the suburbs or country, where customers drive to the restaurant, the specific attractions of the restaurant will determine the kind of crowd that comes. The parking arrangements will be as important as the kitchen! Spaghetti and meatballs at cheerful prices will bring in the young families for an outing on weekends. But where's the Tuesday night business going to come from?

Many restaurants suffer from a feast or famine pattern of business. Wall Street restaurants boom at lunchtime, but die at night. Restaurants of all kinds will normally reckon to do most of their business on Fridays and Saturdays. When competition is fierce, and customers are limited in number, the restaurateur must twist and turn to bring customers in on the other five days and nights.

Established restaurants assume private patterns. Some restaurants always do well on rainy days, while others curse the weather. Monday can be a big day, while Saturdays are dead for many city restaurants.

It's important for new restaurateurs to grit their teeth and accept that some days will be busier than others. Freddie Mills, a world champion boxer of the 1950s, opened a nightclub in London after he retired from the ring. One day he turned up at the joint and asked the doorman how many people were inside. "Two or three," he was told. "Oh my God!" cried Freddie. A few minutes later he was found dead in his car, having shot himself.

The weekly average is the significant figure. Weather, holidays, and TV programs can play havoc with expectations.

Business people who pay by credit card and charge their expenses to the company are by far the most preferred customers in the industry. At the top end of this section is a small group which simply doesn't care how much it spends in restaurants. This is the $150 a head area, which is so rarified that it hardly concerns the average would-be restaurateur. Any restaurateur undertaking such an enterprise must have nothing left to learn, because the risks—which are precisely due to the inflexibility of an "up market operation"—are great. Having to call Italy at four in the morning to get the latest price on white truffles can pall, too.

Fortunately, the restaurateur has to appeal to the great American middle class. This includes youngsters enjoying a vigorous social life and oldsters who have to keep a close eye on expenses. Professional couples giving a spouse a break from kitchen chores can be good customers, too. In recent years the appearance of these couples sometimes known as DINKS (Dual Income No Kids) has boosted the number of those who regularly dine out. A couple who've been workaholicking all day will prefer to dine out, rather than run that dreaded "extra lap"—the chore of preparing the evening meal. The intense desirability of attracting such customers to your restaurant speaks for itself.

The closer a restaurant is to a city center or tourist attraction, the greater the likelihood of a bustling passing trade. To attract the custom of people who will pass your way only once (but may recommend you to visiting friends), it's important to be in clear view and to display a menu. Who hasn't strolled along a street lined with restaurants, looking at the menus, checking out the fare and, most important, the prices? In French resorts, restaurants clearly display the set menu for 20 francs, the menu for 40 francs, and so on, so it's easy for potential customers to make up their minds.

In the country, almost everyone who goes to a restaurant will drive some distance to it. In cities, with restaurants on almost every block, it will often be absolutely necessary to attract customers from outside the neighborhood. To do this, there must be some advertising and promotion.

In France, astonishing though it may seem, it has been statistically demonstrated that 68% of the population *never* visit a restaurant. Outside Paris, where distances and commuting are less of a problem, many workers go home for lunch. Most factories have subsidized cafeterias, as do most universities and schools—often of enormous size.

No research exists in the United States to reveal how many people never go to restaurants. But one third of the population never drinks alcohol, and despite the exhortations of the advertising industry, a majority of houses in America do not contain one drop of alcohol. People go out on the town to drink.

They also go out to talk business, to celebrate, to exchange views, to seduce, and not infrequently to eat. There has never been more disposable income available than there is today, and every inhabitant of the United States is a potential restaurant customer.

But a restaurant has to do more than supply the means for the consumption of fat, protein, and carbohydrate if it wants to pack 'em in and make money!

RAISING
THE
WIND

START-UP MONEY:
HOW TO GET IT

Avid readers of business magazines—and every budding business person should be an avid reader—will often find themselves confused, as they read the exciting report of how some brilliant entrepreneur spotted a hole in the market, risked all, worked hard, and finally achieved success. An important question is often left unanswered: namely, where did the successful entrepreneur get the money to start the business, be it restaurant, flight simulator franchise, flea deterrent for household pets, or whatever? Buried in the text, this burning question is often answered with a glib facility which helps no one. "With a million dollar loan from her father-in-law" or "using the idle resources of his existing factories" are common phrases.

This doesn't really help the person who wants to get started in business, except to illustrate that an awful lot of the competition is way ahead before he or she even starts. Some business people will go so far as to say that getting the start-up money is the hardest part of any enterprise, since the economy of the western world is growing constantly, and all you have to do is not get it terribly wrong, as distinct from getting it absolutely right.

Inheritance

Most wealth is inherited. This is a simple fact of life. This doesn't refer only to Rockefellers but to everybody. The single biggest purchase most people ever make is a home. Death of parents and the proceeds from the subsequent sale of their house is usually the largest sum of money most people will ever see. The cash generated by this inevitable event is often enough to enable an inheritor to consider investing her money in a business.

The family is the most common resource for restaurant start-up money. Many restaurants are inherited—there are family hierarchies that do nothing else, especially in France. Sometimes the inheritors are totally ignorant of the restaurant business, but they know a gold mine when they see one and decide to continue with it. As employers, such people have an appalling reputation! Their resentful amateur eye is never on the doughnut but always on the hole, and they rarely trust anyone—customers or employees. Where the inheritor has grown up in the business, however, happiness often reigns. Family-run restaurants, especially on the continent of Europe, enjoy the best reputations.

There's nothing to stop anyone marrying money or marrying a restaurateur.

Savings

Since wages and tips in busy restaurants are good, many people are able to go into business on the strength of their savings, with perhaps some help from the bank or partners. A hard-working waitress in a busy restaurant can easily earn $400 a week at the age of 23. If she lives inexpensively and has no hobby or interests outside her job—which is commonly the case—in ten years she may have saved $100,000.

This may not be enough to open a 50-seater licensed restaurant, but it's certainly a respectable amount of money to show to a bank manager or to potential partners. If she then marries a waiter with equal savings and similar ambitions, and they take their joint savings to the bank, they will be in an excellent position for getting a loan, if they require one, in order to set up shop.

A large number of restaurants are started by such people. They're often well qualified. Sometimes their view of the world and getting on with people may be a bit stunted, and restaurant work isn't renowned for bringing out charm in people. But they'll have a deep-rooted feel for how a place should be run, and that's a bonus. They can always hire someone with personality to "front" the place.

Bank Loans

Bob Hope defined a bank as a place that will lend you money, as long as you can show them that you don't need it. Someone else compared a bank with a friend who lends you an umbrella, but wants it back as soon as it starts to rain.

In fact, the system by which banks lend money is pretty cut and dried, with only a small area in which bank officers can exercise judgment and advise superiors or the board that the entrepreneurial risks under consideration are worth taking.

Restaurants are considered a high-risk business. Even a proven track record of success in the industry will not always impress banks. They will require collateral, such as your house or any other asset you may have, before lending you money. One budding restaurateur was required to cash in stocks and shares to raise cash for the bank's approval. The restaurant foundered, but the stock went on to incredible heights.

Banks are reluctant to lend money to anyone who is leasing a property. They see no security for their money in a lease. Also, they usually will not lend money for the purchase of secondhand or leased equipment. They're often amenable to lending money to buy new equipment, however, for obvious reasons—the stuff probably has resale value.

Small Business Administration

These bureaus regard restaurants as high risk. But they may act as security for a bank loan if you can impress them with your experience and chances of success. If you're a war veteran or handicapped, they'll look upon you with an even kinder eye. They are federally funded.

Loan Shark

In every major city there are quiet, sincere loan sharks who'll lend money at rather steep interest to budding restaurateurs, for little or no security. Their service can lead to deep waters, and they should be avoided except by those who are adept and experienced in the art of dealing with such people.

PROS AND CONS
OF PARTNERSHIPS

References to owners in press and advertising often disguise the truth. As often as not, the "owner" whose beaming face shines from the advertisements owns only a small percentage of the business, but is paid a salary in addition to receiving a share of the profits. This owner's a "working partner."

Because the capital investment is so huge, and because life is so short, many would-be restaurateurs will contemplate going into business with a partner. It can be an embittering experience. It can also be a great success. A majority of restaurants are owned by more than one person, despite whatever impression may be given in advertising and press gossip.

Many restaurant workers want to own their own place. It's the obvious step at a certain point for an ambitious person. A very highly paid chef or maitre d' might be content with his earnings, but if not, the ceiling he inevitably reaches at some point may be frustrating. He'll want to go it alone, and he may have acquired a following over the years. While having a following can obviously do no harm to a new restaurant, it doesn't guarantee success. Customers like a change, but they won't always be willing to trek to a new and inconvenient location.

One of the clichés of the business is "nobody has enough friends to make a restaurant successful!" The oft-heard cry, "I was in advertising for 20 years—I know literally thousands of people, and they all know me!" is a common and sometimes wistful one. An abundance of friends, however, may well give a restaurateur a nucleus, and if she's smart, or if her friends give her restaurant a good report, she can build on that.

Restaurant employees with ambition should make sure they get around and talk a lot about their plans. Eventually they're bound to have enough contacts to find partners and put a team together. Some leave with the blessing and a helpful loan from their employers—as long as there's no question of a swift transference of customer loyalty! One bartender was slightly disgruntled when he was suddenly saddled with a partner who had talked the boss into allowing him to work with no pay, simply in order to learn the ropes. He cheered up a little when he learned that his pupil wouldn't be taking a share of his tip cup. But, as it turned out, they got on well enough to proceed with a joint restaurant venture that was an enormous success.

Potential partners, perhaps more correctly referred to as investors, are often ignorant of the restaurant business. They will delude themselves that common sense is the best guide and that what they learned in Business 101 or Economics 102 will provide all the answers. But restaurants are quirky businesses.

However, they can hardly be blamed for their nervousness, as they are being called upon to part with that to which it's hard to say good-bye. Bold planning often makes them nervous. If you propose a family restaurant, then you'd better show a plenitude of the breed in the area and demonstrate that you'll need quite a few parents and children consuming items which, by their very nature, cannot command a high price to cover your inevitable overhead.

Potential investors and partners are most frequently made nervous by what appears to them to be an unsuitable location. "You want to open a restaurant on that street? But there are already six restaurants on the block!" they'll whine. It's up to you to evaluate the case. Maybe it's a good thing, because the area has a reputation as being a place where you have a choice of places to eat. Or maybe the area's saturated, and you risk getting lost in the wash.

Another disincentive can be the lack of other restaurants in the area! "Who the heck's going to come here for dinner? There aren't any other restaurants. Do other restaurateurs know something we don't know? No theater, no movies, no businesses."

When seeking partners you may find yourself caught in the age old dilemma. Which comes first, the discovery of the acceptable location or the raising of the money? You'll often find that potential investors and partners will agree in principle to go into business with you when you find what they consider a suitable premises. Sometimes, to your frustration, you'll find what you absolutely know to be a suitable premises which, unfortunately, doesn't appeal to your potential backers.

But, in fact, the necessity of coldly evaluating the suitability of premises serves as a useful and protective exercise. You really will have to think it through and be able to present a solid case for opening a business. Not only will you have to convince yourself and your spouse. You'll have to convince people who are highly suspicious of the scheme's viability.

Multi-Partner Restaurants

Some restaurants have 25 or more partners. Some are silent, while others operate the restaurant and draw a salary as well as a percentage of the overall profit. In California and New York, where show biz, restaurants, and real estate are almost merged, there are several restaurants owned by show biz people who come and go as workers, according to the vagaries of their careers. Such restaurants afford a lot of fun—to their owners, at least! Unfortunately, few have ever proved truly successful. There's a lack of focus and continuity. Faces change, and varying degrees of efficiency cause the service and quality to vary uncomfortably, too.

Too many fingers in the pie can lead to a general dilution of effort. Sometimes it's by no means clear who's in charge. There are often employees who will take advantage of this kind of situation in order to carve out their own little niche. This ensures that they make a profit but will do no good to the business as a whole. That's the principle of divide and conquer.

A disagreeable aspect of the restaurant business for many is the use of authority. All businesses require figures of authority, but somehow this is more apparent in restaurants. Authority is only palatable when it is quite clear who's in charge, and that person exerts authority in a cheerful, acceptable manner.

Partnership Disasters

Sadly, the worst partnership disaster is probably the most common: one partner runs away with the takings! It happens all the time, and such is the flow, flux, and anonymity of American life that the thieves usually get away with it. Some make a profession of it, moving from city to city, and suburb to suburb for years, looking for suckers.

No matter how formally and precisely the agreements are drawn up with a lawyer, if the cash has disappeared, getting it back will always be a problem. Obviously, when you are choosing a partner, the lawyer who was a college classmate or the man who's owned the local gas station for the last 20 years is likely to prove a better bet than the nice character from California whose past is misty, but who is so obviously a regular guy that you can only assume it's been a clean and happy one.

Con Artists

Don't think it can't happen to you. The restaurant business abounds with them. The con artist's usual props are good clothes, a ready smile, a deep compassion for the human race in general, and a ludicrously sentimental attachment (to which they will readily confess, wiping away a furtive, uncontrollable tear) to kids and dogs. Not uncommonly they'll actually *have* a spouse, two super kids, and a dog which they'll trail around as zealously as a detective with a pipe in an old-fashioned mystery thriller. Without being in the least bit sanctimonious, or holier than thou, they'll reveal a deep moral commitment, coupled with a sad contempt for the cynical superficiality of most people today.

Nothing's ever overlooked. They'll work long hours, never be late, and never be too proud to bus a table when the place is busy. "Let's get some turnover here!" they'll say sharply. Occasionally, a faintly reproving brief frown will appear as they insist on some minor but apparently important point. And you'll hear about the horror you've just been saved from. They're pros and have seen it all. With such figures at the helm, how can anything go wrong?

Then, suddenly, the money's gone, and they're gone, too—lock, stock, and barrel. A call to their mother in Seattle will get you nowhere. Her child hasn't been heard from in years.

Working and "Sleeping" Partners

Another part of the minefield features two partners who actually operate the restaurant, while the other partners hope for a return on their investment. The "sleeping" partners will come to the restaurant regularly, often bringing friends to show off the place and help build business. But then they realize that, though the place is a roaring success, they're not getting a very good dividend.

They demand to see the books. These are duly produced. It then transpires that the working partners' expenses include season tickets to the opera, yacht and golf club subscriptions, and so on. These are all plausibly explained under the general heading of public relations. But the two Porsches? Well, you have to drive to work in the morning, right? And what about this extraordinary bill for uniforms? Well, yes, the working partner's tailored clothes are sort of buried in there, too, but heck, they have to look the part!

In other words, those who are actually handling the incoming cash are in the best position to use it. Again, the only way to prevent this kind of exploitation is to have the agreements cut and dried before the bonanza begins.

When this sort of confrontation comes to court, as is not uncommon, the IRS takes a friendly interest. In fact, all parties concerned can hope to be accorded a special little niche on the IRS computer which will ensure close attention at all times—forever.

Friendships

Relationships between former friends can deteriorate alarmingly. Sometimes the feuds between partners become public knowledge. Actor Michael Caine and restaurateur Peter Langan owned a relentlessly advertised London restaurant for society swingers and would-be swingers (who naturally far outnumber the truly qualified brethren). These two gentlemen publicly abused one another's reputations. According to the local gossip columns, these epithets went along the lines of "He's a mediocrity with halitosis" and "He's a 24-hour-a-day drunk"—all nice, grown-up stuff (*New York Post*, page 6, Thursday, May 12, 1988). Whether it increased business or not is a fact known only to their accountants. It is totally possible that a significant number of potential customers, alerted to the fact that a visit to the restaurant might enable them to touch the hem of Caine's jacket, would grab their wallets, call up their friends, and go over. With luck, the great men might condescend to start a verbal battle before their very eyes. But what any of this has to do with food is anybody's guess.

PARTNERSHIP SUCCESSES

Happily, success is by no means uncommon for restaurant partnerships if the participants have some experience of business generally, or of the restaurant business specifically, are keen to make money, and are prepared to work hard to get it. Partners often find each other from the rank and file of the industry. Waitresses marry bartenders, pool their savings, and go to it.

Sometimes matches are made in heaven, where the owner of a successful flower shop, a butcher's shop, and a laundry becomes friendly with a local actor who wants to put her earnings to commercial use. They dovetail in blissfully. The practical business side is managed by one partner, while the mystical elements are provided by the other.

Those matches, which are forged upon the anvil of necessity, are less likely to result in wedded bliss. But as long as the partners are talking civilly, there's always hope.

The restaurant business particularly attracts people who are cursed with a burning certainty that, if only the management will do *this*, all problems will be resolved. In this context, there is only one problem under discussion—the need to bring in customers. When a convinced amateur meets a worried professional, the atmosphere can sour swiftly. And sometimes, the injection of money into new formats and advertising won't solve the problem either.

Perhaps the best recipe for a successful partnership is the same as the traditional one for a happy marriage: "Before marriage you should keep your eyes wide open. After marriage, you should keep them half shut."

An Ideal Marriage?

One well-known operator inherited a restaurant from his father, which he promptly destroyed through hopeless mismanagement. He then did the same to five more businesses. Even his father's reputation (they were a fine old Long Island Italian family) would no longer inspire people's confidence in him. At last, he got a couple of lawyers with money to burn, who decided they'd like a restaurant. At about the same time, Our Hero married the executive editor of a popular illustrated magazine. Four pages of luscious pictures and praise in the magazine, representing thousands of dollars worth of advertising space, but presented as editorial feature material (as so much advertising is), soon saw him on the path to glory. Alas, the building had a short lease and was eventually demolished. The marriage lasted only a little while longer.

FINANCIAL PLANNING

Some restaurants are crowded from the day they open, but most need to acquire patronage over a period of time. The rule of thumb is that restaurateurs should have enough money to cover all overheads for a year, assuming no profits whatsoever. The business picture usually emerges a lot sooner than that, however, and it would be unusual to see a failing business taking a whole year before changing its operation or closing down! Few restaurateurs will undertake the risks involved unless they're pretty certain that there's business to be done.

A reminder: Running out of operating funds before the business goes into profit is one of the *prime reasons* for failure. It's simply no good trusting to luck—the competition is too fierce. The degree to which you're prepared to gamble your money and that of others must be finely gauged.

In observing the industry at large, it's apparent that the more a place twists and turns for new gimmicks to get people in, the shorter the time before it suddenly isn't there anymore. The business is fickle, and it isn't as easy as it looks. But ordinary rules of business common sense apply quite a lot of the time.

Certain expenses or overheads are inescapable and must be paid every month. These are often referred to as the "nut." Once they're paid, some of the cash coming in will be profit. The number of weeks you calculate you can pay this nut, without any recourse to the income you may or may not have is the number of weeks you have to make it.

Rent is usually the largest sum to be paid, except where the restaurateur is blessed with ownership of the building. The next biggest bill is usually the meat bill, followed by produce, alcoholic beverages, general groceries, and fish. The nice thing about these bills is that the bigger they get, the more you must be selling, so in one sense, the bigger the better!

Payroll is a regular overhead. The chef is usually the highest paid employee in the operation, where the owner is also the manager. Where a general manager, as distinct from an assistant manager, is employed, his or her salary will often approach that of the chef. If a figurehead hostess is employed, who might be a local celebrity with a following, she might be paid quite highly, depending on whether or not she receives tips. If she is supposed to be too much of an executive to accept tips, then she will need more salary. One well-known and successful restaurant employs the retired maitre d' from one of the most famous ocean liners and pays him the princely sum of $50 a night. He gets tips and eats as well as the chef allows him. Thus, after a plate of chicken wings and yesterday's leftover rice, he spends the evening recommending gourmet delights. Porters, dishwashers, and chef's helpers usually get minimum wage, with a bit more if they help the chef to prepare food.

Waiters, waitresses, and busboys are generally paid the legal minimum, since the bulk of their income is from tips. Bartenders are usually paid a little more on the grounds that their tips are somewhat less than the others. Every restaurant has a different situation. In some, the bartenders do little but prepare the drinks—they're more a "service bar" than a "front bar." Sometimes they get a kickback, sometimes the house pays them a bit extra.

Staff can be increased or decreased at will. Few employees in the restaurant industry have any kind of contract, except occasionally the chef. Some are protected by unions, which guarantee minimum wages and conditions.

When tax is withheld, paychecks for employees who must declare their tips are often very small. So the fact that a restaurateur employs, say, ten people may seem a bit daunting at first, but when you consider the minimal paychecks most of them are getting, it doesn't look so bad!

Bills

Some of the bills the restaurateur may have to pay after actually opening for business are as follows:

> Rent of premises
> Rent of some equipment
> Meat
> Beer
> China and glassware
> Wine
> Cutlery
> Liquor
> Sodas
> Produce and fruit
> Payroll and taxes
> Fish
> Cheese, cakes, desserts
> General groceries
> Straws, sipsticks, cocktail napkins, etc.
> Matches
> Linen (or paper equivalent)

Uniforms

Insurance (several kinds)

Accountant

Lawyer

Office supplies and expenses

Stationery

Computer hardware

Telephone

Printer (menus, etc.)

Advertising, publicity, promotion

Liquor license, business license

Garbage pick-up

TV, musicians, entertainment

Flowers and plants

Exterminator

Knife sharpener

Light bulbs

Equipment repairs and maintenance

Electricity

Gas

Bathroom supplies

Cleaning materials

The "Go" Position

"More haste, less speed" sometimes applies, but for the restaurateur with limited funds it's *essential* to get into business as soon as the means are available. "We opened too soon" is a common accusatory cry. But most restaurateurs will agree that about five minutes after you are able to serve a hot hamburger and a cold beer, your welcoming doors should be wide open.

You are in the position of an advancing unit that *must* secure a certain landing field before it has any hope of resupply. Your money is going out from Day 1. Your customers are your resupply.

Foreclosure

In the unhappy event that the operation fails, or even if "the operation is a success but the patient dies," it's possible the following notices will be prominently posted in the window.

MARSHALL'S NOTICE OF IMPENDING LEVY AND SALE

Civil Court of the County of Turkeyburger.

J. X. Doe, Marshall

Plaintiff

v

Outtaluck Inc.

By virtue of an Execution issued out of the above Court to me directed and delivered: PLEASE TAKE NOTICE that I have this day LEVIED upon and will expose for SALE at PUBLIC AUCTION, all the right, title, and interest, which the defendant had on this day, or at any time thereafter, in and to the following described chattels, sufficient to satisfy the execution together with the Marshall's fees and expenses.

INVENTORY

Entire contents of restaurant, bar, disco, club, including all kitchen equipment, refrigerators, stoves, tables, chairs, glassware, bar counters, piano, electronic equipment, workbenches, ice machines, bar stools, cash registers, speakers, videos, desks, cabinets, washbasins, vacuum cleaners, racks, and lighting systems.

Pay in full 48 hours before sale. Date of sale will be advertised at your expense. Execution and fees: $99,999 plus expenses and interest.

A further sad note may say:

The landlord has possession of these premises pursuant to a Warrant of Eviction issued by one of the judges of the Civil Court. For information, contact landlord.

You may come across such notices in the boarded-up windows of failed restaurants as you search for premises. Some premises seem to spend as much time boarded up as they spend open for business! In one such building on New York's Columbus Avenue, where no less than four restaurants had failed within 12 months, the new owner put up a notice saying:

REWARD

$250 reward for the person who comes up with a name for the new neighborhood restaurant.

Underneath, a cruel wag had scrawled "How about Ad Nauseam?"

Columbus Avenue is to the restaurant industry what the battlefield of the Somme was to the British Army in World War I—a graveyard of ambition and hope. Notices read in its bombed-out premises should be seen as fair warning but taken in stride, like corpses seen by infantrymen as they make their way up the line to battle. Business is a form of war, and there are casualties.

"The wise can learn from a fool, but a fool learns from nobody." There is a certain amount of wisdom to be obtained by studying losers. But you'll do better to study the winners, like the 125-seater restaurant that has become a 1,300-seater grossing more than $30 million a year— Hilltop Steakhouse.

FRANCHISE

In the business section of your local library you should be able to find a book called *Franchise Opportunities*. A section of it deals with eating establishments. There are more than 200 restaurant franchise companies in the United States. **WARNING:** Not all of them are licensed to operate in all states. So don't start fantasizing about your own Casanova's Hickory Barn until you've ascertained that it can be operated in the area in which you wish to do business.

When you buy a franchise, you buy identity. In the privacy of your soul, this may be what you truly seek in opening a business of your own. Whose identity do you want? If you find your brow puckering, welcome to the club. Franchise does have that effect. Some work tremendously. Some are disasters.

But, while franchise may not immediately appeal to your Rick-like dreams, it is certainly worth considering. After all, you could cut your teeth on a franchise and then go on to greater things. There's no reason why you shouldn't imbue your Casanova's Hickory Barn with your own inimitable touch. They may supply you with fluorescent salad dressing, but there's no reason why you shouldn't concoct one of your own. Of course, that fluorescent salad dressing may be the one thing your patrons seek, after having encountered it on a blissful Miami vacation.

Why are there such things as franchises? Let's say, a clever cook invents a machine that makes hot, crisp mango-bangos, which sell at a terrific rate and profit, especially to the background of tango music and Walt Disney designs on the walls. Unfortunately, the inventor can't be everywhere, so others are allowed to spread the gospel. They must find their own premises and pay the rent, and in return, they are allowed to imitate the inventor's brilliance. In return they receive up to ten weeks of training, advice, and possibly some equipment, with regular counseling from corporate managers, etc.

You can buy a deli and sandwich franchise for $7,500, a pizza place for $70,000, a Roy Rogers for $150,000–$170,000, or a "Tony Roma's: A Place for Ribs" for $415,000. It should be noted that, even in New York, you might be able to get your *own* doors open for $400,000, if you were lucky in your choice of premises. But do you want to cling to the coattails of Casanova? Or do you want to be yourself?

A warning note is struck by the fact that few franchise companies offer any financial assistance. "Never spend your own money" is a favorite maxim for some entrepreneurs, and while its wisdom is obvious, so are its limitations. They'll offer you advice, such as how to prepare the proposal to take to the bank when *you* apply for a loan. They want your money. You are in the position of someone who buys a secondhand car that may prove to be unsound. The dealer may put this right and that right and observe the warranty, if any. But, one thing the dealer won't do is buy the critter back.

Any business requires careful thought, and franchising can be very dangerous. There have been some casualties lately, especially at the cheaper end of the business. You'll do well to talk, observe and, above all, read the fine print of the contract until you understand every word.

Fred P. Ott's, Inc., P.O. Box 16000, 47th & Main Streets, Kansas City, Missouri 64112 (they are *not* registered in all states) franchise their bar and grill "pub-type" restaurants. They think you should be interested in joining them if:

■ You have some restaurant experience and have always wanted to have your own place.

■ You are an investor trying to involve someone else in the restaurant business (i.e., a parent looking to set up a son or daughter in an exciting venture, or a member of an investors group looking for a good place to invest your pooled funds).

◼ You are a restaurant manager who wants to be in business for yourself, but you cannot raise the capital required to open an independent operation. You know you could with a strong franchise relationship behind you, however.

◼ You are a real estate developer who wants a Fred P. Ott's as part of your project, and you are willing to hire the right person to manage the business for you.

FIVE

EQUIPMENT
AND
DECOR

EQUIPMENT—
OLD OR INHERITED

If you take over an existing restaurant, as is likely, you may inherit an amount of basic equipment. It isn't free; you paid for it. You may reject it, of course, in favor of new equipment of your own preference. But you may still have to pay for it. There are considerable savings to be made from using inherited equipment, even though it may sometimes look depressingly old and decrepit and quite out of sympathy with your brave new hopes.

Many a restaurant boasts a shiny Espresso machine bought sec-ondhand ten years ago, still going strong, having paid for itself several times over and yielding a handsome profit ever since. This is increas-ingly a good profit item, even though making espresso and cappucino is a difficult job, unpopular with the waiters and waitresses. Brand-new machines can be expensive.

A practical eye is required. A deep-freeze is a deep-freeze, as long as it works, whether it's brand-new or 20 years old. A refrigerated storage room, called the "walk-in box," is a standard requirement and, again, if it's serviceable, why replace it at considerable expense? In this age of disposable items, where there's always pressure from suppliers to replace existing equipment with new, a lot of bargains are overlooked.

Any old refrigeration equipment that proves unreliable and beyond cheap local repair, however, should be replaced promptly. A breakdown on a Friday night could result in a great deal of wasted food—including expensive items such as shrimp, lobster, and fish—by the time the mechanic arrives on Monday morning. You may discover that the comforting words *24-hour service* don't really mean much after all, as you encounter the disembodied voice on the answering machine, or the harrassed manager who isn't quite sure where the repairman is, but will have him call the minute he shows up. Servicemen don't come cheap, either.

The standard gas range with its large oven, gas burners, and grill is another item often inherited, and science has done little to improve the basic design since it was invented. They can get very dirty, but that's often the only problem. Some would say the older the better, because they're made more solidly. There's a French proverb, *On fait de bonne soupe dans une veille marmite* (You can make good soup in an old pot), but this proverb is rarely used in connection with culinary matters!

The budding restaurateur with no flair for mechanics or machinery should try to have as a friend someone who really understands refrigerators, air conditioners, pipes, toilets, stoves, gas, and electronics. Salvaging dilapidated equipment is part of the folklore of the restaurant business. "I took one look at that beat-up old refrigerator and my heart sank. Then Joe looked at it, and poked around. He discovered that all it needed was a new part and a good clean and it worked perfectly."

Your equipment must relate to the kind of business you envisage. A new owner on New York's famed Columbus Avenue, where restaurants are many but satisfied diners are few, solemnly hoped to feed a seating capacity of 80 people from a three-ring stove. A really sharp chef with a limited menu designed for speed could do it, but this place couldn't. Its menu featured items that simply take time to cook, such as duck and fish *en papillotte* (fish cooked in paper). It flopped, in spite of its brilliant corner location, and soon became a French sweater store.

NEW EQUIPMENT

Brand-new equipment is the most expensive kind. The bank will be more inclined to lend you money for new equipment, but you'll pay top price. Sometimes equipment can be leased. Any of the dozens of restaurant industry newspapers will tell you where equipment can be obtained. Companies are also listed in the phone book.

In the New York-Connecticut-New Jersey-Pennsylvania area, for instance, the *Restaurant Exchange News* (P.O. Box 473, New City, New York 10956) will show you where you can obtain everything from cutting boards to full bar and kitchen installations and printed menus. *The Food Service Product News* (Young/Conway Publications, 104 Fifth Avenue, New York, New York 10011) advertises products from all over the country.

If you obtain permission to convert a premises for restaurant use, you'll have to start from scratch, and the cost can be daunting. But if you are prepared to put in time searching, there are restaurant equipment bargains galore to be obtained. As we saw in the grim example of the Marshall's Notice, restaurants do sometimes fail, and their equipment is often sold. "It's an ill wind that blows nobody any good!"

By telephoning around and checking local newspapers, you can soon discover the local situation. The newspaper advertising department can steer you in the right direction, and you may be amazed by the low prices. Available equipment can range from a complete carved wooden bar to enough cutlery to feed the five thousand.

Remember that there's constant wastage through breakage and souvenir stealing, so that a bargain price on 100 ashtrays may be a good deal, even if your restaurant only needs 30 to cover every table and the bar. You'll use them all eventually.

A word to the wise: When an interesting sale of restaurant equipment is in the offing, the word goes out way ahead of time. If you live in a major city, you must understand that there's a whole network of people with ears permanently close to the ground. They live to open restuarants. They have no other plans in life. So the sales are often rigged, or the best items are siphoned off discreetly before the advertised day of the sale.

The other small point—which can be a nightmare—is that the purchaser is responsible for the prompt removal of the goods. This means a truck and helpers to carry the stuff. It also means you'll need someplace to store it. Storage can be expensive, as can truck rental. And if you think you can get a garage in the suburbs at short notice, you may be in for a shock.

Again, we are back to the importance of planning ahead. Ideally, the painting and refurbishing of your premises should be finished on the day of the sale. Thus, one stage of setting up the restaurant neatly dovetails into the next, with minimum loss of time and minimum expenditure. Sometimes you'll be lucky!

If you're not, and you have to store your newly-acquired bargain equipment at your premises, you'll just have to work around it until you get to the point where you can put it where it belongs.

A lot of ingenuity goes into making cheap things look quite expensive, and, except in deluxe restaurants, most people don't expect to dine off classic china using heavy silver cutlery. The bent fork is a common sight in many restaurants. But, if you propose to charge $3 or more for a glass of white wine, the glass shouldn't look too cheap. And there is currently a heavy emphasis on visual presentation of food. As the current wisecrack has it, "When I looked at the food on my plate, I didn't know whether to eat it or frame it!"

THE WONDERFUL WORLD OF LAUNDRY

Many restaurateurs are inclined to wax both lyrical and mystical on the subject of laundry costs. Why this bill should hurt any more than any of the others is a mystery, but it seems to. It can be an irritatingly large weekly bill. There are laundry services that supply everything from cooks' aprons, pants, jackets, and white hats to tablecloths, dish mops, napkins, and towels. A cliché of the industry is the sight of the owner solemnly taking home a bag of restaurant laundry to wash at home.

A clean, white tablecloth does have a nice appeal, as does a colored and checkered one. Linen napkins add a touch of luxury. Humbert Humbert, the main character of Nabokov's *Lolita*, a bit of a snob who'd been brought up in a luxury hotel, pined for the "cool, rich linens of the Mirana Hotel" as he wiped his lips with pink paper! Using cork or paper coasters for wet-bottomed glasses can often give a tablecloth a sporting chance of being used again, as can an adroitly placed flower arrangement or ashtray. It can be a little dispiriting for customers, though, when a slight shift of the table arrangement reveals a nasty stain.

In expensive restaurants, you will notice that the waiters or waitresses, often have an elaborate drill for changing tablecloths and setting up the table again in an amazingly short time. The tablecloths are folded just so, for swift deployment, and the napkins are in place, too. If they don't do this quickly, they'll get a frown from the boss, and (this is what really spurs them) if a new party arrives without a reservation, the hostess looks round the room and seats the people at the table that's ready. It's called table turnover.

Sometimes customers are happy to wait until a table they prefer is made ready. Some tables are more attractive than others. Waiters are inclined to get the sulks when customers sit at dirty tables, as they are sometimes wont to do, because this makes the task of setting up more difficult. They adore disciplinary maitre d's who ask the customers to wait to one side until their preparation is complete. Many customers enjoy this, too. It's all part of the ritual choreography of the joyous experience. It gives them an opportunity to show how incredibly gracious and understanding they are, and it also provides an opportunity for them to gaze round the dining room to see if there's anyone there they know or would like to know.

Laundry Alternatives

Restaurateurs twist and turn to reduce their laundry bills. It's not unusual to find expensive fresh flowers in abundance with paper tablecloths and napkins. There's something inelegant about having great swathes of noisy paper unraveled before your very eyes. It's unlikely that many people ever notice this. But some will, and if these happen to be the kind of people whose custom you seek, then you'll do well to think long and hard about linen versus paper.

For casual dining, a happy compromise is often reached by having plastic, wood, or even marble tops, which can be easily wiped clean—often with the help of a little discreet and judicious spillage from a water glass by the busperson. If the napkin provided is of high quality, absorbent paper, and if it's emblazoned with the restaurant's logo, this can be effectively attractive and inexpensive, too. For full effect, a flower in a Coca-Cola or Perriér bottle will do the trick.

All of these considerations are reflected in the restaurant's prices. Any potential diner knows perfectly well that if, on pressing her nose to the windowpane, she sees dazzling white tablecloths, then she'd better be ready to dig deep into her pocket. City dwellers are often driven crazy when their out-of-town friends ask to be directed to a "not-too-expensive white tablecloth restaurant."

DECOR

For the modest fee of $75,000, Gigi de Frabazonia will fly in from Rome and design for you a unique restaurant which may, or may not, be so enchanting that people will come just to see it, and the heck with the food. However, it's possible to put together a perfectly acceptable restaurant without spending too much money on decor.

A simple theme is fun and can add charm to a place. There's no doubt that a chilled glass of dry sherry will taste better in a Spanish courtyard than in a plastic diner, just as a fine brandy tastes better from a snifter than from a styrofoam cup. With a little flair, miracles can be achieved.

There's nothing wrong with lining the dining room with Topolski originals, as at the Carlton Tower restaurant in London, or with Hollywood studio memorabilia, as at Maxwell's Plum in New York. It definitely adds to the pleasure of the dining experience, but it has to be paid for.

Some cynical diners believe that the difficulty of getting a slice of lemon for their fish or a large spoon for their soup is directly proportional to the emphasis placed on decor—and who's to say they're wrong? It is certainly irritating to a customer to note that, although the theme, logo, and ambiance have been carried through to the nth degree by a designer who has long since departed the premises, your white wine is warm and there's no mustard in the house.

Most food critics grade the restaurants they review in terms of food, ambiance, and service. Decor obviously affects ambiance. Design also affects service.

DESIGN

The object of all design in restaurants must be to provide the maximum delight to the customers, while efficiently serving as many customers as possible.

All restaurateurs juggle these three factors constantly. Some emphasize efficient service, others are big on ambiance, and others just crowd people in wherever they'll fit.

Hard though it may be to believe, many people like being crowded. Perhaps it gives them an illusion of being involved in some kind of group experience. It's common to see people standing in line to get into a crowded restaurant while disdaining the empty one next door, which is apparently just as attractive. It seems at least possible that many people prefer crowds to space. The higher up the market you go, in general, the more space the customer is allowed to occupy for the duration of his meal.

There's something to be said for every method. A red tablecloth, dimmed lights, and a candle in a bottle can seem very atmospheric when you're young, in love, and have had a glass of wine or two. Despite its banality, this favorite scheme hasn't stopped working yet. Why rack your brains for new ideas when old ones still work well?

A new factor in this area is the wise insistence of some people on not having to smell other people's cigarettes. In some states, all restaurants are now required to designate smoking and nonsmoking areas. Despite dire warnings, a majority of regular restaurant customers smoke. There was a time when the most important prop for a film star was the cigarette, and the timely exhalation of a jet of smoke was as important as getting the musical crescendos in the right places. Among many diners, the tradition continues. Occasionally, the joke's on the health buffs. They are in the hot and crowded part of the restaurant, while a comfortably spread group of smokers have large tables, discreetly separated!

As you study various restaurants, you'll soon begin to notice how some manage to make every table reasonably attractive. Some offer a good view, others offer privacy. Kitchen and restroom entrances are discreetly situated around corners, and so on.

Many restaurants are unattractively stark, especially when you find yourself looking at an oblong room, with square tables lining three and a half walls, with three or four round ones in the middle, and a bar occupying what's left of the wall space. It costs very little to break up this starkness. It can be done by partly partitioning some of the tables or putting potted plants here and there. Thus, the effect is cosy, inviting, and gives a sense of offering more value for the money. McDonald's is ideal for some circumstances, but for social or business intimacy, a more confined space, perhaps with lower lights, is often a better idea.

Some premises offer roofs or courtyards, and very little needs to be done to cheer these areas up. The main enemy is usually the pipes and other functional bits and pieces which have to go somewhere and are, unfortunately clearly visible to diners. For some restaurateurs, a happy solution has been simply to paint the pipes or other offending obstacles in gay colors, defiantly suggesting some obscure school of art. A very real danger is the sudden release of unfortunate odors in the dining area, and this must be prevented.

In cities, it's sometimes possible to obtain permission to extend premises onto the sidewalk to form a sidewalk cafe. This privilege has to be paid for, and may necessitate the presence of our old friend, the discipline-conscious maitre d', to tell incoming customers "Dinner Only!" in order to avoid the occupation of an expensive piece of real estate by people who will not consume more than $3 worth of food or drink during four hours spent people-watching.

Clever design can actually exploit bare walls at no great expense. By placing lights adroitly, for instance, you can give the appearance of being on a film set, which many will find agreeable.

Allowing your restaurant to be used as an art gallery can solve decorating problems and be fun, too. Artists display their work, which is for sale. Sometimes the restaurateurs will charge a commission, sometimes not, depending on their commitment to Art. The changing scene will give regular customers something to talk about.

Empty space is decorative in itself at times. However, Frank Lloyd Wright's concept of "powerful emptiness" should not be taken too much to heart by restaurateurs. Any space not occupied by people eating or drinking is losing you money. Most restaurateurs will admit their dining rooms are a little cramped, but they excuse this on the grounds that to sacrifice even one table, they'd have to increase prices. They will usually diplomatically fail to add that it's been scientifically proved that diners who are crowded and subjected to noise will eat faster, thus enabling tables to be turned over more rapidly.

Somewhere between the tourist cabin of an airplane and the spacious baronial hall, an acceptable compromise must be found. As a rule of thumb, it's generally figured that people are optimally accommodated at three to the square yard. That's how to work out your seating capacity. Don't forget there must be at least some space between tables to permit access by customers and waiters.

SIX

THE
BAR

PROS AND CONS

There is no law that requires you to have a bar of any kind in your restaurant. Nor are you obliged to serve alcoholic drinks. Some restaurants, usually stuffy and expensive, have only a token bar to oblige the occasional customer who might like a drink while waiting for others to arrive or while the table is being prepared. In this kind of restaurant, which tends to have strict reservation systems, delays are usually short. The token bar will usually not have more than four stools, if indeed any at all, and either the maitre d' or one of the waitresses will serve the occasional drinks required. It isn't uncommon to find a restaurant with no bar at all. The owners often definitely do not want a "bar crowd," and they may feel they're not missing any trade because their customers drink heartily enough at the tables.

It must be understood that the profit on alcholic drinks is enormous. The current price of a glass of white wine is about $3. That is exactly the price of a gallon jug of one of the most popular table white wines in the U.S., and 25 to 30 glasses of wine can be squeezed from one bottle. This is a profit mark-up to make even importers of Italian shoes envious! Even with generous "free pouring"—a fairly common procedure—a bottle of vodka, gin, or any spirit will yield the same profit. Fancy drinks such as piña coladas and strawberry daiquiris are excellent profit items. You can charge a lot for them. Customers don't mind because they see all the activity with the blender and various ingredients, but they really don't cost much to produce. They are quite popular with bartenders because they provide an opportunity for a song and dance that can bump up the tip. Noisy blenders are good conversation killers, too, and sometimes an order for six piña coladas will be welcome since it will interrupt the extended first chapter of some customer's life story on its third rerun.

FOOD AT THE BAR

You can also serve food at the bar. Many restaurants start offering the full menu at the bar, only to find that this stretches waiters, waitresses, and bartenders too much. "Suzy, could you check on that steak for the bar, please?" the bartender will plead helplessly, "And could you bring me a set-up? Dressing on the side for the salad, by the way. Did I write that? Sorry." In the end they usually get organized and offer a bar menu, of those things which are least prone to complication and most quickly delivered. If the bartender then has a small supply of knives, forks, napkins, and salts and peppers handy, it can work very easily. People alone often prefer to eat at the bar rather than sitting at a table. Of course, flexibility is all, and if the place isn't busy, there's no reason why full service shouldn't be offered. This is a matter for trial and error.

Hot snacks and appetizers can be a welcome little moneyspinner at the bar and attract regular customers who really don't want the full treatment. But, for no very good reason, this often causes resentment in the kitchen. "They're paid to do the job," you may retort. But a sulking chef can do terrible harm—sulking for a month, turning out lousy food, losing customers, and causing your most efficient waitresses to quit before you get the message.

The practice of putting out nuts and dubious bits of cheese and crackers on the bar is a much debated one. Customers usually love it. But it has its drawbacks. It's extremely unhygienic, though most of the hands that dive in and out are probably clean. Cockroaches and mice simply love bar nibbles. There're always plenty dropped for them!

People who can eat things for free are likely to spend less. If that little corner which might be nicely filled by a $4 slice of chocolate cake has already been filled by cheese nibbles, you've lost a sale. Even at the tables, you'll often hear a veteran instructing a novice not to put out too much bread as it may reduce the customer's appetite.

Every bar that puts out a generous selection of nuts and cheese nibbles, and hot hors d'oevres at cocktail time, will attract some customers who eat everything in sight but drink little. Some owners have fits of guilt about drink prices, and feel they must show a little mercy by offering their drinking customers something to nibble. Cheese, nuts, and nibbles are surprisingly expensive and rapidly consumed. Cheap compromises both look and taste unappetizing.

The theory that salty tidbits will induce thirst doesn't work for some reason—perhaps it has something to do with the fact that sodium intake is essential for the proper absorption of water. Too little salt in the system is more likely to induce thirst than too much salt, as anyone who's suffered even the mildest level of heat exhaustion can testify.

Some diners will resent the drinker's laughter wafting over the dining room from the bar; others will love it and enjoy people-watching. It is entirely a matter of choice. Sometimes the best of both worlds can be achieved by having separate rooms, or at least a separating wall or rail—well disguised by potted plants, of course.

SERVICE BAR

In the average 50–200 seat restaurant, one end of the bar is called the service bar. In larger establishments it's often a separate bar, possibly out of the dining area, like the kitchen. From here, the servers get their drinks for their table customers. Sometimes, to cover the busy period, you'll need an extra bartender. In really busy bars, with ten stools or more, you may need two all the time.

Often the cash register on the bar is also the main register for the tables, too, so that the bar is an important focal point of operations. A very common situation is that of "too much work for one, not enough for two." But that's the name of the game. Most bartenders would rather sweat a little than split their tip cup down the middle!

The emphasis at the service bar is on speed, getting the drinks made, so the servers can move on to their other tasks. It's now common practice for the waiters or waitresses to help themselves to glasses of white wine, since this is the single-most common request in any bar not catering exclusively to a beer-drinking crowd. Occasionally waiters or waitresses will abuse this practice either by drinking too much wine themselves or by selling it in a private transaction and pocketing the money received.

You will do very well to sacrifice a small amount of profit and give your customers a decent glass of table wine. They notice, even if they don't always mention it.

Since the service bar is often hidden from view, it's possible to get away with murder by serving cheap substitutes for what has been ordered. This is a short-sighted policy that will win no friends. While it may be cute to give the cheaper MacDickensian's Old Malt instead of the rather more expensive Famous Grouse and to feel superior when the customer doesn't notice, it's a small victory and an unworthy one.

Having said that, at really busy restaurants where the customers seem to relish being treated like cattle, bartenders are often instructed to pour cheap brands, no matter what is ordered. They get away with it most of the time. Some owners fill expensive brand bottles with cheaper liquor at dead of night for the extra small profit involved. Sometimes a bartender who simply cannot find anyone to go downstairs and bring up a bottle of a popular vodka will simply fill the bottle from another source. Vodka, of course, is the drink where subterfuge is the easiest, since they all taste much the same, in spite of the huge variance in prices.

A few years ago, a magazine surveyed several bars to find out how much vodka they were putting in their Bloody Mary cocktails. In some well-known restaurants, they found that *no* vodka was put in the cocktails from the service bar.

Amusingly, there was no speculation as to why this should be so. Presumably most people thought it was just a straightforward "rip-off." Now, mean though many of them are, few owners would instruct their bartenders to omit vodka from a popular cocktail entirely. The decision to deprive customers of alcohol does not derive from a concern for their health. Omitting the vodka from the drink, while charging full price for it, helps to make up for drinks given away free "on the house" and helps to keep up the profit. The Bloody Mary is tailormade for this deception since, with tomato juice, Tabasco, Worcestershire sauce, salt, pepper, horseradish, and sticks of celery all vying for attention, the shot of bland liquor isn't greatly missed—until the drinker is suddenly surprised to find himself remarkably sober after several drinks!

SUPPLIERS

Your liquor suppliers will provide you with lists, order forms, free pens, ashtrays, sponges, water jugs, and all sorts of useful bits and pieces. You will need more than one supplier, unfortunately, because not every supplier has every brand available. This is yet another legal artifice to maintain as much control as possible on the industry.

In the United States, as in many countries, the liquor lobby is a powerful one. They control huge fortunes. Producers of alcohol enjoy household names in their own countries and worldwide. In France, everyone knows Hennessey, Chateau Rothschild, Möet Chandon, etc. In Spain, Gonzalez Byass, Riscal, and Domecq are famous. The English are well represented, too, with their scotches, gins, and beers. In England, a true vertical monopoly exists in the wine and spirit trade. The huge corporations own the breweries, the vineyards in Europe, the bottling plants and warehouses, the liquor stores, the pubs, the restaurants and, increasingly, the hotels. It would serve no great purpose to try and alter this, however, as the system would be hard to dismantle, and it would be for a fairly empty principle anyway, since capitalism tends toward monopoly, whichever way you shake the kaleidoscope.

If, in the United States, all suppliers were allowed to carry anything, there would soon be a vertical monopoly and a dangerous increase in the already enormous economic power of certain elements.

BAR INVENTORY

Here is a partial list of what a well-stocked bar might carry:

Rye or American whiskey: Seagrams 7, VO, Crown Royal, Canadian Club, Southern Comfort, house

Scotch whisky: Dewars, JB, Cutty Sark, Johnny Walker (Red and Black), Chivas Regal, Glen Livet, house

Rum: Bacardi (light and dark), Black, Gold, Myers, Mount Gay, house

Gin: Beefeaters, Gordons, Tanqueray, house

Vodka: Smirnoff, Finlandia, Absolut, house

Sherry: Tio Pepe, Harvey's Bristol Cream

Tequila: Cuervo

Irish whiskey: Bushmills

Cognac and brandy: Remy Martin, Courvoisier, Apricot, Cherry, Armagnac, house

Cordials and liqueurs: Campari, Grand Marnier, Calvados, Bailey's Irish Cream, White Mint, Green Mint, Chartreuse, Kummel

Vermouth and wine cocktails: Lillet, Dubonnet, Cinzano, sweet and dry house

Champagne: Möet, Taittinger, Korbel

California white wine: Chardonnay, Puligny Montrachet

California red wine: Cabernet Sauvignon, Zinfandel

German white: Moselle, Riesling

French red: Beaujolais, Pommard

French white: Chablis, Pouilly Fumé

Italian red: Valpolicella, Chianti

Italian white: Soave Bolla, Pino Grigio

Rosé: Tavel, Anjou (or house white with a splash of house red in it)

House wine: red and white in half-gallon jugs

Beer, bottled: Heineken, Budweiser, Amstel

Beer, keg: Budweiser, Watneys

Soda: Coca-Cola, Diet Coke, Seven-Up, ginger ale, tonic, seltzer

Juices and bottled waters: Perriér, orange, grapefruit, tomato, cranberry, pineapple

Miscellaneous supplies: Worcestershire sauce, Tabasco sauce, salt, pepper, cherries, olives, onions, lemons, limes, oranges, milk, cream, coconut cream, sugar, nutmeg, straws, stirrers, napkins

The full list of possibilities would require a separate volume, as you'll discover when you start getting suppliers' brochures. *House* means the brand selected for general pouring when no brand is specified. It's usually the cheapest available, but it doesn't need to be. Experienced diners and drinkers will note with approval the use of a popular brand such as Dewars scotch or Gordons gin for general issue at no extra charge.

When you look at a well-stocked bar, the array of bottles may be bewildering. Be assured, however, that the contents are basically the same. Ethyl alcohol is the common ingredient in all intoxicating beverages. (It should not be confused with the industrial methyl alcohol that sometimes finds its way into Christmas party punches, killing a few and blinding others, or into backstreet brands of Italian grappa.) The other ingredients—the juniper berry flavoring in gin, the caramel coloring in scotch, whisky, rum, and brandy, and the hundreds of chemicals—give each liquor its individual flavor and, some say, its individual effect.

Cocktails

You may ask yourself whether some of the more obscure brands are used much. The truth is they're not.

So what are they for?

The answer is simple. There is an occasional demand for most of them. The first drink served from any bottle on a bar pays for the whole bottle! While awaiting its next customer, and its debut as a profit item, that dusty bottle of Old Czechoslovakian Boar's Brandy will take up little space, be decorative if dusted from time to time (or not, according to the preferred ambiance), and give barflies with uneventful lives something exciting to discuss. But sometimes obscure products are foisted on gullible owners by unscrupulous salesmen.

Also, from time to time a liquor company will mount a huge advertising drive featuring some kind of cocktail: Horse's Neck, Long Island Iced Tea, Pink Squirrel, Fuzzy Navel, and so on. If demand is sufficient, you might as well buy the ingredients and serve it.

Most of the cocktails in the Bartender's Guide belong to a dim and distant past. The chances of being asked for a French 75, a Sazerac, or a Bronx cocktail are slim. Some cocktails, such as a Banzai or a Long Island Iced Tea, are aimed at the young and are dangerous because their sweet taste conceals a large amount of alcohol. (Sometimes, when a bartender finds an excuse not to make these kinds of drinks for a bunch of giggling youngsters, he's not being old and boring. He's avoiding the problem of vomit all over the bar and the restrooms, the need to con some taxi driver into taking the kids away, and, most important of all, the responsibility for putting a poorly controlled high-speed projectile into orbit.)

Opinions differ as to how cocktails came into existence. Some say it was to disguise the appalling taste of moonshine liquor during Prohibition, and there may be something in that. But the basic reason is to disguise the fairly horrible taste of alcohol by adding something fruity, bubbly, sweet, or all three. Alcohol is very much an acquired taste. Ask a child to taste whiskey, and you'll get groans and splutters— a reaction far removed from the adult's glow of satisfaction as the first martini slips into place, i.e., into the bloodstream.

But there's also an element of theatre. There used to be what were derisively called Hollywood bartenders, who would make a tremendous show of juggling with the cocktail mixer, often throwing it from hand to hand or over and over in the air. And bar customers love the sound of their own voices as they specify a brand for their martinis, give silly instructions like "shaken, not stirred," "in and out" (put a drop of vermouth in the glass, then throw it out), "in a chilled glass," "with olives" (plural), or "Face east, hold up the glass and whisper

'Vermouth.'" It's all a bit pathetic, but the restaurant industry invented this claptrap with one purpose in mind: to increase sales. And it works. Movie buffs will recognize some of this from the movie *Cocktail*.

Mercifully, the current repertoire of cocktails is comparatively small. Drinking habits seem to be centralizing throughout the western world, and hard drinking is getting a very bad press in the age of jogging and bottled water.

Liquor salesmen will do their best to load you up with every bottle they can sell. "Sale or return!" they'll say with those warm smiles that make you shiver. "Tell you what, just put a bottle of this new product on the bar and see how it goes, huh?" When a public holiday or strike is imminent, they'll exhort you to back yourself up with enough supplies to survive a siege. They are to be pitied, but they must be resisted.

RESTRICTING INVENTORY

The busier you are, the more space you need and the less time you have to talk to salespeople and do bookwork. Of course, at the expensive end of the market, where prices are irrelevant and the customers compete to see how much they can spend, a huge wine cellar with necessary staff may be appropriate. But restaurants like Windows on the World with inventories of thousands of wines need no advice from anyone.

There are hundreds of beers on the market, with newcomers all the time. Gino's, a popular, inexpensive restaurant on New York's Lexington Avenue, carries two beers only, Heineken and Budweiser. This not only reduces storage problems but narrows the area for discussion in a busy joint. Other luxury restaurants only offer Lowenbrau, in spite of enormous advertising pressure from nonalcoholic beers and the new "lite" beers.

The frenzy to find a wine from a huge list, which happened to run out weeks ago but was not replaced by any of the assistant managers, can generate a lot of stress. Other tasks are held up while the search goes on and the frowns and curses mount. It is not unknown for frustrated waiters to start screaming like wounded animals at the tops of their voices at the thought of having to tell a customer they don't have the wine she ordered, thus, perhaps, endangering their tip.

The daily liquor list—the list of bottles that need to be replaced on the bar before commencement of business to bring it up to par—

consists largely of white wine, vodka, rum, gin and scotch in swiftly descending order of magnitude—eight bottles or jars of white wine, four bottles of vodka, and only one of everything else!

No matter how large the wine list, the same old favorites will sell day after day, while the obscure or more expensive ones are often ignored. Inevitably a backlog of these wines will accumulate, and eventually they can be used for pouring or offered as "Specials." Sometimes a wine that simply won't move for $10 will fly from the racks at $18, and there's enormous fun to be had with this kind of price juggling.

Storage space is always at a premium in restaurants. Beer and white wine take up precious refrigerated space. Bottles that don't have to be refrigerated must be stored securely in a room that locks. Two things that have an uncanny attraction for light fingers are cash and hard liquor.

Beer on Tap

If the apparatus for keg or tap beer is in place, it may be wise to continue its use. The profit on keg beers is huge. Some think the sight of pump handles on a bar is a little down-market or unchic. Again, it's the boss's decision.

It really isn't that much bother. Once in a while you'll have to pay to have the pipes cleaned out. It's many years since, in a freak accident, a metal spigot blew from the keg and killed a poor bartender stone dead. The apparatus is now much simpler, but the keg must be connected to the pipes properly. All that hissing can be a bit unnerving, but if you follow the instructions, which should be prominently posted in your beer cellar, there's no problem. Make sure your supplier shows you exactly how to connect it, and pass the information on to as many others as you can.

Make sure you understand exactly what delivery entails. The keg should be delivered inside the building right down to the place where it's connected. If it isn't, you're in trouble, because those kegs are dangerously heavy. Just to cover yourself against occasional hitches, you should be assured, also, that any difficulties in tapping or connection will be attended to by the beer suppliers. In the majority of cases, the delivery man will take care of everything without a murmur, have a drink on the house (possibly one of many in the course of a day), and depart in peace. But sometimes they're neglectful. Don't get the kegs mixed up. Trying to tap a keg with a line designed for a different attachment can be messy, particularly if you achieve a halfway fit, which will mean endless leaking and hissing.

Sodas and Mixers

Many restaurants now use a soda gun instead of storing cases of bottled sodas. The line comes up from the cellar, through a little hole in the floor, and into a black plastic nozzle. Tanks of syrup, which combines with carbonated water, are connected to the system and are piped upstairs to the bar. On the nozzle are little buttons marked S for soda, T for Tab or tonic, Q for quinine, G for ginger, W for water, and L (lemon) for Seven-Up—or some variation on this essential and highly profitable theme. You press the button and out squirts the required soda. This is a good profit item, though the quality is possibly not as high as that of bottled sodas. You'll notice in more expensive bars (the kind where the drinks are $5 and the bill is presented concealed in a leather book) that whole fresh bottles of soda are usually served. Murphy's Law requires that both draft beers and sodas will go "out" at the least convenient time, usually when you're busy. All the more reason, then, to make sure that just about anyone can change a keg or put in a new container of soda in a couple of minutes without fuss.

LIQUOR CONTROL

Liquor control is easy. You keep a record of everything delivered, possibly by entering it into your computer. You decide your bar and wine rack par, in other words, the amounts and kinds of bottles you want instantly available on the bar. For instance, you'll probably have two bottles of vodka in the "well" or "ready rack," which is suspended for easy grabbing by the bartender at about knee level, with six back-ups in the cupboard. So your par for vodka is eight bottles.

Every day, either at close of business or before the beginning of business, the bartender or manager counts and lists all the empty bottles, which have been neatly arrayed on the bar for easy counting. This is the liquor list. A full bottle is then issued against every empty. Sometimes the bartender gets the liquor room keys and does this herself.

Where the owner is paranoid about theft—a not uncommon state, as we shall see—a manager issues the booze.

Since liquor is, or should be, rung on its own special key on the cash register, you can easily compare the money you took in for liquor with the amount you issued to the bar. This enables you to work out your percentage profit, or PC. Usually this will soon strike a level from which it will not deviate much in the course of a year. While the level of business may vary, from New Year's Eve at one extreme to New Year's Day at the other, the percentage profit should be fairly constant. When there is a sudden large difference from the norm, something is probably wrong. This could be the result of overgenerous pouring, or stealing, or an unhappy combination of the two.

However, neat though this sounds, it sometimes breaks down. The liquor list will call for the issue of a bottle of Old Dickens Gin, but the delivery has been delayed, and there isn't any in the cellar. A solemn note is made, but it gets lost. Such OD as remains on the bar is used up, then six weeks down the line, the delivery is made. So the bartender asks for six bottles, though he has no empties to show. Thus, that week, an unusual amount of OD gin has been issued for no noticeable return in the cash register. Yes, it balances out over the months, but it looks a bit funny if you take a weekly reading. Multiply this by 100 brands and you'll see that the scope for chaos is great.

Sometimes a bartender will neglect to "marry up" her bottles so that the next-day shift starts with three bottles, each of which contains a tablespoon of vodka. When she counts her empties she'll have three more than usual. There are also bottles that get broken and stolen, and bottles of wine that have to be poured down the sink for one reason or another. There's a trickle of alcohol to the kitchen, too, for cooking and refreshment.

In large establishments there's no problem because they employ a wine steward or even a "food and beverage manager" to take care of inventory. But what happens at the size of restaurant under discussion, in practice, is that the owner develops an instinctive idea of just what's going on, what's being issued, and how much cash is coming in. With practice and time, some owners can just glance at the pile of orders in the kitchen and the level of empties and guess to within $100 how much money has been taken in. Of course, even if the inventory goes haywire, the amount of cash paid out for liquor is recorded so that if an owner wants to know the story of every nickel and dime, and has the time and patience to work it out, it can be done.

Initially, while business is building, one hopes to see an ever-increasing pile of dupes and truckloads of empties. But at some point, most restaurants rise to a level of business from which they don't vary much. This can be a blessing because it's only by constant comparison of income figures that the restaurateur can tell whether the business is on course or not. A steady increase calls for little action, beyond hiring more help, until it reaches a point where expansion can be considered. But a downward track on the sales graph, which persists even after considerations of weather, taxes, stock market disasters, holidays, and new competition have been made, calls for action.

Types of Liquors

Owners don't have to be experienced bartenders, but it certainly won't hurt. It will help them to supervise the bar better and reduce dependency on the expert knowledge of the bartender. At the very least, they should know what drinks are all about. Knowing how to shake cocktails, once in a while they can take off their coat and step behind the bar at rush hour. Then both customers and help will join in an admiring chorus of "What a boss! Doesn't mind lending a hand when it's busy!" This is the stuff of which Rick's dreams are made.

Grain Spirits. Whiskey, gin, and vodka are grain spirits. Their different characters stem from the type of grain used and various additives, such as coloring for all whiskies and juniper berries (among other fruits and herbs) for gin. In the case of scotch, aging plays a part. At the distillery where the grain spirit is produced, some of it is bottled as vodka, while the rest is flavored and becomes gin. Of all spirits, vodka is quite the purest, closely followed by gin, and this undoubtedly accounts in part for its immense popularity. It's a "clean" drink, so they say, and less likely to give you a headache because of its lack of congeners, (the technical name under which ingredients other than alcohol spirits are grouped). Some believe it has less of a telltale smell than other drinks, another social plus. Vodka is sometimes made from distilled potato juice, and there is a small interest in flavored vodkas from behind the Iron Curtain, including Pepper Vodka.

Wine Derivatives and Liqueurs. Campari, Vermouth, Cinzano, Dubonnet, and several other brands are flavored wines. Most liqueurs are simply flavored brandies, in spite of the arcane nonsense about secret recipes known only to the abbot himself, to be divulged to his successor with his dying breath. Inevitably, cheaper versions of the most expensive liqueurs have been devised, notably in the area of the orange flavor. Grand Marnier and Cointreau are the tops, but Curacao, Triple Sec, and several others will do for cocktails.

Brandy. Brandy, Cognac, Armagnac, Marc—all generally referred to as brandy—are made from the distilled juice of the grape, not the grain. When stored in wood (for up to 40 years, after which it tastes too "woody") cognac matures, acquiring a deeper and more complex taste. Once bottled, cognac doesn't change. Caramel is added to deepen the color and keep it constant, as it is in whisky. An "old" and expensive brandy may actually contain a very small amount of really old brandy in a generally much younger blend. Calvados is the distillation of apple juice, sometimes called applejack or apple brandy. It can be made legally at home in France, and is very strong.

Fortified Wines. Port, sherry, Madeira, and Marsala are fortified wines. They've had brandy added to them. Originally, this was done to maintain stability during transit, but now it's just part of the style. Spanish Manzanilla sherry is probably the driest (least sweet) drink in the spectrum. It's actually a bit too dry for American tastes. Sherry sales have slumped in recent years, even in England, which used to take 70% of the product. Recently it was admitted that the whole range of sherries had been considerably sweetened in the hope of improving sales.

Though delightful and generally of high quality, fortified wines have been crowded out by the heavy advertising of other products and changing drinking habits. Very few offices offer visitors a glass of sherry or Madeira and a slice of seedcake at eleven in the morning these days, and port after dinner puts a considerable strain on a liver that has to accompany its owner to work the next morning.

Wine

As with restaurants themselves, an elaborate theater and folklore have been built around the subject of wine. In recent years, wine consumption in the United States has increased dramatically. There seems to be a view, which manufacturers of hard liquor dispute, that alcohol consumed as wine is less harmful than that which is consumed as whiskey. The ordinary, if fickle, dynamics of fashion have had something to do with it, too.

Wine needs to be stored at a cool consistent temperature. Ideally, the bottles should be on their side so that wine and cork are in contact. Lots of wine are sometimes available at discount prices, but lack of storage space can sometimes be a problem.

Wine production in the United States is at an all-time high, principally in California and New York. Domestic wines are often of good quality, a fact reflected in their surprisingly high cost. After an outbreak of a vine disease called phylloxera damaged the vines of Europe, they were replenished with vines brought in from California, in a classic example of the New World being brought in to redress the balance of the Old.

There are literally thousands of names of wines. But they're all made from the juice of grapes that have been allowed to ferment, not infrequently with a little scientific encouragement. To produce white wine, the grape skins are removed from the vat immediately; for rosé, they're removed at a certain stage of fermentation; and for red, they stay to the end. Champagne is white wine that has been made to ferment a second time, resulting in bubbles.

Most wine improves with age, either in bottle or cask, but only up to a point, and some wines are best drunk young. Red wine is usually drunk at room temperature, which improves its flavor. But even the French often drink red wine chilled, especially the young Beaujolaís. White wine is best drunk chilled, as is rosé. Drinking some of the white wines warm will sometimes expose unattractive tastes, and there is no doubt that chilling can cover a multitude of sins.

An endless number of books are written on the subject, and it is possible to study wine at some colleges in New York and California. The University of Bristol in England awards a degree called Master of Wine. In this book there is only space for some basic information.

The science of wine, or oenology, is undoubtedly a fascinating one. It attracts a fair number of know-it-alls, bores, and pundits who are ever-anxious to impart their greater understanding at great length, even to people who aren't desperately interested in the subject.

In Burgundy in the fall, mortars are fired to break up rain clouds as the selected grapes are left on the vine until the last minute in order to increase their fruit sugar content, until they achieve something called *pourriture noble*, or noble rottenness. In Germany, the best and latest grapes are called *Trockenbeerenauslese*. Sherry gets its unique flavor from a yeast called *saccharomyces elipsoideus beticus*, and the solera system, whereby young sherry is continuously added to old, so that the combination will assume the characteristics of the older wine, is a fascinating showpiece of the vineyards at Jerez, Spain—along with the drunken mice. Bismark vowed to drink 12,000 bottles of champagne in his lifetime, and he may well have succeeded.

If you are interested, there is a whole world to explore. Some vineyards are open to the public on occasion, and many magazines and radio stations have their own wine correspondents. The best way to get to know wine is to drink it and reach your own conclusions.

The broad classifications of wine are red, white, rosé, and fortified. Most restaurants feature a selection of French wines such as Burgundy reds (Chateauneuf du Pape, Pommard, etc.) Burgundy whites (Chablis, Puligny Montrachet, etc.) Bordeaux reds or clarets (Mouton Cadet, Chateau Lafite—very expensive) and Bordeaux whites, some of which, like Graves, are dryish and others of which are very sweet, such as Sauternes, of which Chateau Yquem is the most heralded and the most expensive. The design of the bottles used for Burgundy and Bordeaux wines is slightly different, which can be helpful.

Then there are the Italian wines—reds such as Chianti and Valpolicella, and whites such as Soave Bolla and Pino Grigo. Most German wine is white, much of it sweet and loaded with chemicals; some of it, such as Bernkasteler Doktor, is sublime and therefore expensive. Spanish wines are common, as are wines from Yugoslavia, Hungary, Morocco, Argentina, and Chile. A very impressive quality has been reached by the Australian wine industry.

However, American wines, especially the California whites, win prizes all the time, and the French certainly don't disdain them. Indeed, several French firms, notably Moët Chandon, have bought interests in the California wine industry, to everyone's benefit.

Wine Mystique. The enormous folklore of wine was created by the English in the eighteenth century, as part of that robustness that accompanied the burgeoning wealth of the newly industrialized society. Some of it corresponds to those absurd French phrases used by the Victorians, which no Frenchman ever heard such as *nostalgie de la boue*, meaning a longing for mud or the low life. However, if the 'milords' liked to play, the French were far too good-humored to stop them or interfere with trade.

One of James Thurber's cartoons for *The New Yorker* shows a man, pouring wine and remarking: "It's just a charming little domestic Burgundy with little or no breeding, but I think you'll be amused by its presumption!" The vocabulary has increased since then to include such descriptions as flowery, foxy, fruity, and so on. Wine buffs call a wine's aftertaste its "finish" and often describe a wine as having a blackberry or black currant finish. This isn't surprising since black currant wine, called cassis, is commonly added to red wine to cheer it up. It's also added to white wine to make a cocktail called a Kir, after a Burgundy mayor who devised the mixture to make some of the local wine more palatable.

Such is the enormous proliferation of wines that it would be naive not to suspect a tiny element of flimflam here and there in the vast industry. While wine names are strictly controlled in Europe and elsewhere (*appellation controle*), those vast tankers full of Spanish and Moroccan plonk which roll through the French countryside at night are all going somewhere.

Chemicals

The wine industry will fight to the last round to prevent legislation requiring that ingredients be listed on labels. For obvious reasons, they don't want to spoil the image of healthy naturalness and laughing peasants joyfully treading the grapes.

An increasing number of bottles can now be seen bearing the words "Contains Sulfites." This is only half the story. The average bottle of wine contains more than 1,000 organic compounds, some in miniscule amounts. The main ingredients are alcohol (12%), water (85%), and sulfites (3%), as well as very small amounts of urethanes (a carcinogen) and histamines.

Glycol and methanol are sometimes used, with occasional deadly effect by unscrupulous manufacturers. Because the resulting mix tastes so awful, only the poor are at risk from these concoctions. American soldiers are said to make cocktails from aftershave and antifreeze, which contains glycol (its sweet taste can confirm suspected radiator leaks), but it's hard to understand why they should.

Most wine is routinely filtered through sulfur to stop it from rotting. Red wine is brightened with potassium and white wine with cyanide.

If you consider what happens to grapes when they're left out of the refrigerator, it's easy to understand that wine is fundamentally unstable, and it wouldn't be very good business not to use the wonders of science to help it along. Apart from anything else, it wouldn't travel.

The purpose of these revelations is not to deflate the mystique of wine but to get the subject into perspective. Wine manufacturers may be shooting themselves in the foot by encouraging snobbery and superiority. Many potential consumers are intimidated by the whole business, as is shown by the acute embarrassment felt by some people in a restaurant when they're given a great leatherbound wine list and invited to choose.

If wine is ever to be made a mass market item, it will have to be reduced to the folksy level of beer. For the moment, it remains an almost exclusively bourgeois product, which, fortunately, is the main area of appeal of most restaurants.

Most restaurateurs try to keep a small list of wines which are simply described, e.g., Sanfrandino Puligny Montrachet—a light, dry white wine with a hint of fruit, ideal with fish, chicken, and veal or for casual drinking.

In general, restaurateurs will do well to *demystify* all aspects of wine and food, except at the $150-a-head end of the market, where baloney seems to be best appreciated. Most Americans out to dine want to have fun and, while they may have a healthy interest in the new and unusual, they don't want to be lectured.

Once the average wine-loving customer has gotten over the shock of the price, the delights of Bernkasteler Doktor '78 or Chateau Lafite '73 will be so apparent as to defy verbal description. To a wine lover, the old story of the man who kept a vintage bottle of Tokay specifically to be administered at his death bed isn't a bit ridiculous!

SEVEN

THE
KITCHEN

PROFIT MARGINS

The kitchen is undoubtedly the hub of most restaurants, despite the common heartfelt cry from amateur restaurateurs: "I don't make any money on the food, only on the bar!" How anyone can say this is mystifying when a salad sold for $3.50 often contains only 50 cents worth of material, even at retail prices. But it is a common cliché of the trade and perhaps a symptom of the amateurishness of many of its practitioners.

The wise words of the executive who recently replied to a writer's complaint that, although the world price of coffee had gone down, the price of coffee in the supermarket had gone up, may be significant in this context. "If coffee beans suddenly cost *nothing*," he said, "the price of a jar of instant coffee would remain the same." No matter how cheaply you buy your food supplies, you still won't escape the other overheads that must be financed from your income.

True, the kitchen overheads in terms of payroll and materials alone are heavier than those of the bar where, as we have seen, a 1500% profit isn't unusual. Also, some food items are much better "profit items" than others. But the restaurateur must take the overall view. After all, even though food profits may not be in themselves tremendous, if you don't serve food, you don't have a restaurant!

The two biggest bills you'll ever have to pay, after your rent, are the meat and/or fish bill and the liquor bill. Selling cooked food at a profit takes a certain skill. But the steak priced at $10 on the menu has usually cost the restaurateur no more than $2. Many steakhouses are actually owned by butchers, in order to provide a heavily marked-up retail outlet for their goods.

At the more expensive end of the menu, in the area of carefully and expertly prepared special dishes, the profit margin is just as healthy. If you serve Chicken Kiev, for instance (that's the one where, at the prick of a knife, melted butter spurts from a sewn-up chicken breast), there's preparation time involved, and the people who do the work command full salaries—that is, their income isn't subsidized by tips. In other words, there's a labor cost.

CHEF POWER

For some reason, the area of food intimidates restaurant owners who are not themselves trained chefs. Apart from the general lack of control and confidence this attitude creates, it often leads to a dangerous psychological imbalance in the running of the business: the owner is in awe of the chef. An owner who can't do the chef's job can succumb to a ludicrous dependency. To an extent this isn't unreasonable. If this important end of the business is well taken care of, no one can be blamed for wanting to keep a key employee happy, even if this does mean that the employee gets away with murder, as most chefs do.

The restaurateur knows that, by lifting the telephone, any member of his staff can be replaced within the hour—except the chef. The new waiter, busboy, hostess, maitre d', manager, cloakroom attendant, car valet, porter, or dishwasher may not be the employee of one's dreams, but they'll help to muddle through a shift. Finding and replacing a chef can be a nightmare. "Better the devil you know . . . " the boss will say with a sigh. "At least the chef's *fast* and can get the orders out promptly." Sadly, speed of production is often a better qualification than quality.

All too often, these factors result in chefs being able to rule the roost. They'll come in drunk, go home drunker, insult the staff with dirty talk far beyond the usual, harmless badinage, make enough smoke to cover a divisional river crossing, and generate enough noise to drown out even the loudest pianist or juke box. Few customers are ever likely to return for a repeat experience.

Once in a while a chef'll go berserk and actually attack someone. Anyone will do, no particular employee is at risk, unless it's a waiter who insists, on the customer's behalf, on getting what was ordered, or a waitress who's kept silence in the face of his filthy insults. A recent dreadful murder case in California involving the chef of a famous restaurant raised a few eyebrows, and had a few people wondering what kind of people lurked behind that swinging kitchen door. (It was a revelation that this prince of the skillets, who was often invited to come out and discuss the recently consumed meal with the customers, had very little money in the bank, despite a high salary, and didn't even have a driver's license.)

Bearing in mind the profusion of deadly weapons in the average kitchen, from meat cleaver to frying pan, the dangers are obvious. The optimum freak-out point for most chefs is when a dish is returned to the kitchen, either as a reject or requiring further treatment, or an order arrives just as they're about to start closing up the kitchen. Many owners will insist that late arrivers be served, even though they lack the courage to go into the kitchen and smooth the chef's feelings. Some owners have rigid "last-order times," but many can't resist the opportunity to take in a bit more cash. It's what they're there for, after all. When owners are chefs, they'll sometimes volunteer to do the cooking themselves, and if in the process they build up a clientele who insist on arriving late for that special treatment, well, it serves them right.

All of the above applies just as much to the unshaven short-order cook with the bleary eye and the drooping cigarette (usually always in the mouth, miraculously never growing shorter or longer despite the fact that it's alight) as it does to the brilliant young chef whose picture is in society magazines, who studied under the great prince of the kitchen, Coglioni di Medici, and is being paid $60,000 a year plus bonuses.

The question arises, would a nasty chef be easier to deal with if tipped by the waiters and waitresses? The answer is probably yes. But how many people are they supposed to take care of? They've already got to tip the bartender, the busboy, and possibly the captain. Though it's no longer common, the old hands used to tip the chef quite routinely for getting their orders out promptly and not giving them too much of a hard time. Nowadays a bottle of beer snitched from the bar and brought as a peace offering is more usual. On Cunard ships at one time, a waiter could not put in an order unless he first tipped the kitchen. Management looked the other way, as it continually must in the union-dominated Merchant Marine.

Although the management skills required of the restaurateur do not exceed those required of the most junior NCO in the army, few restaurateurs seem to possess them. What is worse, they don't seem to learn them. There can be no doubt that the best and most successful restaurants are run either by well-educated people who've learned the relevant skills, or people steeped in the business who just happen to have natural management ability. It's a shame because there's rarely a requirement for more than routine common sense and diplomacy.

In order to maintain the edge of authority and reduce stressful dependency, restaurateurs, if they are to accumulate any specialist knowledge at all, would do well to address their training time to food, more than any other area of the business. Many owners will freely criticize every aspect of their operations except the sacrosanct domain of the kitchen. In comparison, everything else is easy. Some restaurateurs find dealing with people difficult. But attractive young people who can work as hosts are easy to come by, if this is the case. They tend to burn out fast in the least attractive job in a restaurant, but they're as easy to replace as a Napoleonic army after a disastrous battle.

For obvious reasons, it's not in the interests of highly paid chefs to reveal just how easy cookery is, once one becomes aware of how food is supposed to look and taste when it's "done right." The trade guards its secrets jealously, but they don't take much working out. With a little practice, you'll find you can even open clams.

This is not to put down the art of cookery. (However, chefs themselves are notoriously skeptical about their "art" and often cite, as their favorite meal, "fried eggs and french fries" or "a nice juicy hamburger." Some of this is probably a bit tongue in cheek, of course.)

But too many owners are totally intimidated by kitchen problems. If they get into the subject seriously, they'll soon learn the ropes, and they'll get better results in the kitchen, too.

Bakery is really the only branch of cooking that takes kowledge and practice. Amateur flair and beginner's luck will get you nowhere in this department. You have to practice and get it wrong a few times before you eventually get it right. But in the end, you'll find you can do it.

It is extremely unusual for employees to be allowed to sample the whole menu in restaurants, even though they're solemnly expected to be able to describe dishes and advise customers. People who work in good quality gourmet restaurants, and are allowed to eat what they want (which would be highly unusual), find everything tastes the same after a while.

This demonstrates the consistency of the chef's work, and is in fact to be encouraged. Regular customers will know what to expect. If you think about it, although all the tastes of home cooking are well known in most families, you really wouldn't want it any different.

Variety is the spice of life. Everybody likes a change occasionally.

Finding a reliable chef who isn't too much of a prima donna can take forever. Many restaurateurs do not embark upon their business project until and unless they have first secured the services of such a person, knowing the pitfalls which may await them. That's another reason why you should get around, meet people, and make friends in the business. When the chef is a partner—and capable, pleasant, and not too neurotic—things often go a lot better. The waiters and waitresses have to be a bit more on their toes, but they often get treated better and are less subject to stress, which makes them a better sales staff.

It can be an unhappy business, full of petty hatred and jealousy. This is almost invariably a result of personality deficiencies in the owner or manager. The brutal truth is that some unhappy restaurants do excellent business anyway. But if an owner wants to stay happy and reduce stress, then putting together an efficient crew motivated by more than the ordinary need to do a job isn't a bad idea. Also, there can be no doubt that when staff morale descends below a certain level, the effect on business can be disastrous. Customers will pick up the "vibes," and they often won't endure them. Remember, customers can be prima donnas, too, and they certainly don't want to be surrounded by misery when they're out relaxing and enjoying themselves.

KITCHEN STAFF

A typical kitchen crew for a restaurant that seats up to 150 people would consist of a chef (probably the highest paid person in the place) and two helpers. One of these may enjoy the title of salad maker, the other will be the dishwasher. Both will be required to carry out various duties in the course of their shift. The dishwasher will be required to run occasional errands, and, in places too small to employ a busboy, clean up mishaps in the dining room. The saladmaker may have to do anything from cutting strawberries to opening clams. It's a good idea to instill a daily routine so that everything gets done automatically, but this shouldn't be done in such a way as to suggest that, outside the regular tasks, nothing else needs to be done. Though most employees will smilingly oblige The Boss, you can't always be there. The cry of "it's not my job!" is the last thing the chef or manager wants to hear, in any of the mild emergencies which inevitably occur in the course of a day.

In some places the power of the chef is such that many odd jobs are sloughed off onto the waiters and waitresses, from making up their own salads to whipping the cream.

The kitchen crew arrives early in the day in order to set up, not just for the day, but for the evening dinner shift as well. Sometimes they'll have to prepare food for a "special" that won't actually be featured for a couple of days. At around 5 P.M., they are relieved by the night crew, whose chef may be less skilled, and thus worse paid, and who only has to dish up that which has been prepared earlier by the day chef. Of course, where, as is hoped, both lunch *and* dinner become very busy affairs, this routine may have to be varied. But patterns of business soon assert themselves. Except in busy travel and tourist areas, there's usually a calm patch in the afternoon when the restaurant can recuperate and various tasks can be accomplished.

Sometimes a state of mutual hatred exists between the two crews.

Most commonly the bone of contention is simply that the job that should have been done has not been done. Once more, it's the job of the owner or manager to mediate and make sure that the show goes on.

DECIDING THE MENU

This is something the owner and chef work out between them. It will conform to the standard repertoire of cooking with individual touches. These may be provided by local produce and tastes or some special skill of the chef. When you're inspired to experiment, you can feature a dish as a "special." Then, if it's a success, you can make it a regular item.

Ease of production must be borne in mind at all times. If the chef turns out a particular dish which is a bit fussy and time-consuming, but which is always a sell-out, then there's obviously a case for featuring it. But you don't make work. There's enough to do just attending to the basics.

You should constantly review the menu. Some owners do this very consciously by doing a breakdown of what's ordered every day. If you sell 40 chicken pot pies, but only three barbecued porks, then you may consider dropping the less popular item.

Also, you should be aware of what gets eaten heartily and what gets left on the plate. Hopefully, the waiters will tell you this, but some may not notice. Sometimes the size of portions needs to be changed. The wonderful science of "portion control" is all about how much you give for the money.

Menu Changes

It's important that the waiters and waitresses learn instantly those items that have run out. If word of mouth doesn't work, then you should have a blackboard outside the kitchen to list the items no longer available. Otherwise, busy waiters may find themselves making wasted trips and apologizing to customers. They hate this as it lessens their psychological domination over the scene—and not infrequently takes the edge off their tip, too. (You might also post a list of all persons who, due to some former misdemeanor, may not be served in the restaurant.)

Food Quality

Restaurant haters complain that restaurant food is rarely as good as home cooking. This is generally true. Cooking a meal for two or three people, under no great pressure, with a knowledge of how people like their food and with a natural wish to please, is entirely a different task from cooking for hundreds of customers. The chance of finding a used bandage in your chicken pot pie is clearly quite small at home. In a restaurant where many people have had their hands in the preparation of a hundred pies, with regular interruption, obviously the scope for horror is greater. And, inevitably, some of those pies will contain tastier meat than others.

One might expect that a commercial chef, with nothing else to do but prepare food, unlike many a working parent with children, would turn out *better* food. In some restaurants, usually the more expensive ones, this is sometimes the case. Expensive restaurants hire more staff in order to increase quality. In the average restaurant, the chef hardly has time to sit down during the entire shift.

Reluctant customers often complain about limited menus (hamburger, cheeseburger, bacon burger, chopped sirloin, steak, flounder with stuffed crab, eggs of any style, etc.). On the other hand, it's irritating to go to a restaurant for lunch and find they don't feature a standard item like steak, french fries, and salad, but are crowded with chi-chi items. An ideal menu should be like a popular symphony concert program, offering the possibility of a familiar and tuneful overture, a warhorse symphony or concerto by one of the great composers, something from the less-played repertoire, and perhaps a lightweight, jolly finale. In other words, something for everybody.

Customers learn what to avoid. "Fried" often means deep-fried in a thick, tasteless batter that hides the protein within. Duck is almost invariably a disaster—to get it right just takes too much time and attention. Pastry dishes, rather a challenge for the domestic cook, are often phoney, ready-made tasteless pie crusts inserted on top of separately prepared mini-stews. "Baked on the premises" in many cases ought to read "Faked on the premises." "Flounder stuffed with crabmeat" is another phoney description of a deep-frozen favorite that finds a home on many a mediocre menu. Few buy twice. A common and depressing customer's cry is "I only order the things the restaurant is least likely to get wrong."

Even the most hard-bitten restaurant hater, however, cannot deny that some things are better in restaurants and would be hard to cook at home. Steak and prime ribs, for instance, require more heat than is comfortably generated in a small apartment—hence, the popularity of the backyard barbecue. Also, the quality of meat supplied to restaurants is generally superior to that obtained in supermarkets or even the ordinary butcher's shop.

The quality of food depends on two factors: the skill with which it's prepared, and the basic quality of the foodstuffs used. To this might be added the perception of novelty factor. Food cooked by someone you don't know has the advantage of a different and original touch. Though mom's sure touch will always be the best, a change will often refresh the palate and perhaps make mom's food taste even better when next sampled. It need hardly be added that "Hunger is the best sauce." The most demanding gourmet will not disdain the yacht club bar hamburger after a cold morning's sailing.

The chef has weapons to help enhance and intensify the taste of food. Salt and sugar are notorious among them. So is monosodium glutamate, which is sold under several brand names. Many people don't realize that even the best chefs will use this sparingly, but some use it with such a heavy hand that it actually affects people who either are, or imagine themselves to be, allergic to it (it's a fashionable allergy) and gives them a headache. This often results in the earnest request (usually in a Chinese restaurant where the chemical is commonly used in vast quantities) for "No monosodium glutamate!" In this event, the waiter or waitress can only nod acquiescence. The food has probably been prepared for ages, and having the temerity to bore the chef with such frivolous instructions might get one fired—or even killed—on a bad day.

Many chefs lean heavily on cream, a clever move because most American homes don't use it a lot, especially since people have become aware of cholesterol. When real whipped cream (as opposed to the commonly used aerosol stuff, which would be put to better use for shaving) is added to strawberries or good chocolate cake, a glimpse of heaven may be vouchsafed. Heavy cream can be added to soups with good effect, too.

The simple addition of a pinch of curry powder, or some other herb or condiment, can transform a dish from the banal to the superb.

So far as mechanical devices go, after the fierce and instantly applied fire of the restaurant stove, the blender is probably the most useful tool. It can be used, for instance, to whip up really tasty desserts quickly.

Food Sources

With tedious regularity, when "great" restaurants are written up and gushed over by the media—an event usually caused by the restaurant's public relations firm, not the excitement of the editorial staff—sooner or later there will be a reference to the heroic owner or chef getting up at 4 A.M. in order to go to the food markets to select the very best items for the esteemed customers. This scenario has its origins in France, where there really are food markets that open very early, which are often full of housewives, restaurateurs, and excellent food. They are well worth a visit when in France, if you can stand the sight of pigs heads on sticks, or blinded rabbits, at crack of dawn.

In terms of validity, it's about on a par with the common whine of the sincere and dedicated please-use-me-as-your-ego doormat restaurateur: "I treat my customers like guests in my own home!"

It's true that there are markets that open at unearthly hours in major American cities and that it's often a case of "first come, first served." They are all worth a visit. But the necessity to attend them has long passed. Food wholesalers, sometimes called purveyors, have longstanding business arrangements with producers to provide them with all kinds of food, from swordfish to radishes, of best—and lesser—quality.

Consequently, if you are in the hands of a good supplier, there really shouldn't be a problem in this area, and you needn't lose any sleep. This doesn't mean you should lose sight of quality control. Most wholesalers are ordinary business people, and they want to keep their customers. But the world is full of wise guys, and if some purveyors (or their delivery staff) see you as a sucker, they won't give you an even break. All incoming goods should be checked carefully against the invoice. If you fail to do it once, you may become a "mark." In many restaurants the highly polished scales in the basement are regularly used to check quantities. One owner, briefing his manager before taking off on vacation, was heard to say, "Oh, yeah, the lobsters. They come in on Tuesdays. Reject a couple, whether there's anything wrong with them or not. Send them back. Keep the bastards on their toes!"

In passing, you should insist that your suppliers deliver the goods at reasonable times, preferably before the commencement of business. Diners in silk and satin, lips poised to consume a *bonne-bouche* or to deliver a *bon mot*, don't want their restaurant experience spoiled by the sight and sounds of food being delivered.

This only affects the gourmet end of the market, but some foods are also genuinely in short supply, and not only white truffles. Only three percent of a steer qualifies as "prime." This represents about 30 pounds of beef. One steakhouse owner, when questioned about expansion, replied, "I don't know if I can get enough heavy prime to do more." Only two out of a hundred steers are graded "prime." Other foods, are, of course, seasonal. With modern shipping and growing techniques, however, almost everything is always available.

Phoney Foods

"All that glitters is not gold" runs the proverb. Looking for better profits, food suppliers have come up with some ingenious methods and substances.

Most foods have to meet a legal definition set down by the FDA. This is what brings about such wondrous items as a well-known company's canned product called "Pork & Beans." When the can is opened, a square inch of pork fat can be seen floating on the beans, which may themselves be of extremely mixed ancestry. This makes it, legally, pork & beans! One might also quibble at the can marked "Spaghetti and Meatballs" which contains but *one* meatball, and that heavily laced with filler. Where is Ralph Nader when we really need him?

"Fresh fish" is defined as that which emerged from the waters no more than five days ago. Clearly, this definition doesn't cover those solid chunks which emerge from the deep freeze. But there's nothing to stop you calling your Salmon Special the "Catch of the Day."

Veterans of Economics 101 will recall that, whenever a product becomes prohibitively expensive or in short and uncertain supply, substitutes will emerge—hence, plastic for rubber, and polyester for cotton and silk. The food industry has its share of alternatives, too. Atlantic pollack is treated, shaped, and flavored to resemble crabmeat, lobster, and even scallops. When you see a "Lobster Crab Sandwich" for $4.50 on the menu, the one thing you can be sure of is that you aren't getting crab or lobster. And "stuffed with crabmeat" is usually a joke. Often it's a case of the substance being a mere shadow of the description. Though purists may quite rightly object to this, the small print of the law allows considerable leeway of definition, and it would require both the wisdom of Solomon and millions of dollars in lawyer's fees to make small points. It is a fact of life that the definitions of certain foods are much looser than would be permitted in, say, Aircraft Safety Regulations.

Having said that, the currently popular substitutes for expensive shellfish are much cheaper, of good quality, and certainly the happiest compromise by far in this league. The worst is possibly ersatz caviar, but everyone will have their favorites, good and bad. The truth is that many manufactured foods are so good, and attractive in price, that even a chef with the purest motives will be a fool not to use them. Canned consommé or beef broth can be mixed with other ingredients to great effect, and those little beef or chicken stock cubes can work wonders, too. While *real* mayonnaise is a delight to the connoisseur, it's a pain in the neck to make and is actually a bit exotic for the average American taste. They far prefer bottled mayo.

It's possible that many old folks may recall with amusement the disgust with which many postwar youngsters greeted fresh eggs, after having known only the powdered variety.

There are many yarns told about the things used in certain foods. Kangaroo meat was found in hamburger meat in New York several years ago and the tall story industry seems to date from that time, though it's most likely cyclic. Very few meats are an effective substitute for beef, and most of the stories belong to the apocryphal group that includes the one about granny dying in the car and the car being stolen, corpse and all. A favorite is the one about the discovery of a skinned corpse in the street that later turned out to be that of a chimpanzee. Investigation revealed that it had died in a local zoo and fallen out of the truck that was delivering it to a hamburger factory, in keeping with a longstanding arrangement for the disposal of dead animals. Horsemeat, quite commonly eaten in Belgium and France (and definitely not "worth a detour," as they say in the *Michelin Good Food Guide*), is too sweet to pass muster.

While most of these stories are nonsense, anyone who ever sees frankfurters being made will think twice before they eat another one.

It has often been said that if people had to do their own slaughter and butchery, we would all be vegetarians—a sentiment which will ring true to anyone who has ever attended a Middle Eastern market and seen animals casually hacked to death before the customer's eyes.

Although canned ham is almost invariably meat from a pig, it is often made up of scraps that have been pounded, shaped, colored, and flavored to give it a farmyard look. Often the genuine article, real ham, or real crabmeat, is prohibitively expensive for your price range. Sometimes you have to settle for acceptable, rather than the best.

Some restaurateurs, notably the quick turnover kinds, are quite unscrupulous about the food they use. What they describe as veal is really pork, and what they call calf's liver is steer liver.

When you immerse yourself in trade magazines, you will be amazed at the ingenious devices and foods that exist to enable you to quickly serve food that gives the impression of having been cooked with tender, loving care over a long period of time. They vary from the acceptable to the ghastly.

The proof of the pudding is in the eating. But the truth is that the American consumer often happily accepts food which even the *English* would disdain, let alone the French. The desire for speed is, of course, the enemy of good eating, but it's here to stay, and it won't go away. The restaurateur must come to terms with it.

Grocery List

Here is a typical, partial list of groceries from the computer of J. G. Melon, a highly successful New York restaurant. It's moderately priced with a large choice of genuine cooked-on-premises items and an interesting wine list that changes regularly to allow regular customers to experiment. If you don't recognize each item and know what it's for, you should.

artichoke heart
anchovy
A1 sauce
angostura bitters
beef broth

beans:
  black turtle
  dark red kidney
  navy
  lentil
  split pea
baker's spray
barley
clams
cranberry juice
cherries
capers
chutney
Coco Lopez
cornstarch
condensed milk
Dijon mustard
flour
graham crackers
grenadine
horseradish
jam
ketchup
lemon juice
lemons
Lea & Perrins
maple syrup
Melfry
mayonnaise
muffin mix
olive oil
ripe olives
cocktail olives

cocktail onions
pasta:
   fettucine
   tortelline
   penne
   lasagna
   linguine
   spirals
   pignoli
pineapple juice
Rose's lime juice
rice
saltines
sugar (three kinds)
Sweet 'n Low
tart shells
Tabasco sauce
tomato puree
tomatoes (whole, plum)
tomato juice
tuna
vanilla extract
vinegars:
   wine
   white wine
   malt
walnuts
spices:
   basil
   bay leaf
   chili powder
   cinnamon
   cloves

cumin

curry

Coleman's mustard

nutmeg

oregano

paprika

parsley

pepper (ground, white)

salt

tarragon

thyme

EIGHT

THE
DINING
ROOM

The dining room is the most important part of the restaurant from the customer's point of view. Except in those restaurants designed to allow the customer a view of all the fascinating goings-on in the kitchen, it's just about all they see.

The dining room is the stage where they enjoy their restaurant experience. It's also where they buy the goods and spend the money.

SEATING POSITIONS

Many restaurateurs are not gifted with any particular aesthetic sense. However, there is nothing to stop you from sitting in every single chair in the room at least once and taking in the view. This may lead to the use of a discreet screen or the repositioning of a "bus station"—the corner where back-up linen and cutlery and condiments are kept, and where dirty dishes are dumped, pending the accumulation of a sufficient amount to make it worthwhile taking them to the dishwasher.

MUSIC

It's usual to have some kind of music in the background in these electronic times. There are repeating eight-hour tapes that will help drive your staff insane before their time. "Music soothes the savage breast," and the researcher who discovered that people consume more against a musical background has a lot to answer for to people who hate recorded background music. Traditionally, music drowns the sound of people slurping soup, just as wine "cuts the grease." Why shouldn't your customers enjoy a little aural satisfaction, along with the oral, tactile, dentile, and olfactory sensations you're throwing into your bargain package?

VENTILATION AND HEATING

It's not a bad idea to open all the doors and windows once in a while to freshen the air. Visiting a poorly ventilated, basement club-restaurant after ten straight days of Christmas parties, when all the amateur drinkers have been out to play, will convince you of the wisdom of this. Most people have a dual attitude to cooking smells. Sometimes they're appropriate and welcome, sometimes not. In general, kitchen smells should not be allowed to leak to the dining room, to ruin the effect of all that citrus cologne and musky perfume. Fiercely efficient ventilation is a good investment.

The larger the room and the higher the ceiling, the more problems you'll have. Sometimes the thermostat controls have to be locked so that only selected personnel can alter them. Nothing kills a dining room faster than a cold draft, so if you have tables near a door, make sure it's a double door with a heater. An insoluble problem of the industry is the fact that those who are rushing around at work are automatically warmed, while the seated customers are not. But you can't have a room with two temperatures. Sometimes the Montagues are sweating while the Capulets are freezing, and vice versa. One solution is to put the air conditioner on for a while, then turn it off, and so on, so that all of the people are happy some of the time. And a good antiseptic gargle before retiring can help prevent colds . . .

Perhaps the worst smell a diner can encounter is the lingering evidence of the exterminator's visit, which is not uncommon, especially in old buildings. Cigarette smoke also can be a problem, but again, efficient ventilation can help enormously. There are machines to disperse cigarette smoke. None of them are worth a damn unless they are switched on long before the smoke becomes a problem. You need an air flow. In some states the new separation of smoking and nonsmoking areas required by law will save nonsmokers from the worst effects. It is cigarettes that have been solemnly lit, then placed in ashtrays to smolder, or incorporated in an intriguing pose in an air current leading right to someone's nose that are the worst. Don't be surprised to see people eating and interspersing mouthfuls with puffs at cigarettes. Would they do that at home, you may wonder? It's only one of a thousand wondrous things you'll see before you're through with the restaurant business.

Some restaurateurs like to spray the place with Forest Zephyr and similar products. Where there's emphasis on fresh flowers, they will provide a masking and pleasant smell, as they used to at funerals in the days before refrigeration.

The floor should be vacuumed if carpeted, and mopped if a hard surface, at least once a day. A quick once-over between lunch and dinner will do no harm either. Garbage tends to accumulate in the bar area and should be cleared regularly. Discreetly placed garbage bags should be emptied promptly, too, especially when they contain wet stuff, because they'll soon start to smell and also become harder to handle.

The presence of breathing bodies, the majority of whom are smoking, will cloud and discolor mirrors, windows, and walls. Yvonne Scherrer, proprietress of the luxurious and highly successful Devon House restaurant in New York, closes for two months a year. During this period the restaurant is painted top to bottom. Not every restaurant can afford to close for such a period. Most will be obliged to paint and mend during the small hours of the night between closing and opening.

A dustpan, broom, mop, and bucket should be placed where they are instantly grabbable, so that spillages and other accidents can be cleaned quickly with minimum disruption of business.

RESTROOMS

You, or your manager, or someone should check the restrooms regularly. Strange things happen in these places. Going into a restroom just before closing to find someone stark naked sitting on the toilet snoring happily because they think they made it home is so commonplace as to be unremarkable. More important is the possibility of nasty mess which will curb the appetites of innocent customers. The busboy or dishwasher is a likely candidate to clean up, but it's amazing how often the manager or even the owner has to do it.

In very expensive restaurants and nightclubs, the restrooms, especially the ladies', often attract attention. The attendants frequently become mother-figures, ever ready with a repair kit to take care of the missing button, tear, or spillage. Some well-known women restaurateurs got their start this way—and many a movie star, too. If you build an upscale clientele, it will do no harm to indulge them with a few chic touches, like linen towels and interesting soap, as this costs little and gives a nice impression.

CLEANLINESS

In a restaurant, as in a hospital or indeed any busy household, cleaning up has to be a continuous process. A successful restaurant is inevitably a busy one and there's a continuous flow of dirty dishes, ashtrays, and general refuse which must be removed well before it becomes offensive. The best way to keep on top of things is to establish a routine. At

4 P.M. the busboy checks the bar garbage, replacing the garbage bags where necessary. Either on closing or before opening, the floors all get mopped and swept. Mondays somebody does the front window, Tuesdays somebody cleans the bar mirrors, and so on. Apart from being efficient, this method will eliminate the dismal habit some owners have of wandering about the place with a long face that only comes to life with a snarl when they discover something that needs cleaning.

Owners who prefer the philosophy of *oderint dum temerant* ("Let them hate, as long as they fear")—and they are by no means in short supply—will naturally ignore this observation.

MENUS

Menu design is often appalling. Many menus are unclear, cluttered, misleading, and, worst of all, out of date. Murphy's Law insists that the one item which has been discontinued, but which has not been deleted from the menu, is the one which will be most frequently requested. Thus the waiters or waitresses are irritatingly "one down" from the word *go* because they have to explain and disappoint. Blackboard menus are a good idea in saloon-type restaurants, but they should be checked regularly for legibility.

A neat dodge available to restaurants with computers is to make small alterations in the menu every day. You can have special dishes of the day while retaining your permanent menu. By changing the specials and the date, you can give a very encouraging impression of having had a dawn conference at which the offerings of the day were carefully considered. It's good theater.

Menus can be presented in a dozen ways. Ideally, you should strike a happy compromise between practicality and decorativeness. Where the menus can be wiped clean, they should be, and where they have to be replaced from the printers, a reserve should be held and dispersed before the ones available become too dog-eared, soup-stained, and greasy.

Verbal Menus

In the spirit of offering theatrical entertainment, many restaurants insist that their waiters or waitresses tell their customers about the Daily

Specials. Many diners find this ridiculous. They get the giggles when some charming would-be actor secures their attention and then addresses them with all the aplomb—replete with meaningful, engaging glances and occasional witty asides—of Gielgud doing Mark Antony's funeral oration. They feel sorry for the shy youngster who gazes at a point in mid-infinity and rattles off the specials by rote, with occasional stammers and blushes at some unfamiliar word.

Many diners forget what was said halfway through the peroration, descend with glee upon a trapped victim, and crossexamine to death, or demand a recapitulation followed by further explanation. Others couldn't give a damn what they're going to eat anyway—they're there to talk sex or money. Some will be too drunk to care.

The bottom line question is: How does this affect sales? Trial and error can prove things one way or another.

But isn't it simpler to change the menu every day on the computer, and have a few copies made? Or have regular specials on different days with detachable slips that can be clipped to the standard menus?

Another current fad in some restaurants—one that smacks of the think tank, restaurant consultants, psychologists, and theme merchants, rather than the result of any common sense consideration—is the business of waiters identifying themselves with a gay "Hi! I'm Craig, and I'm your waiter tonight."

This phoney bonhomie creaks horribly when the chicken arrives rare and the steak burned, and the martini sits on the service bar so long, often in painful sight of its would-be consumer, that it's warm and flabby when it arrives. Again, it's for owners to decide in the light of experience, but perhaps, on the whole, a "Thanks, Suzy" on the back of the check should be the limit of the personal touch. The occasional rapport between staff and customers that results in friendship, romance, stardom, adoption, change of will, or a change of job, is a separate adventure, and no generalizations apply.

DUTIES OF WAITERS
AND WAITRESSES

Owners will do well *not* to add casually to the workload of their waiters and waitresses. They don't just show up five minutes before opening time, unless we're talking about the head guy who's been there five years, knows where all the bodies are buried, and, like the 2,000 pound gorilla, sits wherever it wants. If there's no busboy, they have to sweep and mop. They have to fill the salts and peppers, combine the ketchups and mustards, check the menus, set up the tables, bring up the reserve supply of linen, fill the cutlery containers, make sure the milk, the iced tea, and the cream supply are in place, etc.

Every little bit hurts, and as the workload increases, their positive attitude diminishes. They are, after all, your front line salesmen. Every time they go to a table, they have your considerable investment in the palm of their hands. There is no need to explore the importance of just how they feel about *you*, by the way. However, their prime object is to make money from tips, and they usually won't cut off their noses to spite their faces.

A common fault among restaurant staff is that they allow the unusual to dominate their thinking. An encounter with a rude customer will cause a waiter to be rude to polite and pleasant customers. An ungenerous tip will cause frowns and grumbles, whereas a generous one will be accepted without comment. (By the way, any bartender or waitress will tell you that the amount of tips earned in a given shift in an established restaurant will average out almost uncannily, as will the weekly total.) Old hands, who are determined to stay sane in what can be a crazymaking business, give as good as they get to rude customers and maintain a pleasant manner to the others.

It is amazing how frequently in the United States, where so much is made of respecting the individual, restaurant staff are treated with contempt. However, it may be that one should not make too much of the rapport between the staff and customers. No computer has yet decided how important it is, though common sense tells one that a good rapport is probably better than a bad one.

Systems for Waiters and Waitresses

In the kind of restaurant under discussion, the waiter or waitress usually takes the orders and delivers the food. There is a standard (but hopefully not inflexible) drill. Once the customers are seated, they are given menus (if the host hasn't already done so, or if it isn't already on the table or on the wall) and asked if they'd like a drink. If they would, the waitress gets it, then gives them a moment to consider the menu. If they want to order immediately, she waits. If she's busy, she tells them she'll be right back, goes on to something else, and returns. Most people these days understand this choreography perfectly well.

The waiter has a station of several tables, each with a number, which is entered on the check, on the kitchen order dupe, and on the bar dupe where these are required. Bar dupes are a pain in the neck, and a time-wasting ritual, but some owners find them comforting. They are in no sense a security measure, because no busy bartender has the time to compare documentation *and* make two whisky sours, one up one down, a Campari and soda, two piñas, one is a virgin, and could I get a bottle of number 13, that's the funny label, the one with the— oh, we ran out? are you sure?

You should have ready instant contingency plans for combining tables in order to make a two into a four, or a four into a six, up to whatever your maximum is. Leave "Gee, where we gonna put 'em?" to the competition. But when someone calls at 8:30 and says, "We're, let's see, 14. Could you fix us up with a table in ten minutes?" it's unwise to say yes if you really can't cope. In this regard, beware of phoney reservations from pranksters or competitors intent upon sabotage.

Waiters and waitresses are often, but by no means always, backed up by a busboy, who serves bread and butter, clears finished plates, and so on. The busboy gets a cut of the tips, and sometimes there aren't enough tips or weight of business to warrant having one. This means the waiters have more to do and, inevitably, endure occasional delay. Sometimes the assistant manager, hostess, or seating captain helps clear the tables—never a popular chore, especially since the job usually means wearing "proper" clothes, as distinct from cheap and cheerful ones nobody minds getting dirty.

The owner must discuss the requirement for a busboy with the staff, observe, and make a decision in this regard. Many will risk defective service in order to save a small salary. That's their problem.

Every waiter or waitress has a station, and must be prepared to take note of others. Few words are more depressing to a diner than the dismissive "Sorry, that's not my station. I'm not your waitress" from a passing waitress from whom something has been requested. Nor is the qualifying " . . . but I'll send her over right away" very comforting either. The correct response is "Yes, what can I get you?"

A popular system that seems to work very well is the one where there are two sorts of waiters: front men and runners, or floor men and kitchen men. The front man is a combination of captain and ordinary waiter. He doesn't wear a tuxedo, but, having taken the order and placed it in the kitchen, he then assumes a supervisory capacity. The person he supervises is the runner, whose responsibility it is to pick up and serve the food.

The front man has a nice executive feeling—a lance corporal, rather than a private—and some go off on paranoid ego trips. One well-known New York waiter with a Yul Brynner hairstyle (if that isn't an oxymoron) addresses his affluent, but not necessarily educated, customers with opening speeches such as "Hi, lobsters are the special tonight. They're tremendous, and I mean that both literally and figuratively." At this point his victim's jaws drop, the women pull down their skirts and the men straighten their ties. He claims to be the only Choate educated waiter in the world ("a dubious claim," sniffed an Old St. Paulian) and, by reference to his pocket calculator and the reservations book, he reckons to be able to gauge his total tips to the nearest dollar on any given evening before the first customer walks in. Gambling is his downfall.

The runner is saved the horror of having to talk to people, a special blessing if he doesn't speak English, though it's a bore for customers who ask him for a spoon, and get in return a brilliant smile.

In order to ensure that all customers get what they ordered (customers often forget, so it's a good idea to have the edge on them), a system is employed whereby each diner is accorded a number at the table, which is put on the order slip. 1. chicken   2. veal, and so on. If there's one woman in the party, she's number one. If there are more, then number one is always the person nearest the door, or whatever. The system breaks down frequently, but it's fun straightening things out. Little contretemps in restaurants are often more welcome than owners realize. They're part of the adventure and sometimes help to break the ice.

On the whole, this system works well. A thing to note is that the more people you have on the floor, the less in tips each person takes home. Some owners couldn't give a damn; waitresses, they say, are a dime a dozen. If they don't like working there, tough. But continuity is a good thing, and rapid turnover of help may be a turnoff for regular customers, especially if you're doing a lot of neighborhood business.

PAYMENT

Bills, checks, or tabs are collected by the waiters and waitresses or the manager. They should include the total for food and drinks, as well as anything consumed at the bar but not paid for there. It's unusual for bartenders to allow this to happen. Most are paranoid about collecting their dues on the spot. "Can I put this on my table tab?" the customer asks. "Sorry, madam, separate register!" the bartender lies, trembling slightly at the possibility of missing a tip. In fact, most customers who make this request do so because they want to put the whole bill on a credit card, and are quite happy to give the bartender a tip, even though they don't pay the bar bill.

To this total, the local tax, if any, should be added, and then it's not a bad idea to write the grand total in large black figures so that it can easily be discerned. Mistakes in addition, which frequently occur, are usually made when transferring from the single column to the tens. Experienced waiters develop a feel for the amount, however, and will usually doublecheck when, after two sirloins, two apple pies, two martinis, and a bottle of Beaujolais, the bill somehow only comes to $24. In a majority of cases, the money is handed in to the bartender, who rings it up on the register.

Credit Cards

There is little doubt that restaurants which refuse to accommodate credit cards may lose business. It is significant, however, that many do not accept plastic money and still do well. A thought that leaps to the cynical mind is that credit card transactions are recorded with a third party, and this may not always suit some operators. Naturally, a service charge is made by the credit card company, and some restaurateurs resent this. Possibly the most important factor to consider is that some customers are spending company money for business entertainment, and it's highly convenient for them to be able to hand in their credit card bill to the accounts office as a ready-made list of all they spent in a particular month. Tourists also are likely to use them for the convenience.

If, as is likely, you decide to use this service, you'll be equipped with a machine that enables you to check the validity of cards. There are several designs, but they all follow the same principle. You run the magnetic band of the card through the machine, then enter the card number and amount of transaction. A prompt on the screen will tell you when to proceed. In the end you'll be accorded an approval code. If you have this, you are bound to collect your money even if—and many restaurateurs never quite grasp this—you accidentally retain the wrong copy of the credit card carbon slip.

Some cards require a phone call. They are a pain in the neck, because it sometimes takes ages to get through.

As with so many things in the restaurant, it really helps if you can stop dead and, without interruption, show new employees exactly how to operate this very simple equipment. The choice is simple: Show them properly once, or waste time in the future half-showing them again between interruptions, invariably at the busiest times of the day.

Personal House Accounts

Some regular customers like to be able to sign their bills and pay monthly. There's no reason why they shouldn't. Once in a while you'll get beat. But the steak you sell for $20 didn't *cost* you $20 so, unless you are prone to pain from opportunity loss, you haven't really been ripped off that badly. The trick is not to let the bills get out of hand.

There is a breed of professional restaurant scrounger who specializes in running up small bills around the town. At first they pay promptly, building confidence. Then, suddenly, they're not there anymore. *C'est la vie.* In these times, you're bound to get a visit from one of those deadbeats who eat their fill and then calmly tell you they haven't any money. It isn't worth bringing in the police. Let them depart in peace. But don't let them in again. Poor souls, one day they'll pull their cunning stunt in the wrong place, and find themselves being taken quietly backstage and liquidated. Some owners wittily write off these visitors under "promotion."

It's very nice if you can get company accounts, with certain executives authorized to sign. It means you've got yourself some regular corporate business, and that should produce a warm glow. Incidentally, there's nothing to stop you from visiting companies and promoting yourself—an often neglected means of increasing business.

As part of their "restaurant chic" or "restaurant presence"— variations on the theme of restaurant theater—some customers don't even want to sign their bills while they are entertaining at the table. They'll trust you, or your staff, to total it, add a tip, and put their name on it. In the dining room their guests, if they notice, will be impressed ("Does he own the joint?"). Kindly rich parents will sometimes send young daughters and their swains to a restaurant, having first called to authorize them to put everything on their account.

Tipping

A line in "Casablanca" that often elicits a chuckle from some knowing member of the audience occurs shortly after Claude Raines has closed the joint. "Keep everyone on salary" says good-hearted Rick, with a Bogartian, solicitous please-hurt-me-more frown. Since a waiter or waitress's paycheck is sometimes precisely zero, after tax computed on salary and tips, this would be an empty gesture for the tippable staff—though a bonanza for the others. Also, in places like Casablanca and the South of France, it's not uncommon for waiters to be paid nothing. Their tips are their sole income.

In one sense, tipping is none of the owner's business, but you should be aware of the usual systems adopted. Tipping at tables works out at an uncanny average of 8% nationwide. Sometimes tips are pooled and divided equally, after deductions for the busboys, service bartender, and perhaps the captain or hostess. Occasionally this leads to suspicions and grumbles, because some waiters or waitresses are better than others. One who receives an exorbitant tip may not put it all in the "tronc," as it's called in England. Once a business is established, however, the degree of talent will tend to be fairly uniform.

In some restaurants the staff will keep their own tips. This is fine, except that inevitably some stations are more popular than others, and the waiter in the back may fume as tables in the window are turned time and time again while he does a crossword puzzle. Of course, stations should be rotated. But then you have the seniority factor. The waitress who's been with you for three years may automatically get the front station every day, due perhaps to a period of turnover when a procession of newcomers meant that they took the easier stations and didn't stay long enough to graduate. This can lead to unrest among the troops. On balance, the pooling system would seem to be the best.

Sometimes the captain or hostess will get tipped. In old-fashioned Maxim's-type operations where a captain in a tuxedo supervises a station, he expects to be tipped, and the customers are usually well trained. You will notice on the slips for some credit cards that there's actually a whole line marked "Captain" in the gratuities area of the column. Occasionally customers will tip a captain or hostess to get them a table promptly. It's nice if this is done discreetly, because this can lead to bad feeling among the customers and is often forbidden by owners.

Bartenders are tipped an average of 20% to 30%, but with a usual minimum these days of a dollar. There is a greater variation than at the tables, and in general bar checks aren't as big as table checks. However, since the bartender gets a decent wage as well as tips, there's not much room for complaint and, indeed, complaints are rare. The "decent wage" is usually the union scale, whether the restaurant has a union contract or not. In most states this is now around $50 a shift, as opposed to the federally guaranteed minimum wage per hour, which is usually what the other staff get. Many think the bartender's job is the best in the house.

Pros and Cons of Tipping

Many consider tipping demeaning and prefer the service charge system whereby 15% is automatically added to a check. This is normal on the continent, where it was introduced because tips tended to be small or nonexistent.

A few owners exploit the service charge system and do not give their employees an even break. Most people who have jobs that attract gratuities prefer to take their chances. It averages out better.

When European customers arrive, some waiters or waitresses will add on a 15% service charge, knowing it won't be resented. Otherwise there's a chance people might glance at the sales tax and conveniently mistake it for a service charge.

From a customer point of view, the tipping system is a godsend. Some jobs just wouldn't be worth doing if there were no tips involved. What luggage porter is going to struggle across a crowded foyer to grab heavy bags if there's no reward involved? If you're a regular customer and tip well, you'll amass brownie points entitling you to all sorts of extras, possibly including warm smiles when you call for extra butter.

Businessmen are far and away the best tippers, except for movie stars. Women, especially older women, can be mean. The sight of two members of the fair sex itemizing who had what and counting out 15% to the nearest penny is a familiar and risible sight. Occasionally a man will leave a generous tip, but when he goes to get his hat, his woman companion will put some of the money in her pocket.

In Russia, where tipping is forbidden, the service in restaurants is usually as rotten as the food—as many tourists have reported. Strangely enough, in Japan, where tipping also is forbidden, things seem to go smoothly.

Restaurant employees easily lose sight of the way in which everything averages out, and they rarely rejoice when they get an exceptionally generous tip. It's said that "tip" derives from the phrase "to insure promptitude."

The worst aspect of tipping is the mean attitude it provokes. It's unpleasant to see a young waitress's lips curl as she curses some customer for leaving an ungenerous tip. It rarely seems to cross their minds to reflect that the absence of generosity may be a comment on the quality of service. Even if this point is grasped, there may be a whine on the lines of "I know the fish was cold. This damn chef never gets things out together. It wasn't my fault!"

The owner is responsible for declaring employees' tips for IRS purposes. In fact, the IRS (not ungenerously, though they can hardly employ an agent to shadow each waiter as he goes about his duties) allows each employee to declare a daily amount, and this is agreed among the help. The accountant will normally take care of all this for you. While the IRS is generally benign in its attitude toward restaurants, when it descends, its attentions tend to be ferocious. Often, they're in hot pursuit of organized crime money launderers.

In Italy, customers can be stopped within a statutory distance of the restaurant they've just visited and required to show their restaurant bill to the official tax inspector, whose job it is to make sure that restaurateurs are declaring all their takings. Quite who gets prosecuted if the person has lost the receipt or thrown it away is unclear. It smacks of "bad law," but it is a scene tailormade for the next "Pink Panther" movie.

STEALING

Due to the accessibility of cash and goods, stealing, sadly, is common in the restaurant business. Many owners are obsessed by it, especially first generation immigrants. They will solemnly inspect all employees' bags on leaving, and sometimes will not allow bags to be brought in at all. They will require their employees to undergo screening, including lie detector tests, before they're hired. The security firms they hire—presumably retired thieves who've turned state's evidence—will send spies, called inspectors, to restaurants to observe and report.

Their reports may go something like this: "The bartender greeted us with a smile. His appearance was neat and his fingernails were clean. He placed a clean bevnap in front of each customer. Two Beefeater martinis were ordered. They were correctly prepared, chilled, and served with the requested garnishes. The drinks were immediately rung up on the cash register and the check placed in front of us."

Well, whatever turns you on. You probably pay the security firm more than the bartender steals, but there you are.

Many owners appoint spies among both their employees *and* their customers. Their cover is soon blown, though. Far from liquidating them, the other employees will simply warn acceptable newcomers whom to watch out for, in much the same way as the British often leave terrorist leaders alone and under supervision, on the grounds that if they're arrested, it will take months to identify their replacements. A hilarious aspect of restaurant work is that sometimes, a new employee being shown the ropes will also be initiated into the little wrinkles that help to swell the take. Occasionally, a new employee is embarrassed to discover that the staff are stealing *far too much*, and knows that one dreary day everyone will be fired.

Hotels are notoriously paranoid about stealing. Each bottle of liquor delivered is stamped, sometimes invisibly, to insure that only the house booze is being sold. The point is that bartenders have been known to bring in their own bottles in order to show a good PC while actually pocketing most of the bar proceeds. At crack of dawn, assistant managers will take the bar inventory down to a tenth of a bottle. Often as not they have nothing better to do. Maybe some restaurants can afford it, but the average restaurateur probably cannot.

Some larger restaurants are completely computerized. This makes excellent sense once everyone has mastered the system. This replaces the "dupe" system, whereby, having taken an order, the waitress makes out a duplicate kitchen order slip and enters the number of the check, so that later the check and the kitchen dupe can be compared. With the computer, nothing is sent out unless it's entered on the computer, but again, you may have to pay an extra wage for someone to monitor all this. Some restaurants give the waiter a bank to make his own change. Then, at the close of business, he has to pay up for everything he has entered on the computer.

By the way, the computer systems don't come cheap either. Most restaurants wait until they're going strong before investing.

Waitresses can steal in time-honored ways. They'll use the same check over and over, if a common order in the restaurant is two hamburgers and two beers. But what about the dupe they have to put into the kitchen to get the food out and the dupe they have to give the bartender to get the beers? They wait until no one is looking, grab them, and destroy them—or cut the chef in on their ill-gotten gains.

In busy places waiters will give "verbal checks," simply stating the amount and making change from their pockets. But supposing the boss is watching? Then they go to the restroom and make the change there. If they've got the money for a check in their pockets, they may put it on the next credit card they get hold of and keep the cash. But what about when the customer finds she's paid two bills instead of one? Either the waiter will shrug it off ("That's weeks ago. How can I remember?") or won't be working there anymore anyway. Some employees automatically pad their checks with small amounts. Two dollars per check on a busy day can mount up nicely.

Just as liars need to develop good memories, restaurant thieves need to be on their toes, and they'll tell you it's exhausting having to remember what moves they've made.

Bartenders have their wrinkles, too, but the owner can always compare the liquor takings with the amount issued, so it doesn't pay them to be too greedy.

Generally, the happier the restaurant, and the better managed it is, the less stealing there will be. There's no point in being paranoid about it, although a majority of restaurateurs are. If all your employees are in cahoots, they'll cover their tracks carefully and you'll go crazy trying to find suspected leaks. At one busy Columbus Avenue restaurant in New York City, owned by a bunch of show biz celebrities, they automatically fire everybody after three months in the interests of security.

A weather eye on the profits is your best bellwether in this respect. Half an hour spent on your books in a morning will save an awful lot of suspicion and anxiety. In a reasonably happy restaurant, a frown and a tut-tut from the boss to an employee will often curb greediness. "Joe, I must say, the PC doesn't reflect the increase in bar trade we've noticed lately. I wonder why that is?" Or, to translate this into restaurantese, "Mary, the new help. What are they doing? Either they straighten out or I'm going to have to fire the whole lot of them."

Customers are quite capable of stealing, too. It's mainly souvenirs such as ashtrays or attractive showplates, but the box containing the tips is a favorite target, as are tips allowed to sit too long in plain sight on vacated tables.

Ah, the warm, smiling, carefree joy of the restaurant business! One's faith in human nature and love of mankind is bolstered at every turn! If you have ever felt that Mine Host's Falstaffian laugh sometimes had a rather hollow ring, when you become a Mine Host yourself, you'll soon realize why.

HYGIENE, HEALTH, AND SAFETY

The inevitable dangers that exist in any public place where people are gathered, and particularly where they are smoking, eating, and drinking, are too great to allow safety measures to be left to the goodwill and wisdom of owners and customers. The law requires attention to hygiene, health, and safety. It appoints inspectors to check premises at random. If standards are not met, owners will be warned and required to correct their omissions. If violations are not corrected, then premises are closed. However, authorities are generally helpful in these matters and willing to advise businesses on their requirements. With certain notable exceptions that are unavoidable where the deadly hand of bureaucracy lurks, these requirements are based on common sense standards and you should have little trouble complying with them.

POISON SOURCES

A century has passed since Doctor Lister started insisting that hospital doctors should wash their hands after examining a patient and before examining another. The law now requires the following sign to be hung in restaurant bathrooms: *Employees must wash their hands before leaving this room.* Absence of this notice constitutes a violation, though it's unlikely that a restaurant would actually be closed for this reason.

There is no requirement for the sign to be printed in any language other than English. Nor is there any law that requires restaurant employees to be able to read English. Many people from Third World countries do *not* normally wash their hands after visiting the toilet. You will see them quite commonly emerge from a lavatory and go straight back to work cutting vegetables and dipping veal slices into flour! Though this isn't a pleasant thought, salmonella, the most common form of food poisoning and one which can kill the elderly and infirm, is often transmitted by urine. Diarrhea and dysentery often come from feces.

What saves society from regular epidemics of food poisoning is the cooking process. Germs insinuated into food by dirty workers or natural deterioration are destroyed by the heat.

Other germs may be present in food from other sources. Chicken has been targeted as the main source of salmonella in the United States. That's why it should be thoroughly cooked, though it's not unusual in dubious restaurants to see a little ooze of blood as one cuts into a chicken breast! Such a sight is likely to extinguish the heartiest appetite, so make sure your chicken—and all other appropriate items—are properly cooked or you'll lose customers and even risk lawsuits. Apart from the fact that pork tastes better when well cooked (though the French sometimes eat pork chops medium rare!), there is the danger of trichinosis, a common disease carried by pigs which can be fatal to humans. The dietary laws of some religions preclude the consumption of pork, and originally the reason for this may have been practical rather than religious.

The most dangerous food is that which, having been cooked, is then reheated. At certain temperatures germs spring to life with a vengeance, particularly in meat and quite horrifically in sausage. The simple way to avoid this danger is to make sure that food is served either thoroughly cooked and piping hot, or cold. Of course, this leaves your poor old *salade de canard tiède* (a tepid salad of medium rare duck breasts and vegetables) out in the cold, but some gourmets are happy to take a chance.

Fish is a well-known source of poisoning. In Japan the passion for a certain type of fish that just happens to secrete a high amount of botulin accounts for thousands of deaths each year due to inexpert cleaning. Fortunately, there is usually no mistaking fish that has deteriorated, but accidents do happen and even the strong smell of rotting fish might get lost in the jungle of aromas that pervades the kitchen at busy times.

A properly trained Western cook simply follows the maxim "When in doubt, throw it out." But someone from a Third World country may not share our standards of hygiene.

CLEANLINESS

The price of cleanliness is eternal vigilance. Bored assistant managers will usually find time to run inquisitive fingers along picture rails and examine the glasses containing the bar garnishes. Indeed, some of them manage to fill their whole shift doing little else!

Cleaning routines must be established. Cleaning materials must be readily available so that jobs don't get put off and then forgotten. Some things get cleaned every day, others once a week. A list pinned to the employees' notice board will help. Everyone must get into the habit of cleaning up as they go along.

Consumer watchdogs fiercely monitor the chemicals used to promote the growth, or enhance the appearance, of fruit and vegetables. Most people, even strawberry lovers, are happier if these items are washed in running water before being used. Some gourmets require the lettuce in their salad to be washed, and each individual leaf dried, so as not to dilute the salad dressing! The little worms that sometimes cause such alarm and fuss in salads and fruit dishes are sometimes the least harmful things in the dish—and a good source of protein, too!

If you poison people, they may sue you. A famous example of this in recent years was Yul Brynner's successful case against Trader Vic's in New York. He complained that he and his family had become ill after eating spare ribs. No doubt the company was insured.

Any kind of dirt is a potential source of infection. Even basically clean people can have accidents or overlook things. That's why the authorities inspect premises from time to time. A fresh eye will often see what the accustomed eye ignores.

VERMIN AND EXTERMINATORS

The role of vermin in spreading infection is not totally understood. They may be innocent on all counts. But this seems unlikely since we have confirmed beyond doubt that dysentery, malaria, and bubonic plague are transmitted by flies, mosquitoes, and rats, respectively.

In most cities and states, restaurateurs are required by law to employ an exterminator at regular intervals and to post a report in a prominent place for the health inspector to examine. An exterminator recently told me, "Boy, if they ever establish a connection between roaches and AIDS, business will go through the roof!" The same exterminator confessed that he often carried a dead mouse in his pocket, especially when visiting new clients. He would brandish it triumphantly as evidence of his efficiency. Exterminators know where to spray and they have all the proper equipment. They are well worth the $25 they generally charge for a visit because they go all over the premises, usually in less than an hour.

Exterminators often work very late at night, thus sparing customers the smell of insecticide. Their most disagreeable, though efficient, weapon is the glue mouse trap. Sometimes the first person to enter the restaurant in a morning will be faced with the prospect of administering the *coup de grâce* to a live mouse enveloped in glue. The best way of handling this nasty situation is to stick the moribund mouse under the hot water tap.

Few things are more depressing to the diner than an encrusted fork, a clouded knife, or a glass with a smear of someone else's lipstick on it. "It's not my shade!" the complainer will often wittily cry.

Even in the best run establishments, accidents can happen. Though a conscientious bartender will check glasses automatically during work, the light in bar areas is often subdued. So it sometimes happens that a glass is sent from a gloomy bar area to a window table where the lipstick smear is revealed in all its glory.

This is an area where official hygiene requirements and reality collide. Many regulations require a rinse water temperature which is acceptable in the dishwashing machine, but which would cause serious injury to anyone foolish enough to put their hands in it. Thus the bartender, who usually washes many used glasses in the bar sinks, has to compromise. He or she will normally send glasses that have been used for creamy drinks such as brandy alexanders or piña coladas to the kitchen, in order not to grease up the bar sink. But kissproof lipstick will often survive boiling water. Sometimes the electric revolving brushes in the bar sink will remove it, but the best way is to wipe it off with a damp paper napkin.

Some regulations specify which types of detergents must be used for washing up. But detergents sometimes leave a thin film which, though invisible on inefficiently rinsed china, is all too visible on glass. For this reason, many bartenders prefer to use no soap or detergent whatsoever in their sinks. Provided that the water is regularly changed and as hot as can be tolerated by the naked hand, this poses no health threat. But the law may be contravened—if not flouted.

HEALTH INSPECTORS

Fortunately, health inspectors are just regular people. From time to time some of them lose their jobs because they accept bribes. Some owners would rather resort to the bribe than attend to their perfectly simple responsibilities. Such is the cynicism of our times that they persist in believing that corruption is more rampant than it really is. One owner said recently, "It's always tough when two of them come together. The other day I had a guy and a young girl, a trainee. I cornered the guy by himself in the basement. I had two $50 bills in my pocket. I pulled one out and said, 'I'd like to take care of you. Christmas is coming.' 'No, no,' he said, 'I can't take that. I'm a supervisor!' So then I found the girl in the ladies room where she was just making a note of the fact that somebody had removed my 'Must wash hands' sign. 'Why don't you buy yourself a little something?' I said, offering her the money. 'No, no, that's OK,' she said. 'Don't worry, you'll pass!' And I did. It must be the new generation of health inspectors!"

If you don't pass, you may be called in for a hearing. If things aren't put right, you'll be closed.

Restaurants that are closed down are often run by inexperienced people from countries where standards of hygiene are not as high as those in the United States. They are often in old properties that have been infested for a century or more and that suffer from erratic plumbing.

In some cities, retired health inspectors make a living by carrying out unofficial inspections of premises. For $25 they will go over your premises with great zeal—probably more than when they were acting in an official capacity! This will help keep you out of trouble.

GARBAGE AND SANITATION

Restaurants generate vast amounts of garbage. Take a stroll down any busy city avenue around 11 P.M. and you'll see the minions dragging out great black plastic bags. Big restaurants and hotels often use huge metal containers that are specially designed to be loaded onto a truck.

Such is the quantity of restaurant garbage to be collected that the regular sanitation department cannot cope with it. This is where the private sanitation companies come in and, again, if you stroll city streets late at night, you'll see the garbage trucks with private company names on the side.

Don't fuss about finding a suitable company. About three minutes after you sign the lease on your premises, a representative from the company which by long-established custom covers your area will arrive on your doorstep. The fees are about the same wherever you go. Once you've agreed to give them your business (and you'll have to give it to someone!), you'll find you're "protected" from being bothered by visiting salesmen from other companies. A discreet sticker in your front window will indicate to other sanitation folk that everything is taken care of, and there will be no need to incur the risk of nasty accidents by trying to get your business. Private sanitation companies are renowned for their efficiency.

TYPICAL VIOLATIONS

The New York City Department of Health recently released a list of 41 food establishments cited for violating the health code. In addition, it listed six restaurants that were allowed to reopen after correcting earlier violations and three that were closed for having failed to do so. Here is a selection from the list of violations.

Mouse droppings

Flies

Dead roaches and old food under coffee station

Flies and roaches in the kitchen

Old food on walls and floor

Wall tiles missing in bathroom

Material stored improperly

Debris under preparation table

Old food on potato slicer

Glass cracked in kitchen cabinet door

Food stored improperly

Rinse water too cool

Gas burner improperly under dishwashing sink

Kitchen door not secure against rodents

Holes in basement and kitchen walls

No protection certificate

No hairnets for food handlers

Some food too warm

Ice cream scoops not rinsed in running water

Old food on can opener

Grease on shelves

Seams in cutting board

Leaky pipes under sink

Boxes on floor

Improper detergent

Most recent inspection report not available

No guards on fluorescent lights over preparation area

No ventilation in bathroom

Dust on refrigerator fan guard

Ceiling tiles missing

Dishwashing equipment inadequate

Basement door not secure against rodents

Material under sewer line

Flies, grease, and dust on kitchen floor

Grease on work stove and filters

Food and grease on stove and behind equipment

No extermination report posted

Standing water on basement floor

Carbon dioxide tanks improperly secured

No guards on lights

Uncovered garbage

No backflow prevention in basement hose

Seams in table

No soap or towels in employees' bathroom

Faucet leaks in dishwashing sink

Foods kept at improper temperatures

Food uncovered in refrigerator

Live and dead mice in kitchen and storage areas

It's hard to quarrel with any of the above. The 'Grade 1' violations, which can get you into trouble, are immediately health threatening. When the inspectors find a place in an appalling state they will naturally tend to throw the book at the owner. Then you will see violations such as "No chemical test kit." By law, restaurants must have, but not necessarily use, a little gadget that changes color when immersed in wash water, indicating the level of chlorine, detergent, and other chemicals. It is a farcical example of bureaucracy hitting reality, and nobody takes it very seriously unless they're looking for trouble. Another pernickety violation sometimes cited is material stored on unfinished wood.

PERSONAL HYGIENE

Restaurant workers are required by law to be clean, and the restaurant owner is required to provide them with the necessary supplies of soap, towels, and, for the kitchen staff, clean workclothes. Long hair is supposed to be pinned back in the dining room, and actually covered in the kitchen, though this requirement is often ignored.

Sometimes owners will have to be brutally rude in order to correct carelessness. Employees who come to work with sweaty, greasy hair, often straight from their gym, just have to be straightened out. They may cry, but they will be wiser. Sometimes you have to be cruel to be kind. A Maxim's manager in New York caused great consternation by insisting on a military style parade at which shoes and fingernails were checked. As a result, at least *one* area of the restaurant was efficiently run, though what effect this had on business is not known.

Bad breath is rarely noticed—people don't get *that* close in restaurants—but body odor is a common problem. Some owners actually have a little book of rules which employees must read and sign, but how do you know that your employee, especially if foreign born, has really understood that he or she must bathe every day and use a deodorant?

On the whole, personal hygiene isn't a problem in the restaurant business. But in a society bombarded for decades by advertisements for soap, toothpaste, and deodorants, when someone offends in this area, it really glares.

Getting someone to take care of their body odor is a problem for our well-scrubbed times. One method is to make deodorants available free to employees and make a great fuss of it so that, hopefully, everyone gets the message. But they may not. Most of us would rather attack a machine gun post than inform someone that they smell, but sometimes it's the only way other than the last sad recourse, which is to fire the offending person on some pretext—and this happens.

ALCOHOL ABUSE

The health of restaurant workers is important. Alcohol is often available in abundance. You will be doing your help no favors by allowing them unlimited access to it. Many restaurateurs restrict their employees to a drink with their meal and perhaps another on completing their shift. But it is quite usual for alcohol to be forbidden completely. In larger establishments there's little choice because the chance of generosity being abused is very high. Some employers wisely spell out the rules when they hire someone new. Drinking too much on the job is a very good way to get fired.

Alcoholism is common in the industry, particularly among bartenders. The mysteries of this problem have not yet been fully explained, but it's obvious that access to the stuff is likely to accelerate the process. Some bartenders are strict teetotalers, often as a result of revulsion at the sight of what alcohol does to some people, sometimes because they are rehabilitated alcoholics, and sometimes because a clear head enables them to steal more efficiently from customers and the house! Others like a drink in order to put themselves on the same level as their merry customers. This is a dubious reason, especially when the bartender is required to make change for the dining room as well as the bar. The owner-manager who takes regular little sips of wine throughout the day in order to maintain a gentle buzz is a well-known figure in the trade.

The revered chef or cook can usually do no wrong and often is allowed—even encouraged—to drink, sometimes with disastrous results. Chefs are the least supervised of all employees. One often has the impression that some owners live in fear of their chefs. Owners and managers often apply their executive zeal to every area of the restaurant except the kitchen. It's hot in there, perhaps they don't know much about cooking, and, anyway, it's more satisfying to check the cutlery or tell the bartender to get more sipsticks. Part of the chef's privilege stems from the fact that the chef is the hardest employee to replace in a restaurant. All other jobs can be filled quickly. But if you lose the chef who's gotten used to the restaurant and to you, there's a danger of having to endure a procession of incompetent agency temps who are often drunk when they arrive, let alone when they finish.

Owners will have to make their own rules on this subject and decide just how tolerant they're prepared to be. Sometimes you must ignore situations for the sake of a comparatively quiet life.

It will do no harm to repeat that bartenders can be held responsible for the actions of their drunken clients after they leave the premises. Restaurants must be insured against this risk. Some wicked cynics have opined that this is a splendid example of the law business and the insurance business getting together to feather their own nests.

OVERWORK

The job of waiting tables and tending bar is extremely demanding, mentally and physically. Some newcomers to the job are perplexed by this. After all, the work isn't usually heavy, unless there are steps to be negotiated with heavy trays. And it isn't furiously busy for eight solid hours.

But the constant switching of attention from one person to another and from one task to another is mentally taxing. This is transformed into physical fatigue by a means the medical profession would like to understand but does not. How many other jobs require a person to stand, often in the case of a bartender, in a confined space with little room to move, for eight hours a day, sometimes without an opportunity to sit down?

The cumulative effect of unnatural hours also can be a strain. People who don't get to bed until three or four in the morning show and feel all the signs of jet lag, a depressed state of fatigue brought on by disruption of the circadian rhythm, commonly known as the body clock.

It's generally agreed that four shifts a week is plenty in restaurant work. A few owners insist on a four-shift week because they don't like their employees to become bad-tempered and snappy towards the end of their working week. It's common for owners to *order* their help to take a vacation as they approach burn-out. Others, however, especially in French restaurants, insist on a six-day week and they close on Sunday simply because this eliminates the brain-teasing task of organizing a work schedule!

Unfortunately, it's tough to tell an employee with a mortgage and three kids under 18 that the limit is four shifts a week. Employees may feel they need the wages and tips from a fifth or sixth day to make ends meet, no matter what this is doing to their health. Some restaurants enjoy a phenomenal initial success, and when everyone is making so much money, they will want to work every shift they can against the day when business levels off!

The evidence of overwork is easily discerned in some restaurant employees: that hangdog expression, that dreadful shuffle! Most people's memories of restaurant work are of sheer exhaustion. Long after the amusing little incidents have been forgotten, the ache will be recalled.

Again, this is an area where owners must make their own decisions. Some restaurants are very successful and keep everybody smiling by employing part-time students who are delighted to work only two or three shifts a week. With a good crew there's always a fill-in available at short notice, but as an owner-manager you must make sure you're covered, and if things get too disorganized you may have to impose a stricter schedule. Employees usually respond to this situation in a positive and responsible manner. They are happy to have flexible hours so that they can pursue other interests. They won't want to add to your workload and stress by making you feel insecure.

HEALTH HAZARDS

Occupational health hazards include hemorrhoids, varicose veins, sore feet, cuts, burns, and tension headaches. There is sometimes a lot of stress involved, and this is increased when employees are unhappy. Owners may not be in the business of promoting health and happiness, but they will do well to take such steps as they can to keep their employees as happy as is feasible, given the constraints of the working situation. It is not unknown for restaurant workers to move on to jobs that actually *pay less* to get out of an unhappy place or to escape uncongenial hours!

Restaurant workers should be encouraged to wear suitable shoes. How some waitresses get through six or eight hours on a stone floor in silly little slip-on pumps is perplexing. Thick soles and laces are highly recommended.

SAFETY

The most important aspect of safety in a restaurant is the risk of fire. Extinguishers and other equipment, such as asbestos blankets, are usually required by law, emergency exits must be clearly marked, and the maximum occupancy must not be exceeded. Restaurant fires are not remote possibilities. They happen all the time. Fat is spilled, flames spread a little too far from the broiler, kitchen help are inattentive or drunk—the gamut of possibilities is endless.

From time to time the story of the disaster at Boston's Coconut Grove is recycled in the press. It is a salutary tale. Hundreds died in this restaurant fire.

Burns and cuts are an occupational hazard, too, so a first aid kit is essential. Owners should watch for dangerous habits, such as improper use of cutting implements, slamming glasses into the ice instead of using the scoop, and so on.

Cleaners should be trained to make a great ceremony of mopping floors so that everyone knows it's been done. Too many people get hurt because the dry surface they crossed five minutes before is wet and slippery when they return, though there's no visible evidence of the work having been done. Spillage should be dried immediately (this is a good way of getting a last bit of use out of a dirty tablecloth).

Hundreds of people die every year from choking. The most common situation is one in which a person, who's often had a bit too much to drink, gets bored chewing a piece of steak and tries to swallow it as an alternative to inelegantly spitting it into a napkin. Not everyone has attended West Point and been taught that there should never be more in your mouth than can be disposed of with two chews and a swallow. Indeed, watching people eat in restaurants can be a nauseating sight, and there may be a germ of truth in that old joke about the purpose of music in restaurants being to drown out the sound of people slurping their soup. Some people make the food scene in the movie *Tom Jones* look rather tame!

The health department will happily supply posters describing the Heimlich maneuver. If one of your customers begins choking on a piece of food, approach the victim from behind, put both arms around the waist, and jerk your hands and forearms into the victim's stomach in such a way as to induce spontaneous reverse peristalsis. In other words, you make him throw up. Pretty it's not, but many lives have been saved by this method.

PUBLIC
RELATIONS

"Good wine needs no bush" runs the proverb, dating from the time when a vineyard would announce that its most recent vintage was for sale by displaying a bush on the roof. It's true that some of the very best restaurants rely upon word of mouth for their custom, but they're often small, expensive, and appeal to such an elite group that they only need a small pool of customers in order to prosper.

EXAGGERATED CLAIMS

It could be argued that the restaurant industry has brought its love-hate relationship with the public upon itself. Restaurants try to attract customers by exhorting them to believe that they'll get more for their money than just a meal. Worse, they promise things they can't hope to deliver consistently.

Claims are casually made in advertising that can't possibly be substantiated more than half the time, at best. Airlines try to sell their potential customers dreams and experiences, but what airline would dare run an advertisement saying "Our planes *never* crash"? Again, one looks to the world of theater and movies for similar absurdity: "The perfect play" or "If you only see one movie this year."

One restaurant describes itself as "conducive to good conversation." Another runs a radio ad, delivered in a sepulchral voice better suited to lines like "unfortunately, there is no known cure for this disease" which informs the customer that their menu is so constructed as "not to allow you to make a mistake," as though such an event were the end of the world. The plenitude of feeble egos in the industry is such that the cry "I *never* make a mistake!" is a common one.

One restaurant just bluntly promises in its advertising "Int'l celebrities." Could a customer who stayed all night and didn't see so much as a third cousin twice removed of Gianni Agnelli or Andy Warhol claim a refund? Warren Beatty and Elizabeth Taylor can't be everywhere, every chef gets it wrong once in a while, reservation mistakes are made, and sometimes customers are going to have to accept the idea of dining with the unsmart set.

A very good line used by many restaurateurs is: "Sure, Mrs. Onassis and Clint Eastwood are in here all the time. But they don't like a fuss. If people started gaping, they'd leave, and they wouldn't come back. So we just give them that quiet table in the corner there, and treat them like regular folks."

Some restaurants plug the image of exclusivity, often to their eventual chagrin as the public heartily agrees with them and doesn't dare darken their doors.

THE NEED TO ADVERTISE

Life is short, and many restaurateurs will wish to advertise. It's significant that at a certain point of success, many stop advertising, and the sudden reappearance of blurbs for a restaurant that hasn't advertised in years may indicate a dropping off in business or an expansion of space that needs to be filled.

Viscount Leverhulme, founder of the mighty Unilever soap empire, once said, "I know half my advertising is wasted. Trouble is, I don't know which half!"

That was long before the age of market research, but even in the nineteenth century, surely, it must have been possible to draw some correlation between advertising and increased or unaffected sales. Today, no one needs to linger in doubt for long. It's perfectly simple. If you run an ad in a local paper or magazine and business increases, then your expenditure is worthwhile. If business doesn't improve, then you discontinue the ads. It's usually worth a try.

Unless you are in a busy location, with lots of casual "passing trade," you are pretty well *bound* to advertise unless you intend to rely solely on word of mouth—and that's risky. If there's heavy local competition, if you must bring in customers from other neighborhoods, or if you're in the suburbs or country, it's very hard to see how you can let people know where you are and what you're offering unless you advertise. It isn't always an option. Sometimes it's a necessity.

Advertisements should clearly state location, phone number, business hours, credit card facilities, type of food, and sample prices. One of the most elegant advertising formats, though rarely used, is simply to display a sample check for two people with all the relevant information on it, placed on a background photo of the restaurant's dining room.

When you call the advertising departments of the illustrious organs of the press, there'll be no shortage of help. Selling advertising space is murderously competitive, and when *you* go to *them*, they love you. Never forget that advertising is the single most important source of revenue for the whole of the media industry. They need you.

You might also consider local radio advertising, which isn't cheap but is believed by many to be extremely effective. TV advertising is usually out of the question for a single restaurant because it's far too expensive.

PUBLICITY

This is a sub-branch of advertising where you hire a company (very possibly consisting of one person, a dog, and an occasional bit of help from family and friends, but that's okay) to devise ways of bringing you and your restaurant to the public's notice.

One way is to persuade celebrities to attend your restaurant. You'll be amazed at how rich people will simply leap at the chance of a free dinner. If you decide to graciously allow your PR firm's nominees to come and sample the goods, be careful that the surliness of your staff, who may sense that a tip is in doubt, doesn't turn their experience into a bore. You might even promise to tip them yourself, should the movie star and her date turn out to be "stiffs" (i.e., fail to tip). Sometimes you just have to bite the bullet. No figures exist to prove or disprove the value of this kind of promotion, but the feeling is that it's very hit or miss.

PR people will also get you mentioned in gossip columns. Once in a while they'll even get you on TV—very important and a tremendous boost for the old ego. Nothing sells quite as successfully as TV. It's an integral part of the consumer society, a fact sometimes overlooked as people agonize over whether or not it's really a Good Thing.

To find the PR person of your dreams, you should ask around and check the telephone books. If you see a nice article in the paper, you could ring up and ask who handled it. One contact leads to another. PR people can be "retained" quite cheaply at a monthly rate. For about $1500 a month in New York there are several firms that will take care of your affairs imaginatively and efficiently. Obviously, as one moves away from New York, prices come down.

Celebrity Power

If you can genuinely become the haunt of a celebrity or two, and if they are not deterred by publicity such as mentions in the columns, you can earn a useful cachet. One restaurant kept a photographer on duty at all times to snap any celebs who should wander in. But because it was a cheap-and-cheerful blue jeans and hamburgers type of place, and not the kind where you make an entrance, this policy backfired, as the very casualness which the celebs were seeking was eliminated.

A few celebs like a restaurant where they are not stared at. You pays your money and you takes your choice. It's unfortunate that the most common cachet a restaurant builds is as a hangout for "characters"—artists, musicians, actors, and writers. These people may be interesting, but they're also notoriously and frequently broke. Be assured, the business community is the restaurateur's best friend.

In business terms it makes more sense to have people say "Luigi's Tavern, that's the place where all the big names in, fiber optics hang out," because every Rick in town wants Mick, Meryl, and Warren to be among his regulars. There are no known doctor's hangouts or airline pilot's hangouts, though many restaurateurs, when asked who frequents them, will look the world straight in the eye and say "pre-meds, pilots, stockbrokers, and beautiful young models, mostly."

A lot of people are so partied and blurbed-out these days that they're impervious to most of the devices favored by PR agencies (Oh no, not another hot air balloon party!) and if you find you're paying out and seeing nothing for your money, you'll have to think again.

Special Deals

Especially in suburbia, the mom, pop and kids market should never be ignored. Saturdays and Sundays are long days, and schools get out early.

Gimmicks such as free drinks, happy hours, and "With this voucher one person eats free" sometimes work well, but they should be approached with caution. Any right-minded person should be suspicious of anything "free" in this world, anyway.

On the other hand, special prices for "pre-theater" dinners, which will help you fill the restaurant in the early evening when diners are sometimes sparse, are a good idea. The customers feel they're getting good value, and you're looking at customers instead of empty chairs.

Also, you may coax customers to "trade up" to more expensive evenings.

Your most important PR person is *you*. By taking an interest in neighborhood affairs, or joining the local Chamber of Commerce, you can often do yourself some good, and others, too. You need to be a bit steely sometimes, as there will be no shortage of people coming around, asking you to donate to all sorts of worthy causes, and some of them will be of dubious validity. Your ever-ready restaurateur's smile will be taken by some as a sign of weakness. If you feel your customers will enjoy the attentions of panhandlers, and you're content to let them work the crowd you attract, then let them in, by all means!

THE FOOD CRITICS

Lord Byron, whose appetites for other areas of life unfortunately left little time for gourmandism, observed:

> A man must serve his time in every trade
> Save censure—critics are ready-made.

Almost every branch of consumerism now has its professional commentators and its critics. The restaurant industry is no exception. There are several newspaper and magazine reporters who've turned the assignment of restaurant critic into a highly paid profession. To be fair, some critics really know their stuff. They've actually been in the trenches and know when to forgive and make allowances. The best food critics don't file their report until they—or their appointed agents—have been to a restaurant three times.

A good write-up from a major critic can *make* a restaurant. It's hard to prove, but there are enough people with time and money on their hands that the curiosity factor alone will bring people in. The pattern most commonly observed is one where business booms for up to six or eight months after a rave review, at which point being fashionable abruptly wanes. It is at this point that maximum effort needs to be made. The business is vulnerable to whim. Remember, several restaurants are reviewed every week, and others will get interesting write-ups, too.

Reviews and Their Consequences

Many restaurateurs are expert at the game of "in and out." They raise money quickly, move in, and get the doors open in record time. They have enough contacts to get some good reviews, and then, at the height of fame, they sell. There's a luck element here, and it isn't nearly as easy to do as it is to write about it.

A group of three men, all old hands at the restaurant game, recently opened a Yuppie paradise, a sort of brasserie, on New York's Amsterdam Avenue. The restaurant was an instant success, largely as the result of a quite accidental visit and subsequent glowing report from a major critic. They almost immediately opened a similar operation at what proved to be a disastrous location. Imagine their sighs of relief when a large corporation offered to buy them out on the strength of the first successful operation. They could afford to absorb the less glittering performance of the second. After less than 18 months of work, the partners were each $300,000 richer, and they stayed on to operate the business.

Restaurateurs froth at the mouth with rage when they're ill-served by critics. A state restaurant association recently moved to pass a bill whereby restaurant critics should be licensed. This bill was spurred by a restaurateur who claimed a 20% loss of business, due to an inaccurate report. Another restaurateur, who had lost two of his four stars to a well-known critic, sympathized. He opined that a bad review could break a new restaurant. A critic replied, "Restaurateurs and chefs should be licensed. Beyond meeting health department regulations, all any idiot has to do to open a restaurant is spend some money."

Again, the emphasis is on food, when, in reality, there are scores of reasons for going to restaurants, none of which are connected with sustenance and nourishment. Businesspeople go to restaurants to talk business, lovers, or would-be lovers, to talk about love, lusters about lust, old pals to reminisce, lonelies to enjoy the presence of others, jazz lovers to listen to jazz, and countless others to observe some human ritual, such as graduation, marriage, birth, death, retirement, or success. A salesman about to clinch a deal, a swain about to propose, or a writer discussing her novel won't give a care whether they're eating fish gills or donkey liver. They'll be much more impressed by prompt service and a table where they can think, as opposed to one where any conversation is drowned out by the neigh-bores. But food is the only tangible material given, so it's the inevitable focus.

The restaurateur who has a cosy corner location, ample parking, a loud jukebox in one room, laser beam curtain silence in another, Chateaubriand at $10, beautiful, smiling waitresses, famous habitués, handsome, multilingual waiters, quirk-accommodating kitchen staff, and an intensely moving view has nothing to fear from critics. Others may pay them some mind.

A young (intensely talented) chef in one restaurant—where the "lobster cocktail" was a whole lobster at $25 a time—perused an order which had come down the tube from the dining room one night and, after a moment's reflection, called the maitre d'. "Say, Joe," he said. "check out Table 5, will ya? This looks to me like a food critic's order. I'm gonna be real careful with this one!"

A restaurant chain procured a picture of a food critic, posted it on the notice board and instructed its employees that on no account was he to be served. "Very interesting—but stupid!" as Artie Johnson's German soldier on *Laugh-In* used to say. Some critics send friends.

In order to understand just what the critical eye is looking for, what's noticed and what isn't, restaurateurs will do well to read critics' write-ups carefully. Surprisingly, few of them ever refer to the "Rick factor" or the great convenience of the location. They seem to prefer showing off their knowledge of what *carpaccio* should really be like, and whether *trompe l'oeil* decor is really appropriate to the *je ne sais quoi*. You may sniff the unmistakable odor of taurine excrement, but these people are very influential.

Although they comment on service ("the kitchen was very slow") and ambiance ("a romantic, dark cornered room"), they concentrate inevitably on food. Often they apply gourmet standards that are irrelevant to the operation. When they really get going, they say things like: "The raw beef was cut thin as Brussels lace. A tracery of light and fruity olive oil gleamed on the surface. There were a few flakes of parmesan, and then down came a blizzard of white truffle on top of the *carpaccio con tartufi*. It was, explained the man at the inappropriately named Ristorante L'Assassasino in Milan, only simple *cucina del paese*, but it was the closest I wish to come to paradise on this earth."

Bribes

Is it possible to bribe food critics? Of course it is. But not in a crude manner. It has to be subtle . . . done through friends . . . and it ain't cheap.

The bribery of chefs and food and beverage managers is so common that such payments have even been held up in law as legitimate business expenses. Whether your friendly IRS would take a similar view of payments to critics is open to conjecture.

DEALING WITH THE PUBLIC

A tragic by-product of the restaurant industry, or indeed any "people business," is the sheer hatred of humanity engendered in some people who must deal with the public. You see dead eyes set in the glum faces of otherwise pretty hostesses and waitresses, and you endure their gratuitous rudeness. From their expressions you might deduce that their only child has just been ripped from their breast, when in fact all that's happened is that the people at Table 7 have politely asked if they could move to Table 8.

To be blunt, a major reason for all of this is the low caliber of many restaurant employees and the poor management qualities of some owners. Most people shudder at the prospect of having anything to do with the Public. Small children want to be engine drivers, pilots, doctors, nurses, soldiers, actresses, writers, and teachers—not hostesses, bartenders, or maitre d's. Inevitably stress and threat, real or imagined, will reveal personality defects and character weaknesses.

An awful lot of workers in the restaurant business should never be allowed to have anything to do with people. Some feel that this is the age of the repressed, inward-looking loner, happier with electronic stimulus of one kind or another than in the ordinary give and take between people. The dwindling interest in marriage, and the divorce figures, may substantiate this to an extent. Whatever the sociological reasons for it may be, the fact remains that the industry contains an unusual number of misfits. Nevertheless, everybody has to get through the day.

Management Qualities

Management qualities involve:

leadership
relationships with people

stability and stress tolerance

planning and organization

spoken communication

written communication

motivation

flexibility

decisiveness

problem analysis

initiative

originality

You may have fun deciding to what degree some of your favorite restaurant people have mastered these talents. Don't be surprised by low scores.

Management skills may be summarized as follows:

Leadership: getting people to do their best.

Relationships with people: "You don't seem too happy. Is there something you want to get off your chest?"

Stability and stress tolerance: "We're a person short and there are lots of reservations. But we can do it!" "Monday and Thursday were disasters. But the week's average will be okay if we get a busy weekend."

Planning and organization: "We won't need three waiters on Tuesdays. Two will be fine."

Spoken communication: "Terrible weather, isn't it? How about a nice fireside table?"

Written communication: "Dear Mr. Smith: I'm so glad you enjoyed your lunch here. I take pleasure in sending you our new spring menu for your perusal. With so many of your colleagues interested in fishing, I'm sure you'll be amused to hear that world champion Sigi Galoomi has become a regular customer . . . "

Motivation: What the military call "the will to win." First cousin of self-confidence.

Flexibility: "If it rains, don't bother putting out the umbrellas." "If people keep asking for 'Fuzzy Navels,' then make them."

Decisiveness: "That new waitress is terrible. We'll have to let her go."

Problem analysis: "Why do I get these regular complaints from the front station? What's wrong? How can I speed up service?"

Initiative and originality: "There isn't a brunch place for miles. Let's do it. And let's give them a really exciting omelet!"

Employee Qualities

The talent most required of restaurant employees is simply *speed*, not an ability to relate to fellow members of the human race, though this quality will often be welcomed. If you can carry six salads along your arm, or make three piña coladas in 20 seconds flat, the fact that you communicate in four-letter words and grunts and that your knuckles brush the floor as you walk won't matter much. Admittedly, good looks can sometimes help, and, indeed, many restaurants have little else to offer apart from their good-looking floor staff.

That much vaunted quality, leadership, is difficult to apply to employees who, on the whole, would rather be doing something else, thank you, but happen to need a job. In the days when navies were crewed by men who had been rounded up by press gangs, it was the threat of being flogged or keel hauled that made the navy work, not the Mountbattenish charm of the officers.

People Stress (or Combat Fatigue)

The restaurant business is very much a people business, and thus has a heavy built-in stress factor. While you simply cannot run a business like a platoon or a scout company, the happier the crew and the customer-employee relationships, the less stress will be generated. A wise restaurateur seeks opportunities to reduce stress as assiduously as for areas of greater profit.

A small number of precious people actually enjoy the chi-chi aspect of restaurant theatre. "Alphonse knows my favorite table, Luigi knows exactly how I like my linguini" and all that guff. They live for pipsqueak fuss about nothing. Some restaurateurs are better equipped to deal with these monsters than others.

The tragedy is that nine out of ten restaurant customers—who may or may not sometimes fall into a special psychological group— are harmless, undemanding, and nice. They may not always be wildly exciting, but they are rarely obnoxious. Yet the nice often pay the price for the nasty at the hands of incompetent restaurant personnel.

Some might wisely observe that, even if only one in ten people is unpleasant, if you deal with a hundred people a day, that's plenty! But it does seem that a lot of tension and stress is generated unnecessarily. It's an unfortunate aspect of American life that rudeness commands an absurd amount of respect. Behavior that would be laughed out of court in most European countries reduces many Americans to terror, and worse, they take it out on the undeserving.

Everyone in the business has to live with all this. The public is to the restaurateur what the land is to the farmer or the sea to the fisherman. There's no choice but to dig and trawl.

Basically, the majority of your customers are more interested in themselves and their conversations and appetites than they are in the detail of your restaurant. If their restaurant experience is satisfactory in this regard, they'll retain a nice memory of the place, whether the food was good or not.

Greeting

If you employ a maitre d', host, or hostess—and remember that this might well be *your* spot, at least initially—you should remember that the worst thing that can happen to an entering customer is to be ig-nored.

We live in the age of the plastic smile. It doesn't have to warm your eyes; it just has to signal your general agreeableness. "Hi, folks, how are you doing?" is as good a greeting as any, unless you immediately sense (as a good restaurateur should) that "Good evening, sir" will go down better.

It doesn't matter much. A smile and a greeting is what you should deliver. Everyone should keep an eye on the door, and all your employees should be trained to take a general and overall interest in what's going on in the joint, not just in their own corner. The waitress nearest the door and the bartender can greet customers if the host is seating people in the rear of the restaurant.

This isn't only good manners. It's good marketing. The greeting should never be "Sorry, I don't have a table right now," unless it would be patently dishonest to pretend otherwise. Rather it should be "I should have something breaking in ten minutes."

You should instill in your employees the conviction that they must convey an atmosphere of welcome. Customers will not respond well on slow nights to the intimation that they're the partypoopers, the ones who interrupted an exciting game of Name the Show Stopper by their untimely entry and willingness to spend money.

The bottom line is bad training. When things go wrong it's usually the owner's fault.

Reservations

It gives a nice professional air when your telephone is answered politely and smartly, and reservations are taken accurately and cheerfully. "We shall look forward to seeing you!" should be the watchword. "Serious" restaurants, with few tables and high prices, can lose money by keeping tables for someone important, who fails to show, while turning away casual drop-ins.

It's nice to be able to check your book and gauge how busy you're going to be. It makes you feel like you're running a grown-up business.

No Reservations

If, because of its informality and speed of turnover, there's no great point in making reservations at your restaurant, this fact must be admitted in a positive manner. A surly "We don't take reservations" is a negative attitude, often heard, and one which frequently turns would-be paying customers away. It's just as easy to say, "We don't take reservations, but how many are you? Two? For 8 P.M.? There might be a five minute wait, but don't worry."

For large parties of six or more, it makes sense to take reservations, because this may entail moving together several small tables.

The old restaurant con trick of backing people up at the bar so they can spend a little more money while awaiting their tables works fine when you really *can* seat the people in a reasonable amount of time and get those names ticked off the little list in your pocket. Only time and practice will enable you to gauge turnover speed. It isn't always easy, particularly as—yet another cross the restaurateur has to bear— the whole world wants to lunch at 12:30 and dine at 8.

Those unfortunates—and we all travel this dreary road at least once in our lives—who, after drinking far too many cocktails than they really like at the bar, finally realize that they aren't going to get a table before their appetites have disappeared and their conversation dried up anyway, will never return to your restaurant. Not only that, but they'll "bad mouth" it all over town.

Strangely enough, there are some who will be intrigued by the hard-to-get ploy. They actually feel triumphant at being allowed, at last, to spend their money at your table. But this doesn't work with everybody. And even if they do collapse with relief onto a table, the memory of the long wait, and the lurking certainty that someone who arrived after them got a table *before* them, will linger.

Again, time and practice will enable you to read the situation accurately and ensure maximum satisfaction to yourself and your customers.

Dress Codes

If you are bold enough to stipulate a dress code, which usually means jacket and tie for the men, or no blue jeans, then you immediately kiss the bulk of casual diners good-bye before you have even said hello. While the desire to strike a blow for old-fashioned standards may be laudable, it isn't very practical in an age when everyone seems to be competing to be "more laid-back than thou."

Some restaurants have a little brass plate which proclaims rather pathetically "Proper Attire Required." This gives the host a small edge. If unsuitable people appear, he can sometimes turn them away on the grounds that they're not properly dressed. Some restaurants keep a supply of ties and jackets to accommodate those would-be customers who aren't wearing either.

But what do you do when the movie star of the month and her glamorous crowd in their white Reeboks, designer jeans, and designer stubble suddenly appear at your door, creating waves of excitement? What you usually do is make an exception, which can be dangerous.

"Oh, sure, you can go to Rick's in blue jeans—if you happen to be a star!" your neighborhood customers may grumble.

One of the many stock restaurant situations, repeated time after time, features an earnest hostess obeying orders to the letter and refusing to admit Mick Jagger or Dustin Hoffman or some other worthy because he's not properly dressed. When the owner, lurking in the back, discovers this, he reacts with horror. A moment of glory appears about to escape him. He runs down the block beseechingly. "Come home, all is forgiven!" But the celeb has already forgotten the incident and is bound for one of his usual haunts where he knows he won't be turned away.

Another scenario features the owner arriving and seeing a customer improperly dressed. "Go tell that man he has to have a tie," he orders his host bravely, not having the courage to do it himself. The host tries to make his point and is told to bleep off. Suddenly, it's all *his* fault, and the boss still hasn't found the courage to approach the customer directly. As has been discussed, when Italian war hero Gianni Agnelli arrives at "21" in blue jeans he gets in. Like the 2,000 lb gorillas of this world, some celebs can do whatever they want.

If your restaurant proclaims itself in every way as exclusive and expensive, then you may be able to insist on a dress code, and, indeed, if your service and decor are up to it, your clients may enjoy the theatricality of dressing up.

But in an age when many men sit at restaurant tables with their hats on, drinking beer straight from the bottle, you are on dangerous ground trying to educate them. Billy Graham caused sighs of relief when he told the world that it was okay to be rich. But America got the message long ago that it was okay to be a slob. The chewing gum industry is an $800 million industry that employs a lot of people. Somebody out there has got to chew that gum, dammit. And if some of it (usually the green variety) shows up in your ashtrays, you just have to be grateful they put it where no one would sit on it.

"Dressing the Room"

This means putting attractive people where they will be seen to advantage by other customers as they arrive. You put the well-dressed, good-looking Yuppies on a nice table near the door and the grumpy old pair who snarl at each other and complain the whole time in the back.

Sometimes they resent it. You then have to explain that the star table is reserved. They'll then watch it like a hawk and very possibly query whether the people who eventually get the table really had a reservation.

Some celebs are wise to this one and will strenuously insist on being in the back. There are two or three restaurants in New York, however, where the reverse is the case, and the same old faces sit at the same old tables in mutual admiration day after day. The maitre d' who awards the "power table" can always be sure of a good tip. When restaurants are featured in movies, people will ring up from all over the world months ahead of time to reserve the table where Candy Frabazoni and Hank Strutt finally plighted their troth in the Oscar-winning movie, "A Vulnerable Girl."

Visitors from outer space after the nuclear holocaust will open time capsules and marvel at the beauty of the human race as displayed in current glossy magazines. In your early days you may be so glad to have a customer that you make a fuss of people who are *banned* from every other restaurant in the neighborhood on account of their cigars, their loudness, their falling-down drunkenness, their coughing, their spluttering and spitting, or whatever. Then one day, when things are going a little better, you'll see a girl whisper in her escort's ear, while studiously not looking in the direction of the table where dear old Paddy is swishing his dental plate in a glass of water. They'll leave, with vague assurances of "Catch you another time."

So don't be *too* generous with your bonhomie. It may come back to haunt you.

AVOIDING NASTY SITUATIONS

The customer is right 90% of the time. You might as well indulge their whims—you may have promised to in your advertising. But unpleasantness of one kind or another does sometimes occur. Sometimes it's more practical to just look the other way and ride out the storm, rather than escalate the incident by asserting your authority. It isn't satisfying, and you may despise yourself a bit, but you can congratulate yourself on having happily resolved ominous events if (a) other customers haven't been disturbed, (b) there has been no violence, and (c) you've suffered no serious loss of revenue.

Apart from the people who just aren't very pleasant to look at or listen to, you may be unlucky enough to attract a group of mean nasties who are intent on causing trouble. They'll insult your staff, make noise, swear at the tops of their voices, and even throw things around. It must be stressed that this doesn't happen very often, but it happens.

One much-despised owner spied troublemakers in his restaurant whose behavior had once required calling the police. Instead of asking them to leave, he merely warned the staff to make sure they got the money. They didn't get the money, and one of the staff was assaulted. Before the police arrived, they'd run away, full of fun.

Experience has shown that the best thing to do is to wait for nasties to leave, then hope your headache soon subsides and your entire staff doesn't walk out. Your aim must be at all times to minimize the risk of physical violence. Going over to the table and asking a bunch of guys to behave themselves may be just the trigger they've been hoping for. There's no point in being brave and putting your fists up to a man with a gun or a knife. Sometimes you may have a happy arrangement with your local police station, and the pressing of a button will bring help. Some places employ armed doormen—often moonlighting cops. This is an excellent idea, and if you're trying to build a club, it gives members a nice sense of security. Sometimes you can combine host and bouncer in one person, where a tall, strong man also has a congenial manner. Nowadays, quite harmless-looking people are often martial arts experts, and if this talent exists among your staff, it's a useful bonus. But a strenuous effort to avoid trouble is your best bet.

Stick-ups

If you take the view that this sort of thing only happens to other people, then you need read no further. Some restaurants are robbed regularly. In one classic instance, where all the customers were made to lie on the floor at gunpoint while the cash register was emptied, the owner laconically remarked afterwards, "Thank God the Aga Khan had just left!"

The standard drill when approached with a gun or other weapon is to hand over the cash calmly and immediately. You then pray the criminal won't kill you anyway, either for fun or to prevent you from identifying him later in the event of his arrest.

Criminals mark places and stake them out. They observe routines. At 11 A.M. every day the guy with the glasses comes out of the restaurant with a canvas bag in his hand and goes to the bank. What can be in that bag, the criminal wonders.

Knowing this, casually-hired employees will sometimes stage a phoney mugging and hand the bag with the money to a pal. "It was horrible, he had this big gun. I just gave him the money." "You did the right thing, son." Similarly, many a delivery boy has been known to pocket the money for the four deluxe dinners to go and disappear into the night.

Security

On closing, money should be deposited in a hidden safe. The cash register should be left open, whether you've left the next day's bank there or not, so that if there's a break-in, they may get some money but they won't break your register. Some of the new computerized registers cost more than $3,000. You may be insured, but it'll take a day to replace your register, and your premium may go up. The less money there is in the house, the less there is to steal.

The two most vulnerable times of day are opening and closing, when there are few people present and the staff is preoccupied with setting up or closing down. Late at night, when only the bartender and a manager are present, it's a sound precaution to lock the door and only admit known faces—neighborhood people looking for a nightcap, or the porter coming in to clean.

Whenever two or three men come in purposefully, and one stays at the door while another strides briskly to the back, the third man is probably the one who will announce the stick-up. Some of these incidents make hilarious telling after the event—when everyone survives, that is. Sometimes situations grow and grow, with no one aware of what's happening, then suddenly violence erupts. Your best defense is awareness.

ELEVEN
EMPLOYEES

A standard moan among restaurateurs is "You can't get good people." It's true that the restaurant industry does have special problems that dissuade many from working in it. Many people get to a stage where they can no longer take the contact with a demanding public, a demanding owner, and co-workers who really defy belief in their horrific attitude to life and their comrades but who are adored by the boss. Add to this the unsociable hours and the physically tiring nature of the work, and you can still see what people are grumbling about.

The best solution to the general stress is plenty of time off.

In New York and Los Angeles it's easy to recruit people from among the struggling would-be showbiz types. In other cities you are looking for students and part-timers with a few reliable pros. In the country, you'll have to cast your net wide, not only for customers but for employees, too.

Very few restaurateurs exercise any imagination in this area. Many seem to have an unhappy knack for hiring the wrong people all the time, so that it's a running disaster with harder work for the other employees.

Hiring the chef, as has been discussed, is a crucial business and a separate exercise. They almost invariably call their own shots and carve out their own empires. Kitchen staff can be recruited satisfactorily from agencies. You apply trial and error until you get reasonable people. Cloakroom attendants are usually either part-timers or work for the person to whom you've leased your cloakroom concession.

It's the rank and file of waiters, waitresses, and bartenders who present the most problems. There is always a certain turnover among them, and you constantly have to be on the lookout for suitable replacements. They are often poorly motivated, which is a shame, because they really are important in the running of a restaurant—they talk to your customers, they're your PR people and salesreps all in one.

If you can arrange it, it's a good idea to have a limit of four shifts a week for your floor staff. That way they won't get too tired, fed up, and snappy. As has been discussed elsewhere, this may not always yield a satisfactory wage for a married person with responsibilities, but it's often a godsend for younger, single people. They don't feel enslaved, and they have time to do their own thing.

FINDING HELP

Agencies are the single worst source of restaurant employees. There are happy exceptions, but they're few and far between. Sometimes restaurant personnel walk into jobs that are like paradise. But most often agencies supply people for the seedy places way off the beaten track, with quirky suspicious owners and regular cantankerous customers. Such places often deliberately mitigate against the employee's chances of earning decent tips and are *happy* to accept a constant turnover of personnel. Life being what it is, that doesn't prevent such restaurants from being highly successful places of business.

The single best method of recruitment is word of mouth through friends. Just as a waiter and waitress start their job hunt by ringing everyone they ever knew in the business, so must the restaurateur.

Newspaper advertising is okay from a restaurateur's point of view, but it is a notorious nightmare from the employee's point of view. Experienced people simply don't read the Help Wanted columns. Why not? Because when you put on your best bib and tucker and trundle halfway across the county for your interview, you find there are 30 people ahead of you and more coming in. The interviewer will take an intelligent interest in the first two or three people he sees, then the faces blur.

Often the interviewer is looking for sexpertise, not expertise. The restaurant industry isn't the only one in which the job often has been allocated even before the sham interviews start. Why the farce continues is anybody's guess. Sometimes there are internal political reasons for making it look as though a fair effort has been made to recruit external talent. One well-known and well-hated owner of a famous New York restaurant has a running ad in the newspaper and interviews every Monday. What he's looking for is anybody's guess, but it isn't employees. He never hires.

You get a positive *attitude* from people who've just finished training courses somewhere, but often they haven't yet acquired the confidence and zip necessary for a busy, successful restaurant. If they learn fast, and you have the patience to train them, this can work out very well indeed.

Since personal manner and looks are so very important in the business, a very good way of finding a job is simply to make the rounds.

Every restaurateur becomes accustomed to people walking in and asking for jobs. Some are embarrassed, and it doesn't work for them. Some jobseekers are pretty ridiculous, slouching in, chewing gum, not even bothering to take off their sunglasses or remove their earphones, and not able to cite references and experience. Perhaps they believe the main talent is to be cool.

If someone with reasonable "vibes" comes in, you should simply note their name and telephone number. Before long you'll have a large pool of potential employees. When you call them up they may have found a job, in which case you have to call the next.

Unless you're convinced that they're competent, perhaps from having had a word with a former employer, you ask them to come in and "trail"—that is, observe the method of service you use and see how they adjust to it. After an hour of having them around, you should have a good idea of how they'll shape up. If you have an old, established crew, it will be important that the trailer fit in, so you might seek confirmation from your senior waitress or bartender. Some owners pay their trailers, some don't. They never get any tips, but they should at least get a bite to eat.

One well-organized restaurateur has a little booklet printed in which the rules of employment are spelled out very simply—not in an intimidating military style manner. When someone nice comes in looking for a job, he gives them the booklet and asks them to take it home and read it. If they feel they'll be happy, and there is a position open, they can talk a bit more on the phone, then trail and so on. It may sound a bit elaborate, but it eliminates the embarrassment of having to correct people's dress or whatever.

There's no shortage of ancient wisdom to help you lead your staff to glory and get the best out of them. Start as you mean to go on, man should be led as though you led him not. You should at least try to be fair in your dealing, although it won't always be possible. Remember, no man can serve two masters, but many of us have to try. And, masters who make themselves like honey are eaten by the flies.

EMPLOYEES' POINT OF VIEW

Here's what a happy waiter had to say:

I really like this job. The boss knows his stuff and is always cheerful. His wife comes in with the kids sometimes. She doesn't give a damn; in fact, sometimes she wants to gossip when we have work to do! If we need to change the schedule, it's okay as long as we give plenty of notice and make sure our shift is covered. The only thing he hates is when people are late because that gives him one more thing to worry about. He does have his private quirks. Why shouldn't he? It's his movie. But he always makes his points with a smile, so nobody ever gets upset. There's every reason to be prompt, because then you can sit down and have a bite to eat at leisure. You can also have a snack when you go off, if you like, and a drink or two, although he has fired one or two people for overdoing it. He's no patsy! The law doesn't require him to let us have that, but he doesn't mind. We don't have union membership, but we're paid union rates and he gives two weeks paid vacation after a year, even to part-timers like me—I only work four shifts. Boy, it's enough, that place gets so damn busy! But Al the chef is a real nice guy. I think he writes plays or something and he's always talking about writing a cookbook, although we never seem to see much progress. If you make a mistake, as often as not he'll pick up on it and put it straight. If there's something funny about an order, he'll just ask you politely what it's all about. The bartenders are great. They make the drinks promptly for the floor and get the change right. Also, they get our credit card tips right. We don't mind giving them 5% of our tips at the end of the shift. The menu's simple, and there's always plenty of cutlery and linen, so there's no need to get tense about trivia. The money averages out very well.

But an unhappy waiter said:

What is it with this restaurant business? Why does every customer and employee turn into an idiot the minute they walk through the door? What kind of homes could they possibly have come from to talk the way they do? It's gotta be the last bastion of slavery, the way people talk to you. I've hit three chefs, a maitre d', and a customer in my time. Every one of them deserved it. I wish I'd hit them harder. One was in the hospital for two weeks. The customer sent his beef back three times, saying he wanted it cut in a certain way that I couldn't explain to the Chinese chef. Apparently he was a valued customer. Of course, I blew the job, but who cares? And the money isn't that good unless you're at an expensive place, and then there's so much regimentation it's a pain in the neck. I just don't know who I hate most: the customers, the chefs or the owners. Some chefs are animals, the way they scream and shout and cause trouble deliberately. You don't meet a lot of nice ones. But owners are the real weirdos. They are like curios from a psychiatrist's museum, most of them. And even when they're successful, most of them seem to be miserable. Some of their wives are pretty good numbers, too. There was one who used to walk in with a face like stone, look around the place for a moment, then walk up to her husband, who was terrified of her, and say, "There's a fork missing on Table 3." She would announce it like it was the end of the world. He was such a jerk he put up with it. If I could just get off the booze and get some money together, I wouldn't mind opening my own place."

A happy bartender said:

I love the job. The money's great and the crazy hours suit me fine because I'm a night person. The job is my social life, too. I often meet people who are customers on my own time. We go to ballgames and stuff. And yes, I meet a lot of girls. Bartenders are like priests and doctors. Women find us fascinating. Of course, the main thing with me is I'm a people person. The chef's a great guy and gives me anything I want. I give the busboy a few bucks and he does all the donkey work, brings up the beer and ice, and cleans up, too.

DRUGS

As blissful as you want your working conditions to be, you should be alert to employees who seem just a little bit too happy, especially bartenders. They may be on drugs. Worse, they may be selling drugs on your premises, and that's potential trouble. If you're suspicious, you should fire them. If laughing, capering, eternally quipping Joe has a large following at the bar, and a significant amount of money is going into the register, then you may have to compromise. But you should let him know you're aware of his little secret. Hopefully, he'll be circumspect. An unhappy bartender said:

Alcoholics disgust me. I like a drink, but when you find yourself pouring whole bottles of hard liquor into people, and they still appear to be sober, it's scary. The regulars are the worst. They won't stop talking. They're lonely, and it's easy to understand why. Who the heck could put up with them if they didn't have to? Sometimes I give them a couple of drops of (an over-the-counter medicine). They start throwing up in ten minutes and go home. The tips are good, but you always feel you earned them. Sometimes with an alcoholic you can give him the same check twice and he won't notice. A lot of bartenders try to screw up the waiters so that the boss and the managers will concentrate on them and stay away from the bar. I don't do that myself. I need their tips! The element of violence always lurks. I've been attacked, had drinks thrown at me and stuff. Fortunately the people were too drunk to be dangerous, but you might not always be lucky. It's no good saying you shouldn't serve them. How do you know how many drinks they had before they got to your place? They'll often fool you, come in nice and proper, and order a drink very politely. Then, wham, the noise starts, they start bothering the other customers, whatever. You have to throw them out. Then you never know when they might come back with three friends and a shotgun. Owners very rarely back you up in these situations. Indeed, they often create them. I once saw the owner's wife break step and run the length of a bar to drag in some guy. "Dinner for one?" she cooed. Anyone could see he was a bum except her, of course. I thought about letting him have his fun, then leaving it to her to get him out on the principle of "You let him in. You get him out." But I thought better of it and whispered confidentially that the drinks were $6 each, and there was this great bar just round the corner where. . . . Sometimes you have to do everybody's thinking for them, and it's exhausting. By the time I finish my 5-shift week, I'm exhausted, physically and mentally. It takes me one full day to recover. The next day I'm okay, but not exactly full of energy. Then, just as I feel recuperated, it's time to go back to work. I've got to get out of this.

MANAGERS

If good help generally is hard to find, good managers are *really* hard to find. If they know enough to be good managers, there's only a short space of time between achieving that happy status and owning their own restaurant. It can be a dreadful job, involving everything from bussing tables to answering the phone, with a taxed salary but no tips, and only the dubious privileges of not having to wear a uniform and being able to eat from the menu to cheer it up. Some managers work out a few kickbacks here and there, but it isn't common in the size of restaurant under discussion.

You can get the best out of managers by explaining their duties and not making them the culprit for everything that goes wrong. That's if you don't want to take the short cut to happiness and give them a decent salary.

They often irritate other staff members by embarking on a power trip, especially if they have the right to hire and fire. This is usually a bad thing, but it's your movie and it may suit your purposes sometimes.

The area of personnel is the one in which your ideals can be put to best use. There's no doubt that while some miserable restaurants make fortunes, happy restaurants are more likely to prosper. Besides, since you have to spend so much time at work, why not make it as congenial as possible?

The author makes no apology for the occasionally harrowing descriptions of just what goes on in the wonderful world of restaurants. None of them are even faintly exaggerated. Forewarned is forearmed. If you can keep your head when all about others are losing theirs, the restaurant business will make you rich and give you a rewarding and occasionally amusing career.

How can you be a successful restaurateur and still stay sane and happy? The answer seems to be the ability to detach. Take those weekends off, and insist on those vacations. As one very successful restaurateur used to say to his staff, "When I leave, I don't want to be called for any reason whatsoever, unless it's a matter of life and death."

Let's face it, there's a little bit of Rick in all of us!

TWELVE

MAKING YOUR DECISION

There is a certain hollowness about deciding whether or not one is wise in becoming a restaurateur. Very few people do the ideal thing with their lives. The world is full of square pegs in round holes. Some are shunted into careers in which they have no particular interest because they have no particular interest in anything, but are still faced with the necessity of earning a living. Others may long for a career in ballet, but find themselves lured into the world of computers by the fact that there is a choice of seven secure, well-paying jobs awaiting every graduate in computer science. Doctors' sons and daughters don't exactly *drift* into medicine. They simply never entertain the idea of doing anything else with their lives, and the same is true of many military people. Many restaurateurs are also born to the business. Although sometimes efficient, they rarely have enough personality to do more than a mundane job; however, the mundane can be just as profitable as the brilliant.

To call a spade a spade, very few members of what might be called the professional classes enter the restaurant trade. It's a world in which you can succeed mightily with 500 words of English and the ability to count.

THE "UP" SIDE

The attractions of the restaurant business are as follows. The abilities and talents it requires are not very esoteric. You don't have to charm people into laying down their lives for you with hypnotic words. You just have to say "How are you? You're looking good. Gee, what's Steinbrenner trying to pull this time?" to your regular customers. If you're a vet and made lance corporal, you have enough management talent to succeed. Even if you failed at everything else you ever did in your life, you still have an even chance of making it. Apart from local health department requirements, no other qualifications are needed to be a restaurateur. If you call yourself a restaurateur, then that's what you are!

It's a freer free-for-all than most businesses. The business is in a constant state of expansion, apart from occasional hiccups and fashion changes. There has been a shake-out at the lower end of the market due to crazy real estate spirals. Profits can be enormous. There's always the chance of being bought out at a considerable profit.

People who are well adjusted with a reasonably optimistic view of life and possessed of education, intelligence, humor, and a healthy skepticism can do very well in the business and stay sane. They are the sort of people who would do well at whatever they attempted, but, clearly, running your own show is preferable even to a long, safe career with IBM.

It's hard to disdain the "perks" of owning a restaurant. We need not refer to the obvious advantages which the criminal element exploits but to the simple bonus of being able to eat, drink, and entertain on the firm, to say nothing of the deductible expenses for cars and so on. You can also take time off whenever you want.

But beyond the ordinary, practical day-to-day considerations of a restaurateur's life, there's a deeper satisfaction in creating a success.

It's small wonder that so many people from the creative side of life, perhaps having been disappointed in their first careers, find total satisfaction in the restaurant business. That's because their greatest source of energy, their creative urge, is used all the time in different situations. Not only do they have to plan menus and decor, but they have to reach compromises on the personality level, too, like a diplomat.

The respect of your employees and customers can be very heartwarming. The sight of familiar faces who've become regulars at your establishment is a daily confirmation that you're doing something right. This, of course, is one of the major satisfactions of all service industries.

If you get it right, you've succeeded in inventing your own world, and there can be no greater satisfaction than that.

THE "DOWN" SIDE

This is a convenient point at which to begin the list of disadvantages of being a restaurateur. The luxury of being able to carve out your own leisure time may be elusive and hollow. When the cat's away, the mice will play. Unless you are a good manager with the good fortune to have recruited a first-class staff, then you must accept that the business will only run efficiently when you are there in person. Even when you go to the back for a bite to eat yourself, the service on the station out of sight from you will slack off, and customers will start looking around to find the waiter who has become immersed in a deadly game of Show Business Trivia.

The tetchy, pale sight of the restaurateur who has taken the weekend off and decided just to look into the joint on the way home is a cliché of the trade. All worst possible fears are almost invariably confirmed. The lights are set too high or too low. On the front station, a couple with the helpless look of shipwrecked sailors are looking around, holding their menus in a way which suggests they're ready to order—and have been for some time. The music will be blaring heavy metal, not soft rock. Suzie will have her hair down, and Ira will be wearing blue jeans, in contradiction of house rules. There'll be smoke in the kitchen, and some of it will be percolating through into the dining room. There'll be an unusual number of empty beer bottles in the kitchen garbage. Juliette will be polishing off a lobster and a glass of Chardonnay at the back table, heavily involved in a rehash of some movie or other. Where's Pete? He went home early "because there wasn't much business." If the reading on the cash register is a disappointing one, then it will be clear that the nagging fears that have blighted his skiing, sailing, or sunbathing were totally justified. One more step on the road to ulcerdom, bankruptcy, severe depression, divorce, or massive coronary.

Until and unless the near-perfect manager and staff are found, the restaurateur will have to spend far more than eight hours a day on the job. A bitter cliché of the business is that people who are capable of doing a job unsupervised will be in business for themselves anyway, not working for others. This, though clearly an exaggeration, is the general belief. One never hears about the assistance Iacocca, Onassis, Patton, and Napoleon got from their staffs because it isn't good media entertainment. We want heroes! But a leader who cannot successfully delegate whether in business, sport, or battle is less likely to succeed.

True, being in charge isn't nearly as tiring as being in a subservient role, but it still requires a lot of hours of concentration. This concentration is of a curiously harrowing kind, because a restaurateur's day is one of constant interruption. Very few people seem to have the self-organizing ability to finish one thing at a time or to resist phone calls. It's hard to discipline yourself to finish the funny story you're telling a regular customer if you see that the Daily Special is being served without tomatoes and with the wrong fork. Customers in restaurants often get headaches from all the interruptions while they're trying to talk to the boss or the bartender.

An apt metaphor may be borrowed from the mechanical world. As was revealed after a recent bizarre air accident in Hawaii, aircraft are "aged" more by the number of take-offs and landings they make than by the mileage. Thus, an aircraft used for "island-hopping," and comparatively "young" in terms of miles flown, may be comparatively "old" in terms of take-offs and landings when compared, say, with a plane used mainly on the London–New York run. They therefore become prone to metal fatigue at an earlier stage than might normally be expected. And then there are those who believe it's not economical to switch off fluorescent lighting, on the grounds that more wear and tear is caused by switching them on again. Whatever the reason, the constant switching of attention is exhausting.

Some restaurateurs appear to thrive on it, however. They're only happy when problem after problem is brought to their attention to be solved brilliantly with a Solomonlike pronouncement that produces gasps of admiration to their faces, but much groaning and rolling of eyes when their backs are turned.

All restaurant staff are oppressed by the strange antisocial hours. True, for people who're trying to do something else with their lives, this can sometimes be a tremendous advantage, especially if they're fortunate enough to be able to work part-time. But, especially for a married person who enjoys family life, the long absence from home can be a strain, often barely compensated by the cash rewards of a flourishing business. The routine of returning exhausted (stinking of kitchen and cigarette smoke) with no appetite for dinner at home and falling asleep in front of the TV news isn't very good for some people, though there are undoubtedly some who hardly notice. Really late hours, such as those worked by some cocktail waitresses and supper club waiters, do induce a form of jet lag, as discussed, and lead to depression.

The availability of alcohol, and the subliminal effect of seeing so many people drinking it, can be a trap for those whose drinking habits, if any, are not already formed. Alcoholism is common in the business and often ruins it. Many restaurateurs proclaim loudly that they never drink with a customer or that they're never seen with a glass in their hands.

Although it's less of a problem for the owner than it is for the staff, dealing with the public can be a strain. There's a curious tradition, expounded by Hollywood, that it's all right to be rude to restaurant personnel. Every Yuppie worth the name knows how to put down that "snotty" maitre d', despite the fact that most maitre d's these days are more likely to err on the side of overfamiliarity than arrogance. When the hero knocks over the fruit bowl and the apples and oranges roll, to the consternation of the comically distressed waiter, it's considered funny. Some people take a delight in ordering finicky things that cause a disproportionate amount of stress backstage. Maybe their companions are impressed by the masterly approach. You can't kick out everyone you don't like, least of all in the beginning. When you're turning away business, then you can start to be a little more selective.

Any sensible person can see that you should be able to organize yourself around all this. If that's your reaction, then there's hope for you.

It may well be that the unhappy restaurateur laughing on the outside, crying on the inside, is a cliché easily accepted because they're somehow more prominent than the happy kind. If you are wise, you will make the demonstration of that point one of your major goals.

Getting away from the mystical, the major practical reasons for avoiding the restaurant business are the large capital investment required, the chance of losing every penny, and the heavy competition in many urban areas. The brave fellow with $200,000 raised from several sources is in competition with multimillion dollar corporations that will snap up any suitable location that comes on the market and accept a low return on their money for a longer period than the average individual could possibly afford. (Against this may be balanced the more aggressive search efforts of the individual. A sharp, probing eye will often see more than that of a large corporation nodding over its interdepartmental memos and endless meetings.) But there is never any shortage of people looking for suitable premises, and the brokers are every bit as aggressive in their sales tactics as other real estate operators.

QUESTIONS BEFORE DECIDING TO GO INTO BUSINESS

Am I confident of being able to realize a significant profit within a reasonable time, say, a year?

Do I have enough money to cover all financial outgoings for a reasonable period?

Is the location under consideration at least workable? That is, are there no serious negative factors whatsoever, either now or looming on the horizon due to local zoning plans or building?

Have I enough general experience of every aspect of the business to feel completely confident?

Can I keep a healthy amount of leisure time, in spite of the rigorous demands of the setting-up phase?

Can I hire and fire people?

Can I get good, or at least acceptable, help?

Do I know enough about people and life to choose winners over losers?

Am I going to be able to get along with the customers?

What does my spouse think about it all?

Is my partner reliable? How well do we know each other?

What's the competition locally?

Is there a real, natural demand for my restaurant?

If not, am I going to have to bring customers in from other areas by various means?

Supposing everything about the agreed format turns out to be disastrously wrong, am I flexible enough to change quickly?

AS D-DAY APPROACHES

While the day you open is exciting, your *real* opening day occurs when you decide to proceed into business. You must really force the pace to open those doors and get some money coming in. This can be an exhilarating and creative phase which, if you're successful, you'll look back on with surprising pleasure.

There is a lot to be said for inviting friends—if you have enough—for a shakedown evening so that you can see whether or not things work as planned. Unfortunately, all too often such stagings are the signal for all the hired help to quit on the spot. So make sure your friends are not too demanding, and if you can afford it, give your employees at least a nominal tip for the exercise. Seek their opinions, too.

If you do have a massive walk-out, then you'll be glad you kept a list of back-up personnel. Some of them may still be looking for work.

Rome wasn't built in a day. Some restaurants are an instant success, but most take time to develop. You should neither rejoice when you have a good day nor wail when you have a bad one. When you begin to spy growth patterns and familiar faces among the customers, you may permit yourself some self-congratulation.

At the end of every week you should ask yourself three questions:

Did you attract enough customers to meet the average number of "covers" you need to operate at a profit?

Did the vast majority of your customers get what they ordered promptly and to their apparent satisfaction?

Did they pay?

If you can answer yes to these questions, you're in business!

APPENDIX I

WHERE TO OBTAIN EDUCATION IN THE RESTAURANT INDUSTRY

The Educational Foundation of the National Restaurant Association [20 North Wacker Drive, Suite 2620, Chicago, Illinois 60606, (312) 782–1703] has been kind enough to provide the following information.

PROGRAMS IN HOTEL, RESTAURANT, INSTITUTIONAL MANAGEMENT

There are no fewer than 550 places in the United States where two-year or four-year courses may be taken. National average salaries for managers range from $15,000 to $40,000 per annum, with bonuses of $3,000 to $7,500. For chefs, the rates are $23,000 to $35,000, with bonuses of $1,500 to $7,000.

Junior/Community College and Culinary School Programs

The following information was taken from an extensive survey conducted by the National Restaurant Association and the National Institute for the Foodservice Industry. Hundreds of community and junior colleges and vocational-technical institutes were contacted to determine if they had a non-baccalaureate, post-secondary program in the foodservice, hospitality, or culinary areas. The listings included are taken from the information provided by the schools that responded to this survey.

Additional information for most of the schools listed is also available from the NRA and NIFI, including numbers of students and facul-

Information from Appendix I reprinted with permission from The Educational Foundation of the National Restaurant Association.

ty, names of directors of programs, costs, and brief program descriptions. It is suggested, however, that you contact the schools directly for more detailed and most current information available.

All these schools have indicated that they have an educational program directly related to the hospital industry. Included is the title of the program with each school's listing. As you will note, they vary greatly. By and large, there appear to be two general categories of programs: One includes those in the area of *hospitality* (hotel and restaurant) *management,* and a second group concentrates more on the *culinary arts* and *commercial cooking.* Many schools offer alternatives in both of the general categories.

Some of the program titles in the first category include Hotel and Restaurant Management; Foodservice Management; Hotel, Restaurant and Institutional Management; Hospitality Management; Restaurant/Foodservice Management; Foodservice Training; Foodservice Occupations; Food Preparation and Service; Foodservice and Hospitality Education; Hospitality Administration; Restaurant, Club, Hotel Management; Hotel-Restaurant Technology; Travel and Tourism; and Hospitality and Tourism Management.

Among the titles for programs concentrating in the culinary area are Culinary Arts; Commercial Cooking; Chef Training; Culinary Technology; Commercial Foods Preparation; Commercial Cooking and Baking; and Commercial Food Production and Management.

You may find that some of the schools listed also have secondary programs. Undoubtedly, some schools are not listed. No distinction has been made as to whether an Associate Degree, Certificate, Diploma, or other form of recognition is offered.

If you have any questions or comments about this information, please write to:

National Restaurant Association
150 N. Michigan, Suite 2000
Chicago, Illinois 60601
(312) 853-2525

National Institute for the
Foodservice Industry
20 N. Wacker Dr.
Chicago, Illinois 60606
(312) 782-1703

ALABAMA

Community College of the Air Force
Restaurant Management
CCAF/AYL Building 836
Maxwell AFB, Alabama 36112
(205) 293-6447

Bessemer State Technical College
Food Service
P.O. Box 308
Bessemer, Alabama 35021
(205) 428-6391

Carver State Technical College
Food Preparation and Services
414 Stanton Street
Mobile, Alabama 36617
(205) 473-8692

Jefferson State Junior College
Food Service Management & Technology
2601 Carson Road
Birmingham, Alabama 35215
(205) 853-1200

Lawson State Community College
Commercial Food Preparation
3060 Wilson Road, S.W.
Birmingham, Alabama 35221
(205) 925-1666

Wallace State Community College
Commercial Foods & Nutrition
P.O. Box 250
Hanceville, Alabama 35077
(205) 352-6403

ALASKA

Anchorage Community College
Food Service Technology
2533 Providence Avenue
Anchorage, Alaska 99504
(907) 263-1402

Alaska Vocational Technical Center
Food Service and Baking
P.O. Box 889
Seward, Alaska 99664
(907) 224-3322

ARIZONA

Pima Community College
Hospitality Education Program
P.O. Box 5027
Tucson, Arizona 85703
(602) 884-6541

Phoenix College
Foodservice Administration
1202 W. Thomas Road
Phoenix, Arizona 85013
(602) 264-2492

Scottsdale Community College
Hospitality Program
9000 East Chaparral Road
Scottsdale, Arizona 85253
(602) 941-0999

ARKANSAS

Quapaw Vocational Technical
Food Service Management
201 Vo-Tech Drive
Hot Springs, Arkansas 71913
(501) 767-9314

**Southern Arkansas University-
   Technical Branch**
Hotel & Restaurant Management
P.O. Box 3048
Camden, Arkansas 71701
(501) 574-4530

CALIFORNIA

American River College
Food Service Management
4700 College Oak Drive
Sacramento, California 95841
(916) 484-8656

Bakersfield College
Hotel, Restaurant & Institutional
   Management
1801 Panorama Drive
Bakersfield, California 93305
(805) 395-4561

California Culinary Academy
Professional Chef Program
625 Polk Street
San Francisco, California 94102
(415) 771-3536

Chaffey Community College
Food Service Management Training
5885 Haven
Alta Loma, California 91701
(714) 987-1737

Columbia College
Hospitality Management
P.O. Box 1849
Columbia, California 95310
(209) 532-3141

Contra Costa College
Culinary Arts
2600 Mission Bell Drive
San Pablo, California 94806
(415) 235-7800

Cypress College
Culinary Arts Department
9200 Valley View Boulevard
Cypress, California 90630
(714) 826-2220

College of the Desert
School of Culinary Arts
43900 Monterey Avenue
Palm Desert, California 92260
(619) 346-8041

Diablo Valley College
Hotel & Restaurant Management Program
321 Golf Club Road
Pleasant Hill, California 94523
(415) 685-1230

El Camino College
Food Service Management
16007 Crenshaw Boulevard
Torrance, California 90506
(213) 532-3670

Glendale Community College
Food Service & Management Program
1500 North Verdugo Road
Glendale, California 91208
(818) 240-1000

Grossmont College
Food Service Management
8800 Grossmont College Drive
El Cajon, California 92020
(619) 465-1700

Lake Tahoe Community College
Innkeeping & Restaurant Operations
P.O. Box 14445
South Lake Tahoe, California 95602
(916) 541-4660

Laney Community College
Food Preparation & Service
900 Fallon Street
Oakland, California 94607
(415) 834-5740

Los Angeles City College
Family & Consumer Studies
855 North Vermont Avenue
Los Angeles, California 90029
(213) 669-4235

Los Angeles Trade-Technical College
Hotel-Motel Management/Culinary Arts
400 West Washington Boulevard
Los Angeles, California 90015
(213) 746-0800

Merced College
Home Economics
3600 M. Street
Merced, California 95340
(209) 723-4321

Mission College
Hospitality Management
3000 Mission College Boulevard
Santa Clara, California 95054
(408) 988-2200

Modesto Junior College
Food Service
West Campus—Blue Gum Avenue
Modesto, California 95350
(209) 526-2000

Orange Coast College
Food Service & Hotel Management
2701 Fairview Road
Costa Mesa, California 92626
(714) 556-5876

Oxnard College
Hotel and Restaurant Management
4000 S. Rose Avenue
Oxnard, California 93033
(805) 488-0911

Pasadena City College
Food Service Instruction
1570 East Colorado Boulevard
Pasadena, California 91106
(818) 578-7235

Saddleback College
Hospitality Management
5500 Irvine Center Drive
Irvine, California 92714
(714) 559-9300

San Diego Community College District
Food Services/Hotel, Motel Management
3375 Camino Del Rio South
San Diego, California 92108
(619) 584-6568

San Diego Mesa College
Hotel, Motel Management
7250 Mesa College Drive
San Diego, California 92111
(619) 560-2600

City College of San Francisco
Hotel & Restaurant Department
50 Phelan Avenue
San Francisco, California 94112
(415) 239-3152

San Joaquin Delta Community College
Food Service Industry
5151 Pacific Avenue
Stockton, California 95207
(209) 474-5516

Santa Barbara City College
Hotel & Restaurant Management
721 Cliff Drive
Santa Barbara, California 93109
(805) 965-0581

Shasta College
Foodservice & Culinary Arts
1065 North Old Oregon Trail
Redding, California 96099
(916) 241-3523

Skyline College
Hotel-Motel Management,
   Food & Beverage Operations
3300 College Drive
San Bruno, California 94066
(415) 355-7000

Ventura College
Food Management
4667 Telegraph Road
Ventura, California 93003
(805) 642-3211

Yuba Community College
Food Service Management
2088 North Beale Road
Marysville, California 95901
(916) 741-6933

COLORADO

Aurora Public School Technical Center
Food Management Training
500 Buckley Road
Aurora, Colorado 80011
(303) 344-4910

Colorado Mountain College/Alpine Campus
Resort Management
Box 775280 1370 Bob Adams Dr.
Steamboat Springs, Colorado 80477
(303) 879-3288

Colorado Mountain College/Timberline Campus
Ski/Resort Management
Leadville, Colorado 80461
(303) 486-2015

Front Range Community College
Dietetic Technology
3645 West 112th Avenue
Westminster, Colorado 80030
(303) 466-8811

Emily Griffith Opportunity School
Denver Public School System
Foodservice Production & Management
1250 Welton Street
Denver, Colorado 80204
(303) 572-8218

Pikes Peak Community College
Food Management Program
5675 South Academy Boulevard
Colorado Springs, Colorado 80906
(303) 576-7711

Pueblo Community College
Food Service Program
900 West Orman Avenue
Pueblo, Colorado 81004
(303) 549-3306

Warren Occupational Technical Center
Restaurant Arts Program
13300 West Ellsworth Avenue
Golden, Colorado 80401
(303) 988-7470

CONNECTICUT

Manchester Community College
Hotel & Foodservice Management Program
60 Bidwell Street
Manchester, Connecticut 06040
(203) 647-6000

Mattatuck Community College
Food Services Management
750 Chase Parkway
Waterbury, Connecticut 06708
(203) 575-0328

University of New Haven
Hotel/Restaurant Management
300 Orange Avenue
West Haven, Connecticut 06516
(203) 932-7362

South Central Community College
Dietetic Technician/Nutrition Care
60 Sargent Drive
New Haven, Connecticut 06511
(203) 789-7826

DELAWARE

Delaware Technical Community College
Hospitality Management
P.O. Box 610
Georgetown, Delaware 19947
(302) 856-5400

Widener University
Hotel & Restaurant Management
P.O. Box 7139-Concord Pike
Wilmington, Delaware 19803
(302) 478-3000

FLORIDA

Atlantic Vocational Technical Center
Culinary Arts
4700 N.W. Coconut Creek Parkway
Coconut Creek, Florida 33066
(305) 979-6220

Broward Community College
Restaurant Management; Hotel-Motel
Administration
3501 S.W. Davie Road
Fort Lauderdale, Florida 33314
(305) 475-6710

College of Boca Raton
Hospitality Management/Culinary Arts
3601 N. Military Trail
Boca Raton, Florida 33431
(305) 994-0770

Daytona Beach Community College
Hospitality Management
P.O. Box 1111
Daytona Beach, Florida 32015
(904) 255-8131

Florida Junior College at Jacksonville
Hospitality Management
3939 Roosevelt Boulevard
Jacksonville, Florida 32205
(904) 387-8166

Gulf Coast Community College
Hotel/Motel, Restaurant Management
5230 West Highway 98
Panama City, Florida 32401
(904) 769-1551

Hillsborough Community College
Hotel & Restaurant Management
P.O. Box 22127
Tampa, Florida 33622
(813) 879-7222

Manatee Junior College
Food Service-Restaurant,
Hotel-Motel Management
5840 26th Street, West
Bradenton, Florida 33507
(813) 755-1511

Miami-Dade Community College
Hotel, Restaurant & Institutional Management
300 N.E. 2nd Avenue
Miami, Florida 33132
(305) 347-3151

Mid-Florida Technical Institute
Commercial Cooking/Culinary Arts
2900 W. Oakridge Road
Orlando, Florida 32809
(305) 855-5880

North Technical Education Center
Culinary Arts
7071 Garden Road
Riviera Beach, Florida 33404
(305) 848-0692

Okaloosa-Walton Junior College
Commercial Foods-Industrial Education
100 College Boulevard
Niceville, Florida 32578
(904) 678-5111

Palm Beach Junior College
Hospitality Management Program
4200 South Congress Avenue
Lake Worth, Florida 33461
(305) 439-8162

College of the Palm Beaches
Hotel-Motel Management
660 Fern Street
West Palm Beach, Florida 33401
(305) 833-5575

Pensacola Junior College
Dietetic Technician/Hotel & Restaurant
 Management
1000 College Boulevard
Pensacola, Florida 32504
(904) 476-5410

Pinellas Vocational Technical Institute
Culinary Arts Department
6100 154th Avenue, North
Clearwater, Florida 33540
(813) 535-3531

Sarasota County Vocational Technical Center
Culinary Arts/Hospitality Management
4748 Beneva Road
Sarasota, Florida 33583
(813) 924-1365

Seminole Community College
Food Service/Culinary Arts
Hwy. 17-92
Sanford, Florida 32771
(305) 323-1450

St. Augustine Technical Center
Commercial Foods/Culinary Arts Program
Collins Avenue at Del Monte Drive
St. Augustine, Florida 32084
(904) 824-4401

Valencia Community College
Hotel, Motel & Restaurant Management
 Training
P.O. Box 3028
Orlando, Florida 32802
(305) 299-5000

Washington-Holmes Area Vocational
 Technical Center
Commercial Foods Preparation &
 Culinary Arts
209 Hoyt Street
Chipley, Florida 32428
(904) 638-1180

Webber College
Hospitality Management
Route 27-A
Babson Park, Florida 33827
(813) 638-1431

GEORGIA

Albany Area Vocational Technical School
Foodservice Management
1021 Lowe
Albany, Georgia 31708
(912) 888-1320

Atlanta Area Vocational Technical School
Culinary Arts—Commercial Baking
1560 Stewart Avenue, SW
Atlanta, Georgia 30310
(404) 758-9451

Augusta Area Technical School
Culinary Arts
3116 Deans Bridge Rd.
Augusta, Georgia 30906
(404) 796-6900

Ben Hill-Irwin Area Vocational
 Technical School
Food Service
P.O. Box 1069
Fitzgerald, Georgia 31750
(912) 468-7487

Georgia State University
Hotel, Restaurant & Travel Administration
University Plaza
Atlanta, Georgia 30303
(404) 658-3512

Houston Vocational Center
Food Service Department
1311 Corder Road
Warner Robins, Georgia 31056
(912) 929-7750

Macon Area Vocational Technical School
Quantity Food Service
3300 Macon Tech Drive
Macon, Georgia 31206
(912) 781-0551

Savannah Area Vocational Technical School
Food Management
5717 White Bluff Rd.
Savannah, Georgia 31405
(912) 352-1464

HAWAII
Cannon's International Business College
of Honolulu
Hotel Front Office Procedures, Hotel
Management
1500 Kapiolani Boulevard
Honolulu, Hawaii 96814
(808) 955-1500

Hawaii Community College
Food Service Department
1175 Manono Street
Hilo, Hawaii 96720
(808) 961-9432

Honolulu Community College
Commercial Baking
874 Dillingham Boulevard
Honolulu, Hawaii 96817
(808) 845-9138

Kapiolani Community College
Food Service & Hospitality Education
620 Pensacola Street
Honolulu, Hawaii 96814
(808) 531-4654

Leeward Community College
Food Service Program, Vocational Technical
Division
96-045 Ala Ike
Pearl City, Hawaii 96782
(808) 455-0011

Maui Community College
Food Service Program
310 Kaahumanu Avenue
Kahului, Hawaii 96732
(808) 242-1210

Brigham Young University—Hawaii
Travel, Hotel, & Restaurant Management
55-220 Julanui Street
Laie, Hawaii 96762
(808) 293-3580

IDAHO
Boise State University
Food Service Technology
1910 University Drive
Boise, Idaho 83725
(208) 385-1957

ILLINOIS
Chicago Hospitality Institute
Chicago City-Wide College
Foodservice & Hotel-Motel Management
30 East Lake Street
Chicago, Illinois 60601
(312) 984-3211

College of DuPage
Hospitality Administration
22nd Street and Lambert Road
Glen Ellyn, Illinois 60137
(312) 858-2800

Elgin Community College
Hospitality Management
1700 Spartan Drive
Elgin, Illinois 60120
(312) 697-1000

William Rainey Harper College
Food Service Management, Cooking &
Baking
Algonquin & Roselle Roads
Palatine, Illinois 60067
(312) 397-3000

Joliet Junior College
Culinary Arts/Hotel-Restaurant Management
1216 Houbolt Avenue
Joliet, Illinois 60436
(815) 769-9020

Kendall College
The Culinary School
2408 Orrington Avenue
Evanston, Illinois 60201
(312) 866-1313

Kennedy-King College
Food Management
6800 South Wentworth Avenue
Chicago, Illinois 60621
(312) 962-3200

Lexington Institute
Hospitality Management
10840 S. Western Avenue
Chicago, Illinois 60643
(312) 779-3800

Lincoln Trail College
Restaurant Management/Culinary Arts
RR 3
Robinson, Illinois 62454
(618) 544-8657

Oakton Community College
Hotel-Motel Management Program
1600 East Golf Road
Des Plaines, Illinois 60016
(312) 635-1869

Parkland College
Food Service Management
2400 W. Bradley
Champaign, Illinois 61821
(217) 351-2200

Sauk Valley College
Public Services-Food Services
Rural Route #5
Dixon, Illinois 61021
(815) 288-5511

Southeastern Illinois College
Food Service Technology
Rural Route #4
Harrisburg, Illinois 62946
(618) 252-6376

Triton College
Hospitality Industry Administration
2000 Fifth Avenue
River Grove, Illinois 60171
(312) 456-0300

Washburne Trade School
Chef Training
3233 W. 31st Street
Chicago, Illinois 60623
(312) 650-4410

John Wood Community College
Occupational Education
1919 North 18th Street
Quincy, Illinois 62301
(217) 224-6500

INDIANA

Ball State University
Food Management
Home Economics Department
Practical Arts Building
Muncie, Indiana 47306
(317) 285-5931

Indiana University—
  Purdue University at Indianapolis
Restaurant, Hotel, & Institutional Management
799 West Michigan Street
Indianapolis, Indiana 46202
(317) 264-8772

Indiana Vocational Technical College
Hotel & Restaurant Management/
  Culinary Arts
One West 26th Street
Indianapolis, Indiana 46206
(317) 929-4797

Purdue University
Restaurant, Hotel and
  Institutional Management
Stone Hall
West Lafayette, Indiana 47907
(317) 494-4643

Vincennes University
Restaurant and Foodservice Management
1st Street
Vincennes, Indiana 47591
(812) 885-4465

IOWA

Des Moines Area Community College
Hospitality Careers
2006 Ankeny Boulevard
Ankeny, Iowa 50021
(515) 964-6532

Indian Hills Community College
Chef Training, Bakery Training
Grandview & Elm
Ottumwa, Iowa 52501
(515) 683-5197

Iowa Lakes Community College
Hotel/Motel & Restaurant Management
3200 College Drive
Emmetsburg, Iowa 50536
(712) 852-3554

Iowa Western Community College
Food Service Management; Cooking &
  Baking
2700 College Road
Council Bluffs, Iowa 51502
(712) 325-3277

Kirkwood Community College
Food Service Management
6301 Kirkwood Boulevard S.W.
Cedar Rapids, Iowa 52406
(319) 398-5468

KANSAS

Butler County Community College
Food Service & Management
Towanda Avenue and Haverhill Road
El Dorado, Kansas 67042
(316) 321-5083

Central College
Food Service/Home Economics
1200 South Main
McPherson, Kansas 67460
(316) 241-0723

Flint Hills Area Vocational Technical
  School
Foodservice Program
3301 W. 18th Avenue
Emporia, Kansas 66801
(316) 342-6404

Johnson County Community College
Hospitality Management Program
12345 College at Quivira
Overland Park, Kansas 66210
(913) 888-8500

Kansas City Area Vocational Technical
  School
Commercial Foodservice
2220 W. 59th Street
Kansas City, Kansas 66104
(913) 334-1000

KAW Area Vocational Technical Institute
Foodservice Program
5724 Huntoon
Topeka, Kansas 66604
(913) 273-7140

Manhattan Area Vocational
  Technical School
Foodservice & Management
3136 Dickens Avenue
Manhattan, Kansas 66502
(913) 539-7431

Northeast Kansas Area Vocational
  Technical School
Commercial Food Preparation/Restaurant
  Management
1501 West Riley
Atchison, Kansas 66002
(913) 367-6204

Salina Area Vocational Technical School
Foodservice Management
2562 Scanlan
Salina, Kansas 67401
(913) 825-2261

Southwest Kansas Area Vocational
  Technical School
Foodservice Program
2nd & Comanche Streets
Dodge City, Kansas 67801
(316) 225-0285

Wichita Area Vocational Technical School
Food Service Mid-Management
  & Culinary Arts
324 North Emporia
Wichita, Kansas 67202
(316) 265-8666

KENTUCKY

Daviess County State Vocational Technical
  School
Commercial Foods
1901 S.E. Parkway
Owensboro, Kentucky 42301
(502) 684-7211

Elizabethtown State Vocational Technical
  School
Commercial Foods
505 University Drive
Elizabethtown, Kentucky 42701
(502) 765-2104

Jefferson Community College
Culinary Arts
109 East Broadway
Louisville, Kentucky 40202
(502) 584-0181

Northern Kentucky State Vocational
  Technical School
Commercial Foods Program
Amsterdam Road
Covington, Kentucky 41011
(606) 292-2711

West Kentucky State Vocational Technical
  School
Commercial Foods
Blandville Road, P.O. Box 7408
Paducah, Kentucky 42001
(502) 554-4991

LOUISIANA

Baton Rouge Vocational Technical Institute
Culinary Arts
3250 North Acadian Throughway
Baton Rouge, Louisiana 70805
(504) 355-5621

Sidney N. Collier Vocational Technical
  Institute
Culinary Arts
3727 Louisa Street
New Orleans, Louisiana 70126
(504) 945-8080

Delgado Community College
Chef Apprenticeship
615 City Park Avenue
New Orleans, Louisiana 70119
(504) 483-4208

New Orleans Regional Vocational
  Technical Institute
Chef Apprenticeship
980 Navarre Avenue
New Orleans, Louisiana 70124
(504) 483-4666

Nicholls State University
Food Service Management
P.O. Box 2014 NSU
Thibodaux, Louisiana 70301
(504) 446-8111

MAINE

Eastern Maine Vocational Technical
  Institute
Food Technology
354 Hogan Road
Bangor, Maine 04401
(207) 941-4600

Southern Maine Vocational Technical
  Institute
Culinary Arts/Hotel, Motel & Restaurant
  Management
2 Fort Road
South Portland, Maine 04106
(207) 799-7303

Washington County
  Vocational-Technical Institute
Foodservice
River Road
Calais, Maine 04619
(207) 454-2144

MARYLAND

Baltimore's International Culinary Arts
  Institute
Restaurant Skills, Baking & Pastry Skills
19 S. Gay Street
Baltimore, Maryland 21202
(301) 752-4710

Essex Community College
Hotel-Motel & Restaurant-Club Management
7201 Rossville Boulevard
Baltimore, Maryland 21237
(301) 522-1456

Hagerstown Junior College
Hospitality Program
751 Robinwood Drive
Hagerstown, Maryland 21740
(301) 790-2800

Montgomery College
Hospitality Management
51 Mannakee Street
Rockville, Maryland 20850
(301) 279-5185

Wor-Wic Tech Community College
Hotel, Motel & Restaurant Management
Old Ocean City Road
Salisbury, Maryland 21801
(301) 749-8181

MASSACHUSETTS
Berkshire Community College
Hotel & Restaurant Management
West Street
Pittsfield, Massachusetts 01201
(413) 499-4660

Bunker Hill Community College
Hotel/Restaurant Management/Culinary Arts
New Rutherford Avenue
Charlestown, Massachusetts 02129
(619) 241-8600

Cape Cod Community College
Hotel/Restaurant Management Program
Route 132
West Barnstable, Massachusetts 02668
(617) 362-2131

Chamberlayne Junior College
Hotel & Institutional Management
128 Commonwealth Avenue
Boston, Massachusetts 02116
(617) 536-4500

Endicott College
Hotel-Restaurant Management
376 Hale Street
Beverly, Massachusetts 01915
(617) 927-0585

Holyoke Community College
Hospitality Management Program
303 Homestead Avenue
Holyoke, Massachusetts 01040
(413) 538-7000

Laboure Junior College
Division of Dietetic Technology
2120 Dorchester Avenue
Boston, Massachusetts 02124
(617) 296-8300

Newbury Junior College
Culinary Arts Program
129 Fisher Avenue
Brookline, Massachusetts 02146
(617) 739-0510

Northeastern University
Hotel & Restaurant Management
102 Churchill Hall
Boston, Massachusetts 02115
(617) 437-2407

Henry O. Peabody School
Culinary Arts
Nichols Street and Peabody Road
Norwood, Massachusetts 02062
(617) 762-1470

Quincy Junior College
Hotel/Restaurant Management
34 Coddington Street
Quincy, Massachusetts 02169
(617) 786-8777

Quinsigamond Community College
Hotel-Restaurant Management
670 West Boylston Street
Worcester, Massachusetts 01606
(617) 853-2300

MICHIGAN
The Career Development Center
Culinary Arts
5961 14th Street
Detroit, Michigan 48208
(313) 894-0610

Davenport College of Business
Hospitality Management
415 East Fulton Street
Grand Rapids, Michigan 49503
(616) 451-3511

Ferris State College
Food Service/Hospitality Management
South Commons
Big Rapids, Michigan 49307
(616) 796-0461

Henry Ford Community College
Culinary Arts/Hotel Restaurant Management
5101 Evergreen Road
Dearborn, Michigan 48128
(313) 271-2750

Gogebic Community College
Food Service
Jackson & Greenbush
Ironwood, Michigan 49938
(906) 932-4231

Grand Rapids Junior College
Hotel/Restaurant Management; Culinary Arts
143 Bostwick N.E.
Grand Rapids, Michigan 49503
(616) 456-4837

Lake Michigan College
Food Service Management
2755 East Napier Avenue
Benton Harbor, Michigan 49022
(616) 927-3571

Lansing Community College
Food Service & Hotel/Motel Management
419 North Capitol Avenue
Lansing, Michigan 48901
(517) 483-1561

Macomb Community College
Professional Foodservice
44575 Garfield Road
Mount Clemens, Michigan 48044
(313) 286-2000

Charles S. Mott Community College
Food Management
1401 E. Court Street
Flint, Michigan 48502
(313) 762-0440

Northern Michigan University
Institution & Restaurant Management
Thomas Fine Arts Building
Marquette, Michigan 49855
(906) 227-2364

Northwestern Michigan College
Food Services Technology
1701 East Front Street
Traverse City, Michigan 49684
(616) 922-1197

Northwood Institute-Michigan
Hotel/Restaurant Management
3225 Cook Road
Midland, Michigan 48640
(517) 631-1600

Oakland Community College
Hospitality Department
27055 Orchard Lake Road
Farmington Hills, Michigan 48018
(313) 471-7779

Schoolcraft Community College
Culinary Arts
18600 Haggerty Road
Livonia, Michigan 48152
(313) 591-6400

Siena Heights College
Hotel, Restaurant, & Institutional Management
1247 E. Siena Heights Drive
Adrian, Michigan 49221
(517) 263-0731

St. Clair County Community College
Foodservice Management
323 Erie Street
Port Huron, Michigan 48060
(313) 984-3881

State Technical Institute
Food Service Training
Alber Drive
Plainwell, Michigan 49080
(616) 664-4461

Washtenaw Community College
Foods & Hospitality
4800 E. Huron River Drive
Ann Arbor, Michigan 48106
(313) 973-3584

Wayne County Community College
Culinary Arts Program
8551 Greenfield
Detroit, Michigan 48228
(313) 943-4000

West Shore Community College
Hospitality Management
3000 North Stiles Road
Scottville, Michigan 49454
(616) 845-6211

MINNESOTA

Alexandria Area Vocational Technical Institute
Hotel, Motel & Restaurant Management
1601 Jefferson Street
Alexandria, Minnesota 56308
(612) 762-0221

Canby Area Vocational Technical Institute
Food Service Management
1011 First Street West
Canby, Minnesota 56220
(507) 223-7252

Dakota County Area Vocational Technical Institute
Food Service & Chef Management
1300 145th Street E.
Rosemount, Minnesota 55068
(612) 423-8301

Detroit Lakes Area Vocational Technical Institute
Commercial Cooking & Baking
Highway 34 East
Detroit Lakes, Minnesota 56501
(218) 847-1341

Duluth Area Vocational Technical Institute
Food Service Management
2101 Trinity Road
Duluth, Minnesota 55811
(218) 722-2801

Hennepin Technical Centers
Cook/Chef
1820 North Xenium Lane
Minneapolis, Minnesota 55441
(612) 559-3535

Mankato Area Vocational Technical Institute
Cook/Chef
1920 Lee Boulevard
North Mankato, Minnesota 56001
(507) 625-3441

University of Minnesota Technical College-Crookston
Hotel, Restaurant & Resort Management
Highway 2 and 75, North
Crookston, Minnesota 56716
(218) 281-6510

Moorhead Area Vocational Technical Institute
Chef Training
1900 28th Avenue South
Moorhead, Minnesota 56560
(218) 236-6277

Normandale Community College
Hospitality Management Program
9700 France Avenue South
Bloomington, Minnesota 55431
(612) 830-9300

**St. Paul Public Schools Technical
  Vocational Institute**
Restaurant-Hotel Cookery
235 Marshall Avenue
St. Paul, Minnesota 55102
(612) 221-1300

Willmar Area Vocational Technical Institute
Chefs Training & Food Service Management
Box 1097
Willmar, Minnesota 56201
(612) 235-5114

916 Vocational Technical Institute
Chef Training
3300 Century Avenue North
White Bear Lake, Minnesota 55110
(612) 770-2351

MISSISSIPPI

Hinds Junior College
Hotel, Motel & Restaurant Management
3925 Sunset Drive
Jackson, Mississippi 39213
(601) 366-1405

Meridian Junior College
Hotel & Restaurant Management
5500 Highway 19 North
Meridian, Mississippi 39305
(601) 483-8241

**Mississippi Gulf Coast Junior College—
  Jefferson Davis Campus**
Hotel, Motel & Restaurant Program
Handsboro Station
Gulfport, Mississippi 39501
(601) 896-3355

The Northeastern Mississippi Junior College
Hotel, Motel & Restaurant Management
Cunningham Boulevard
Booneville, Mississippi 38829
(601) 728-7751

MISSOURI

Crowder College
Hospitality Management
Neosho, Missouri 64850
(417) 451-3223

Jefferson College
Hotel/Restaurant Management
Hillsboro, Missouri 63050
(314) 789-3951

Penn Valley Community College
Lodging & Food Service Management
3201 Southwest Trafficway
Kansas City, Missouri 64111
(816) 932-7600

**St. Louis Community College at
  Florissant Valley**
Dietetic Technology
3400 Pershall Road
St. Louis, Missouri 63135
(314) 595-4426

St. Louis Community College at Forest Park
Hospitality Restaurant Management
  Department
5600 Oakland Avenue
St. Louis, Missouri 63110
(314) 644-9749

State Fair Community College
Food Service Management
1900 Clarendon Road
Sedalia, Missouri 65301
(816) 826-7100

Three Rivers Community College
Hospitality Management Program
Three Rivers Boulevard
Poplar Bluff, Missouri 63901
(314) 686-4101

MONTANA

Missoula Vocational Technical Center
Commercial Food Preparation
909 South Avenue West
Missoula, Montana 59801
(406) 721-1330

Western Montana College
Institutions & Resort Management
710 S. Atlantic
Dillon, Montana 59725
(406) 683-7011

NEBRASKA

Central Community College
Hotel & Restaurant Management
P.O. Box 1024
Hastings, Nebraska 68901
(402) 461-2458

Metropolitan Technical Community College
Culinary Arts
P.O. Box 3777
Omaha, Nebraska 68103
(402) 449-8400

**Southeast Community College-Lincoln
  Campus**
Food Service Management
8800 "O" Street
Lincoln, Nebraska 68520
(402) 471-3333

NEVADA

Clark County Community College
Restaurant Foodservice/Hotel Management/
  Casino Restaurant Management
3200 Cheyenne Avenue
West Las Vegas, Nevada 89030
(702) 643-6060

Truckee Meadows Community College
Food Service Technology-Trade
& Industry Division
7000 Dandini Boulevard
Sparks, Nevada 89512
(702) 673-7000

NEW HAMPSHIRE
New Hampshire College
Culinary Institute
2500 North River Road
Manchester, New Hampshire 03104
(603) 485-8415

New Hampshire Vocational Technical College
Culinary Arts
2020 Riverside Drive
Berlin, New Hampshire 03570
(603) 752-1113

University of New Hampshire
Thompson School of Applied Sciences
Food Service Management/Culinary Arts
Barton Hall, Room 105
Durham, New Hampshire 03824
(603) 862-1073

NEW JERSEY
Academy of Culinary Arts
Atlantic Community College
Black Horse Pike
Mays Landing, New Jersey 08330
(609) 625-1607

Atlantic Community College
Hospitality Management Program
Mays Landing, New Jersey 08330
(609) 625-1111

Bergen Community College
Hotel/Restaurant Management Program
400 Paramus Road
Paramus, New Jersey 07652
(201) 447-7192

Brookdale Community College
Food Service Management
Newman Springs Road
Lincroft, New Jersey 07738
(201) 842-1900

Burlington County College
Hospitality Management
Pemberton-Browns Mill Road
Pemberton, New Jersey 08068
(609) 894-9311

Camden County College
Dietetic Technician-Food Management
Box 200 B
Blackwood, New Jersey 08021
(609) 227-7200

Career Center
Cape May County Vocational Technical School
Food Occupations
Cresthaven Road
Cape May Court House, New Jersey 08210
(609) 465-2161

Hudson County Community College
Culinary Arts
161 Newkirk Street
Jersey City, New Jersey 07306
(201) 656-2020

Middlesex County College
Hotel, Restaurant & Institution
  Management Department
155 Mill Road
Edison, New Jersey 08818
(201) 548-6000

Ocean County College
Food Service Management
Toms River, New Jersey 08753
(201) 255-4000

Salem County Vocational Technical Schools
Culinary Arts
R.D. #2, Box 350
Woodstown, New Jersey 08098
(609) 769-0101

NEW MEXICO
Albuquerque Technical Vocational Institute
Hospitality & Foodservice Management
525 Buena Vista SE
Albuquerque, New Mexico 87106
(505) 848-1700

NEW YORK
Adirondack Community College
Commercial Cooking/Occupational Education
Bay Road
Glens Falls, New York 12801
(518) 793-4491

The Culinary Institute of America
Culinary Arts
P.O. Box 53
Hyde Park, New York 12538
(914) 452-9600

Erie Community College
Food Service Administration
Main and Youngs Road
Buffalo, New York 14221
(716) 634-0800

Fulton-Montgomery Community College
Food Service Administration
Route 67
Johnstown, New York 12095
(518) 762-4651

Genesee Community College
Hospitality Management
One College Road
Batavia, New York 14020
(716) 343-0055

Herkimer County Community College
Food Service Administration
Reservoir Road
Herkimer, New York 13357
(315) 866-0300

Hudson Valley Community College
Food Service Administration Department
80 Vandenburgh Avenue
Troy, New York 12180
(518) 283-1100

Jefferson Community College
Hospitality & Tourism
Outer Coffeen Street
Watertown, New York 13601
(315) 782-5250

Fiorello H. LaGuardia Community College
Dietetic Technician Program
31-10 Thomson Avenue
Long Island City, New York 11101
(718) 626-5468

Mohawk Valley Community College
Food Service
Floyd Avenue
Rome, New York 13440
(315) 339-3470

Monroe Community College
Food Service Administration
1000 East Henrietta Road
Rochester, New York 14623
(716) 424-5200

Nassau Community College
Hotel/Restaurant Technology
Stewart Avenue
Garden City, New York 11530
(516) 222-7500

New York City Technical College
Hotel & Restaurant Management Department
300 Jay Street
Brooklyn, New York 11201
(718) 643-8386

New York Institute of Dietetics
Food & Hotel Management
154 West 14th Street
New York, New York 10011
(212) 675-6655

New York University
Foodservice Management Program
239 Greene Street, 537 East Building
New York, New York 10003
(212) 598-2369

The New York Restaurant School
The New School of Social Research
27 W. 34th Street
New York, New York 10001
(212) 947-7097

Niagara County Community College
Food Service/Professional Chef Option
3111 Saunders Settlement Road
Sanborn, New York 14132
(716) 731-4101

Onondaga Community College
Foodservice Administration & Hotel
  Management
Route #173
Syracuse, New York 13215
(315) 469-7741

Schenectady County Community College
Hotel Technology and Culinary Arts
Washington Avenue
Schenectady, New York 12305
(518) 346-6211

Paul Smith's College of Arts & Sciences
Hospitality Management
Paul Smiths, New York 12970
(518) 327-6218

State University of New York at Alfred
Food Service
South Brooklyn Avenue
Wellsville, New York 14895
(607) 871-6215

State University of New York at Canton
Hotel Technology, Restaurant Management
Cornell Drive
Canton, New York 13617
(315) 386-7011

State University of New York at Cobleskill
Food Service & Hospitality Administration
Champlin Hall
Cobleskill, New York 12043
(518) 234-5425

State University of New York at Delhi
Hotel, Restaurant & Food Service
  Management
Delhi, New York 13753
(607) 746-4189

State University of New York
  at Farmingdale
Food Service Administration/Restaurant
  Management
Thompson Hall
Melville Road
Farmingdale, New York 11735
(516) 420-2000

State University of New York at Morrisville
Food Science Technology
Bailey Annex
Morrisville, New York 13408
(315) 684-6016

Suffolk County Community College
Hotel, Restaurant Institutional Management
Speonk Riverhead Road
Riverhead, New York 11901
(516) 369-2600

Sullivan County Community College
Hotel Technology/Restaurant Management
College Road, Box 269
Loch Sheldrake, New York 12759
(914) 434-5750

Tompkins Cortland Community College
Hotel Technology/Food Service
  Administration
170 North Street
Dryden, New York 13053
(607) 844-8211

Villa Maria College of Buffalo
Food Service Management
240 Pine Ridge Road
Buffalo, New York 14225
(716) 896-0700

Westchester Community College
Hotel & Restaurant Management
75 Grasslands Road
Valhalla, New York 10595
(914) 285-6750

NORTH CAROLINA
Asheville Buncombe Technical College
  Culinary Technology and Motel &
    Restaurant Management
340 Victoria Road
Asheville, North Carolina 28801
(704) 254-1921

Central Piedmont Community College
Hotel, Restaurant Management Program
P.O. Box 35009
Charlotte, North Carolina 28235
(704) 373-6721

Fayetteville Technical Institute
Food Service Management
P.O. Box 35236
Fayetteville, North Carolina 28303
(919) 323-1961

Guilford Technical Community College
Foodservice Management
Box 309
Jamestown, North Carolina 27282
(919) 454-1126

Lenoir Community College
Food Service Management
P.O. Box 188
Kinston, North Carolina 28502
(919) 527-6223

Southwestern Technical College
Food Service Management
P.O. Box 67
Sylva, North Carolina 28779
(704) 586-4091

Technical College of Alamance
Foodservice Specialist
Foodservice Management
P.O. Box 623
Haw River, North Carolina 27258
(919) 578-2002

Wake Technical College
Restaurant & Hotel Management
9101 Fayetteville Road
Raleigh, North Carolina 27603
(919) 772-0551

Wilkes Community College
Hotel/Restaurant Management
Drawer 120
Wilkesboro, North Carolina 28697
(919) 667-7136

NORTH DAKOTA
Bismarck Junior College
Hotel, Motel & Restaurant Management
Shafer Heights
Bismarck, North Dakota 58501
(701) 224-5479

North Dakota State School of Science
Cook and Chef Training
Wahpeton, North Dakota 58075
(701) 671-2201

OHIO
Bowling Green State University
Applied Sciences Department
901 Rye Beach Road
Huron, Ohio 44839
(419) 433-5560

Cincinnati Technical College
Executive Chef Technology/
  Hotel-Motel-Restaurant Management
3520 Central Parkway
Cincinnati, Ohio 45223
(513) 861-9338

Clermont General & Technical College
University of Cincinnati
Hospitality Management
College Drive
Batavia, Ohio 45103
(513) 732-2990

Columbus Technical Institute
Hospitality Management Department
550 East Spring Street
Columbus, Ohio 43215
(614) 227-2579

Cuyahoga Community College
Hospitality Management
2900 Community College Road
Cleveland, Ohio 44115
(216) 241-5966

Hocking Technical College
Hotel/Restaurant Management
Route #1
Nelsonville, Ohio 45764
(614) 753-3591

Jefferson Technical College
Hospitality/Food Service Management
4000 Sunset Boulevard
Steubenville, Ohio 43952
(614) 264-5591

Owens Technical College
Hospitality Management Technology
30335 Oregon Road
Toledo, Ohio 43699
(419) 666-0580

University of Toledo—
Community and Technical College
Food Service Management/Culinary Arts
West Bancroft Street
Toledo, Ohio 43606
(419) 537-3112

Youngstown State University
Dietetic Technology
College of Applied Science & Technology
410 Wick Avenue
Youngstown, Ohio 44555
(216) 742-3344

Youngstown State University
Food & Nutrition/Dietetics
410 Wick Avenue
Youngstown, Ohio 44555
(216) 742-3344

OKLAHOMA

Carl Albert Junior College
School of Hotel & Restaurant Management
P.O. Box 606
Poteau, Oklahoma 74953
(918) 647-8221

Great Plains Area Vocational Technical
Center
Commercial Food Services/Fast Foods
Management
4500 West Lee Boulevard
Lawton, Oklahoma 73505
(405) 355-6371

Indian Meridian Vocational Technical School
Commercial Food Production & Management
1312 South Sangre Road
Stillwater, Oklahoma 74074
(405) 377-3333

Oklahoma State University
School of Technical Training
Food Service Occupations/Culinary Arts—
Baking
4th and Mission
Okmulgee, Oklahoma 74447
(918) 756-6211

Pioneer Area Vocational Technical School
Commercial Foods
2101 North Ash
Ponca City, Oklahoma 74601
(405) 762-8336

Southern Oklahoma Area Vocational-
Technical School
Culinary Arts
Route 1
Ardmore, Oklahoma 73401
(405) 223-2070

Tulsa Junior College
Lodging & Food Service Management
909 South Boston
Tulsa, Oklahoma 74119
(918) 587-6561

OREGON

Chemeketa Community College
Food Service Management
P.O. Box 14007
Salem, Oregon 97309
(503) 399-5091

Horst Mager Culinary Institute
Culinary Program
1316 S.W. 13th Avenue
Portland, Oregon 97201
(503) 223-2245

Lane Community College
Food Service Management
4000 East 30th Avenue
Eugene, Oregon 97405
(503) 747-4501

Linn-Benton Community College
Culinary Arts/Restaurant Management
6500 SW Pacific Boulevard
Albany, Oregon 97321
(503) 928-2361

Portland Community College
Hospitality Department
12000 SW 49th
Portland, Oregon 97219
(503) 244-6111

PENNSYLVANIA

Community College of Allegheny County
Hospitality Management/Culinary Arts
595 Beatty Road
Monroeville, Pennsylvania 15146
(412) 327-1327

Bucks County Community College
Hospitality Services & Chefs
Apprenticeship
Swamp Road
Newtown, Pennsylvania 18940
(215) 968-8225

Butler County Community College
Food Service Management
Oak Hills, College Drive
Butler, Pennsylvania 16001
(412) 282-1235

Delaware County Community College
Hotel/Restaurant Management
Route 252
Media, Pennsylvania 19063
(215) 359-5000

Harrisburg Area Community College
Food Service Management
3300 Cameron Street
Harrisburg, Pennsylvania 17110
(717) 780-2493

Keystone Junior College
Hospitality Management
La Plume, Pennsylvania 18440
(717) 945-5141

Luzerne County Community College
Hotel & Restaurant Management
Prospect Street and Middle Road
Nanticoke, Pennsylvania 18634
(717) 821-1514

Montgomery County Community College
Hospitality Management Program
340 DeKalb Pike
Blue Bell, Pennsylvania 19422
(215) 641-6300

Peirce Junior College
Hospitality Management
1420 Pine Street
Philadelphia, Pennsylvania 19102
(215) 545-6400

Pennsylvania State University, Berks Campus
Hotel, Restaurant and Institution Management
College of Human Development
R.D. #5, Tulpehocken Road
Reading, Pennsylvania 19608
(215) 320-4813

Community College of Philadelphia
Hotel, Restaurant & Institutional Management
1700 Spring Garden Street
Philadelphia, Pennsylvania 19130
(215) 751-8704

The Restaurant School
Restaurant Management/Chef Training
2129 Walnut Street
Philadelphia, Pennsylvania 19103
(215) 561-3446

Westmoreland County Community College
Food Service Management/Culinary Arts
Armbrust Road
Youngwood, Pennsylvania 15697
(412) 925-4000

Williamsport Area Community College
Food & Hospitality Management
1005 West Third Street
Williamsport, Pennsylvania 17701
(717) 326-3761

York Technical Institute
Hotel, Motel Management/Foodservice
   Management/Travel/Tourism
255 W. King Street
York, Pennsylvania 17404
(717) 757-1100

RHODE ISLAND
Johnson & Wales College
Hotel Management/Culinary Arts/Baking Pastry
One Washington Avenue
Providence, Rhode Island 02905
(401) 456-1000

SOUTH CAROLINA
Greenville Technical College
Food Science
P.O. Box 5616—Section "B"
Greenville, South Carolina 29606
(803) 242-3170

Horry-Georgetown Technical College
Hotel, Motel & Restaurant Management
Highway 501 East, P.O. Box 1966
Conway, South Carolina 29526
(803) 347-3186

Johnson & Wales College
Culinary Arts—Southern Division
701 S. Bay St.
Charleston, South Carolina 29403
(803) 723-4649

SOUTH DAKOTA
Black Hills State College
Travel Industry Management
1200 University
Spearfish, South Dakota 57783
(605) 642-6867

Mitchell Area Vocational Technical School
Cook/Chef
821 North Capitol
Mitchell, South Dakota 57301
(605) 996-6671

TENNESSEE
**Knoxville State Area Vocational Technical
   School**
Commercial Food Preparation
1100 Liberty Street
Knoxville, Tennessee 37919
(615) 546-5567

**Nashville Area Vocational Technical
   School**
Commercial Foods
2601 Bransford Avenue
Nashville, Tennessee 37207
(615) 254-9718

Shelby State Community College
Department of Nutrition & Dietetics
P.O. Box 40568
Memphis, Tennessee 38174
(901) 528-6865

State Technical Institute at Memphis
Motel/Restaurant Management
5983 Macon Cove
Memphis, Tennessee 38134
(901) 377-4132

TEXAS
Austin Community College
Chef's Apprenticeship
5350 Burnet Road
Austin, Texas 78756
(512) 454-3673

Central Texas College
Food Service & Hotel/Motel Management
Highway 190 West
Killeen, Texas 76542
(817) 526-1248

Del Mar College
Restaurant Management Department
Baldwin at Ayers
Corpus Christi, Texas 78404
(512) 881-6435

El Centro College
Food & Hospitality Services Institute
Main at Lamar Streets
Dallas, Texas 75202
(214) 746-2202

Hill Junior College
Food Preparation, Service & Management
Box 619
Hillsboro, Texas 76645
(817) 582-2555

Houston Community College
Culinary Arts
1300 Holman
Houston, Texas 77004
(713) 868-0742

Houston Community College
Hotel, Restaurant, Club Management
4310 Dunlavy
Houston, Texas 77006
(713) 868-0775

Northwood Institute—Texas
Hotel/Restaurant Management
P.O. Box 58 FR 1382
Cedar Hill, Texas 75104
(214) 291-1541

St. Philip's College
Hospitality Management/Chef's Apprenticeship
2111 Nevada
San Antonio, Texas 78203
(512) 531-3315

San Jacinto College
Restaurant Management and Dietetic
  Technology
8060 Spencer Highway
Pasadena, Texas 77505
(713) 476-1869

San Jacinto College—North Campus
Baking & Catering
5800 Uvalde
Houston, Texas 77049
(713) 458-4050

South Plains College
Food Industry Management
1302 Main Street
Lubbock, Texas 79401
(806) 747-0576

Texas State Technical Institute
Food Service Technology Program
Building 15-1
Waco, Texas 76705
(815) 799-3611

UTAH
Sevier Valley Technical School
Food Services
500 West 2nd South
Richfield, Utah 84701
(801) 869-8202

Utah Technical College
Foodservice Management/Hotel-Restaurant
  Management/Hospitality Management
1200 South 800 West
Orem, Utah 84057
(801) 226-5000

Utah Technical College
Hotel-Motel/Restaurant Management
P.O. Box 1609
Provo, Utah 84601
(801) 226-5000

VERMONT
Champlain College
Hotel, Motel & Restaurant Management
232 South Willard Street
Burlington, Vermont 05402
(802) 658-0800

New England Culinary Institute
Culinary Arts
250 Main Street
Montpelier, Vermont 05602
(802) 223-6324

VIRGINIA
Thomas Nelson Community College
Hotel, Restaurant & Institutional
  Management
P.O. Box 9407
Hampton, Virginia 23670
(804) 825-2900

Northern Virginia Community College
Hotel, Restaurant & Institutional
  Management
8333 Little River Turnpike
Annandale, Virginia 22003
(703) 323-3457

Tidewater Community College
Hotel, Restaurant & Institutional
  Management
1700 College Crescent
Virginia Beach, Virginia 23456
(804) 427-7100

John Tyler Community College
Food Service Management
Chester, Virginia 23831
(804) 796-4031

WASHINGTON
Clark College
Culinary Arts
1800 East McLoughlin Boulevard
Vancouver, Washington 98663
(206) 699-0304

Everett Community College
Food Technology
801 Wetmore Avenue
Everett, Washington 98201
(201) 259-7151

Fort Steilacoom Community College
Food Service Management
P.O. Box 33265
Fort Lewis, Washington 98433
(206) 964-6567

Highline Community College
Hospitality & Tourism Management
Pacific Hwy. South and South 240th
Midway, Washington 98032
(206) 878-3710

North Seattle Community College
Hospitality & Foodservice
9600 College Way North
Seattle, Washington 98103
(206) 634-4503

Olympic College
Commercial Cooking/Food Service
16th & Chester
Bremerton, Washington 98310
(206) 478-4576

Seattle Central Community College
Hospitality Management/Culinary Arts
1701 Broadway Room 2112
Seattle, Washington 98122
(206) 587-5424

Shoreline Community College
Food Services Technology
16101 Greenwood Avenue North
Seattle, Washington 98133
(206) 546-4789

Skagit Valley College
Culinary Arts/Restaurant Management
2405 College Way
Mount Vernon, Washington 98273
(206) 428-1211

South Seattle Community College
Food Service Management/Pastry
& Speciality Baking
6000 16th Avenue S.W.
Seattle, Washington 98106
(206) 764-5344

Spokane Community College
Culinary Arts/Hotel-Motel Management
1810 North Green Street
Spokane, Washington 99207
(509) 536-7283

WEST VIRGINIA
Community College of West Virginia State
Hotel, Restaurant & Institutional Management
Campus Box 183
Institute, West Virginia 25112
(304) 766-3118

Fairmont State College
Food Service Management
Home Economics/Technology
Fairmont, West Virginia 26554
(304) 367-4271

Garnet Career Center
Commercial Foods
422 Dickinson Street
Charleston, West Virginia 25301
(304) 348-6127

James Rumsey Vocational Technical Center
Food Service Occupations
Route 6—Box 268
Martinsburg, West Virginia 25401
(304) 754-7925

Shepherd College
Hotel, Motel & Restaurant Management
Shepherdstown, West Virginia 25443
(304) 876-2511

WISCONSIN
Cardinal Stritch College
Hotel, Restaurant & Foodservice
Management
6801 N. Yates Rd.
Milwaukee, WI 53217
(414) 352-5400

District 1 Technical Institute
Restaurant & Hotel Cookery; Hospitality
Management
620 West Clairemont Avenue
Eau Claire, Wisconsin 54701
(715) 836-3514

Fox Valley Technical Institute
Hospitality/Culinary Arts
1825 North Bluemound Drive
Appleton, Wisconsin 54913
(414) 735-5600

Gateway Technical Institute
Hotel/Motel Management; Food Service
Management
1001 South Main Street
Racine, Wisconsin 53403
(414) 631-7300

Madison Area Technical College
Industrial Foods
211 North Carroll Street
Madison, Wisconsin 53703
(608) 266-5007

Milwaukee Area Technical College
Restaurant & Hotel Cookery Program
1015 North Sixth Street
Milwaukee, Wisconsin 53203
(414) 278-6255

Moraine Park Technical Institute
Restaurant & Hotel Cookery
235 North National Avenue
Fond du Lac, Wisconsin 54935
(414) 922-8611

Nicolet College
Hospitality Management
Box 518
Rhinelander, Wisconsin 54501
(715) 369-4410

Southwest Wisconsin Vocational Technical
  Institute
Food Service Management
Route #1, Box 500
Fennimore, Wisconsin 53809
(608) 822-3262

Western Wisconsin Technical Institute
Food Service Management
Eighth and Pine Streets
La Crosse, Wisconsin 54601
(608) 785-9267

Wisconsin Indianhead Technical Institute
Hospitality Management—Tourism
2100 Beaser Avenue
Ashland, Wisconsin 54806
(715) 682-4591

WYOMING

Laramie County Community College
Food Services
1400 East College Drive
Cheyenne, Wyoming 82007
(307) 634-5853

Four-year College Programs

The following information was taken from an extensive survey conducted by the National Restaurant Association, in cooperation with the National Institute for the Foodservice Industry. Additional data on these programs is available from the NRA and NIFI, including number of students enrolled, number of faculty, names of program directors, costs, and brief program descriptions. It is strongly recommended that you contact the schools directly for more detailed and current information.

The programs are listed with a commercial emphasis in foodservice—those in the hotel, restaurant, and institutional field. The foodservice industry, however, is quite varied and encompasses hospitals, nursing homes, and other institutions that place a heavy emphasis on dietetics. Therefore, a number of these "dietetic" oriented programs that offer a foodservice management option are listed, flagged with the letter "D."

In the course of this survey, a number of schools reported that they offered post-graduate degrees in these studies—by and large, MS or MBA degrees. These programs are flagged with the letter "M" to the left of their listing for ease of reference.

If you have any questions, or comments about this information, please write:

National Restaurant Association
150 N. Michigan, Suite 2000
Chicago, Illinois 60601
(312) 853-2525

National Institute for the
Foodservice Industry
20 N. Wacker Dr.
Chicago, Illinois 60606
(312) 782-1703

ALABAMA

Auburn University
D Foodservice Administration
Department of Nutrition & Foods
Auburn, Alabama 36849
(205) 826-4261

Samford University
Foodservice Administration
Home Economics Department
800 Lakeshore Drive
Birmingham, Alabama 35229
(205) 870-2011

Tuskegee Institute
Foodservice Management
Department of Home Economics
Tuskegee, Alabama 36088
(205) 727-8331

ALASKA

University of Alaska
Travel Industry Management Program
Department of Business Administration
Fairbanks, Alaska 99701
(907) 474-6528

ARIZONA

Northern Arizona University
Lodging, Restaurant & Tourism
Administration
Campus Box 15066
Flagstaff, Arizona 86011
(602) 523-3657

ARKANSAS

Arkansas Tech University
Hotel Restaurant Management Program
School of Systems Science
North Arkansas Avenue
Russellville, Arkansas 72801
(501) 968-0607

CALIFORNIA

California Polytechnic State University
D Dietetics/Food Administration
Food Science/Nutrition
San Luis Obispo, California 93407
(805) 546-2377

California State University
D Food & Nutrition
Home Economics Department
Chico, California 95929
(916) 895-6805

California State University, Long Beach
D Foodservice Systems Administration
Department of Home Economics
1250 Bellflower Boulevard
Long Beach, California 90840
(213) 498-4484

California State Polytechnic University
Hotel, Restaurant & Travel Management
Department
3801 W. Temple Avenue
Pomona, California 91768
(714) 598-4235

Golden Gate University
D Hotel, Restaurant & Institutional Management
536 Mission Street
San Francisco, California 94133
(415) 442-7215

Loma Linda University
D Nutrition & Dietetics
11234 Anderson
Loma Linda, California 92350
(714) 824-4593

San Jose State University
D Nutrition & Food Service
School of Applied Arts & Sciences
One Washington Square
San Jose, California 95192
(408) 277-2526

United States International University
Hotel & Restaurant Management
10455 Pomerado Road
San Diego, California 92131
(619) 693-4615

University of California, Berkeley
D Nutrition & Clinical Dietetics
127 Morgan Hall
Berkeley, California 94720
(415) 642-2879

University of California, Davis
D Dietetics-Food Service Management
Department of Nutrition
Davis, California 95616
(916) 752-6650

University of San Francisco
Hospitality Management
2130 Fulton Street
San Francisco, California 94117
(415) 666-6771

COLORADO
Colorado State University   M
Restaurant Management
Department of Food Science & Nutrition
Gifford Building
Fort Collins, Colorado 80523
(303) 491-5127

Metropolitan State College
Hospitality, Meeting, Travel Administration
1006 11th Street, Box 60
Denver, Colorado 80204
(303) 629-3152

University of Denver
D   School of Hotel & Restaurant Management
2030 East Evans
Denver, Colorado 80208
(303) 871-2322

CONNECTICUT
University of New Haven
M   Hotel, Restaurant Management, Dietetics
    & Tourism Administration
300 Orange Avenue
West Haven, Connecticut 06516
(203) 932-7362

DELAWARE
Widener University
Hotel & Restaurant Management
P.O. Box 713 Concord Pike
Wilmington, Delaware 19803
(302) 478-3000

DISTRICT OF COLUMBIA
Howard University
Hotel/Motel Management
2600 Sixth Street, NW
Washington, D.C. 20059
(202) 636-5114

FLORIDA
Bethune-Cookman College
Hospitality Management
Division of Business
640 Second Avenue
Daytona Beach, FL 32015
(904) 255-1401

Biscayne College
Tourism, Hospitality Management &
    International Enterprise
16400 N.W. 32nd Avenue
Miami, Florida 33054
(305) 625-6000

College of Boca Raton
Hospitality Management
3601 N. Military Trail
Boca Raton, Florida 33431
(305) 994-0770

Florida International University
School of Hospitality
Tamiami Trail
Miami, Florida 33199
(305) 554-2591

Florida State University
Department of Hospitality Administration
College of Business
225 William Johnston Building
Tallahassee, Florida 32306
(904) 644-4787

Saint Leo College
Restaurant Management
Business Administration
State Road 52 P.O. Box 2067
Saint Leo, Florida 33574
(813) 588-8309

St. Thomas University
Tourism and Hospitality Management
16400 N.W. 32 Avenue
Miami, Florida 33054
(305) 625-6000

University of Central Florida
Hospitality Management Department
College of Business Administration
P.O. Box 25000
Orlando, Florida 32816
(305) 275-2188

Webber College
Hospitality Management Department
Route 27-A
Babson Park, Florida 33827
(813) 638-1431

GEORGIA
Georgia State University
Department of Hotel, Restaurant &
    Travel Administration
University Plaza
Atlanta, Georgia 30303
(404) 658-3512

Morris Brown College
Hotel Management Department
643 Martin Luther King, Jr. Drive
Atlanta, Georgia 30314
(404) 525-7831

University of Georgia
D   Food Service Management
Dawson Hall
Athens, Georgia 30602
(404) 542-2551

HAWAII
Brigham Young University
Travel, Hotel, and Restaurant Management
55-220 Kulanui Street
Laie, HI 96762
(808) 293-3580

University of Hawaii
School of Travel Industry Management
2404 Maile Way, A 303
Honolulu, Hawaii 96822
(808) 948-8946

ILLINOIS
Bradley University
D Foods, Dietetics & Nutrition
Home Economics Department
Peoria, Illinois 61625
(309) 676-7611

Chicago State University
Hotel and Restaurant Management
College of Business and Administration
95th Street and King Drive
Chicago, Illinois 60628
(312) 995-3978

Eastern Illinois University
D Dietetics
School of Home Economics
Charleston, Illinois 61920
(217) 581-3325

Northern Illinois University
D Coordinated Undergraduate Program in
Dietetics
Department of Home Economics
DeKalb, Illinois 60115
(815) 753-1543

Roosevelt University
Hospitality Management
430 S. Michigan Avenue
Chicago, Illinois 60605
(312) 341-3860

Rosary College
D Foods & Nutrition
7900 West Division Street
River Forest, Illinois 60305
(312) 366-2490

Southern Illinois University
Food & Lodging Systems Management
Quigley Hall
Carbondale, Illinois 62901
(618) 453-5193

University of Illinois
M Restaurant Management
274 Bevier Hall
Urbana, Illinois 61801
(217) 333-1326

Western Illinois University
Foods & Lodging Management
Home Economics Department
Macomb, Illinois 61455
(309) 298-1092

INDIANA
Ball State University
Food Service Management
Home Economics Department
Practical Arts Building
Muncie, Indiana 47306
(317) 285-5931

Purdue University
M Department of Restaurant, Hotel &
Institutional Management
Stone Hall
West Lafayette, Indiana 47907
(317) 494-4643

IOWA
Iowa State University
M Hotel, Restaurant & Institution Management
11 MacKay Hall
Ames, Iowa 50011
(515) 294-1730

KANSAS
Kansas State University
Restaurant Management
105 Justin Hall
Manhattan, Kansas 66506
(913) 532-5521

KENTUCKY
Morehead State University
D Food Service Administration
Home Economics Department
UPO 889, MSU
Morehead, Kentucky 40351
(606) 783-2966

Transylvania University
Hotel, Restaurant, Tourism Administration
300 N. Broadway
Lexington, Kentucky 40508
(606) 233-8249

University of Kentucky
Restaurant Management
Nutrition & Food Science Department
205 Erickson Hall
Lexington, Kentucky 40506
(606) 257-7794

Western Kentucky University
Institution Administration/Hotel Restaurant
Management
Academic Complex
Bowling Green, Kentucky 42101
(502) 745-4352

LOUISIANA
University of New Orleans
School of Hotel, Restaurant &
Tourism Administration
New Orleans, Louisiana 70148
(504) 286-6385

University of Southwestern Louisiana
Restaurant Administration   M
Home Economics
USL Box 40399
Lafayette, Louisiana 40399
(318) 231-6000

MARYLAND
University of Maryland
M D   Institution Administration
Department of Food, Nutrition &
    Institution Administration
College Park, Maryland 20742
(301) 454-2143

University of Maryland-Eastern Shore
Department of Hotel & Restaurant
    Management
Somerset Hall—Room 409
Princess Anne, Maryland 21853
(301) 651-2200

MASSACHUSETTS
Boston University—Metropolitan College
Hotel & Food Administration
808 Commonwealth Avenue
Boston, Massachusetts 02215
(617) 353-3000

University of Massachusetts
M   Department of Hotel, Restaurant &
    Travel Administration
101 Flint Laboratory
Amherst, Massachusetts 01003
(413) 545-2535

MICHIGAN
Central Michigan University
Hospitality Services Administration
100 Smith Hall
Mt. Pleasant, Michigan 48859
(517) 774-3701

Eastern Michigan University
D   Food Systems Management/General Dietetics
108 Roosevelt Hall
Ypsilanti, Michigan 48197
(313) 487-2490

Ferris State College
Hospitality Management
South Commons
Big Rapids, Michigan 49307
(616) 796-0461

Grand Valley State Colleges
Hospitality & Tourism Management
Allendale, Michigan 49401
(616) 895-6611

Mercy College of Detroit
Foodservice Management
8200 W. Outer Drive
Detroit, Michigan 48219
(313) 592-6039

Michigan State University
School of Hotel, Restaurant &
    Institutional Management
425 Eppley Center
East Lansing, Michigan 48824
(517) 353-9211

Northern Michigan University
D   Institution & Restaurant Management
Home Economics
Thomas Fine Arts Building
Marquette, Michigan 49855
(906) 227-2364

Siena Heights College
Hotel, Restaurant & Institutional Management
1247 E. Siena Heights Drive
Adrian, Michigan 49221
(517) 263-0731

MINNESOTA
Mankato State University
D   Food & Nutrition
Home Economics Department
MSU Box 44
Mankato, Minnesota 56001
(505) 389-2421

Moorhead State University
Hotel-Motel Restaurant Management
Business Administration
Moorhead, Minnesota 56560
(218) 236-2486

Southwest State University
Hotel, Restaurant & Institutional
    Management
Marshall, Minnesota 56258
(507) 537-7380

MISSISSIPPI
University of Southern Mississippi
Hotel & Restaurant Administration
Southern Station Box 10025
Hattiesburg, Mississippi 39401
(601) 266-4680

MISSOURI
Central Missouri State University
Hotel, Motel Restaurant Administration
250 Grinstead Hall
Warrensburg, Missouri 64093
(816) 429-4362

University of Missouri
Food Service & Lodging Management
Eckles Hall
Columbia, Missouri 65211
(314) 882-4113

NEBRASKA

University of Nebraska
Food Service Management/Restaurant
  Management
East Campus
Omaha, Nebraska 68583
(402) 472-2913

NEVADA

University of Nevada, Las Vegas
M College of Hotel Administration
4505 Maryland Parkway
Las Vegas, Nevada 89154
(702) 739-3230

NEW HAMPSHIRE

New Hampshire College
Hotel and Restaurant Management
2500 North River Road
Manchester, New Hampshire 03104
(603) 668-2211

University of New Hampshire
Hotel Administration Program
McConnell Hall
Durham, New Hampshire 03824
(603) 862-3303

NEW JERSEY

Fairleigh Dickinson University
M Hotel & Restaurant Management
College of Business
Rutherford, New Jersey 07070
(201) 460-5362

Montclair State College
D Food Service Management
Normal Avenue
Upper Montclair, New Jersey 07043
(201) 893-4171

NEW MEXICO

New Mexico Highlands University
Hotel, Restaurant & Tourism Management
Division of Business/Economics
Las Vegas, New Mexico 87701
(505) 425-7511

NEW YORK

Cornell University
M School of Hotel Administration
Statler Hall
Ithaca, New York 14853
(607) 256-5106

Marymount College
D Food and Nutrition
Department of Home Economics
Marymount Avenue
Tarrytown, New York 10591
(914) 631-3200

New York City Technical College
Hotel and Restaurant Management
  Department
300 Jay Street
Brooklyn, New York 11201
(718) 643-8386

New York Institute of Technology
Hotel/Restaurant Administration
207 Simonson House
Old Westbury, New York 11568
(516) 686-7838

New York University
M Foodservice Management
239 Greene Street, 537 East Building
New York, New York 10003
(212) 598-2369

Niagara University
Hospitality Management
Institute of Transportation, Travel
  & Tourism
Niagara, New York, 14109
(716) 285-1212

Pratt Institute
D Department of Food Science & Management
215 Ryerson Street, Room 318, DeKalb Hall
Brooklyn, New York 11205
(212) 636-3586

Rochester Institute of Technology
Department of Food, Hotel & Tourism
  Management
One Lomb Memorial Drive
Rochester, New York 14623
(716) 475-2867

State University College at Buffalo
Food Systems Management
Nutrition & Food Science Department
1300 Elmwood Avenue
Buffalo, New York 14222
(716) 878-5913

State University of New York-Oneonta
Food & Business
Department of Home Economics
Oneonta, New York 13820
(607) 431-3500

State University of New York-Plattsburg
D Food Service Systems Management
Center for Human Resources
Ward Hall
Plattsburg, New York 12901
(518) 564-2164

Syracuse University
Food Systems Management
Restaurants & Institutions
112 Slocum Hall
Syracuse, New York 13244
(315) 423-4553

NORTH CAROLINA
Appalachian State University
Restaurant Hotel Resort Management
College of Business
Boone, North Carolina 28608
(704) 262-2163

D **Barber-Scotia College**
Hotel, Restaurant Management
School of Arts, Science and Business
145 Cabarrus Avenue West
Concord, North Carolina 28025
(704) 786-5171

East Carolina University
D Food, Nutrition & Institution Management
School of Home Economics
Greenville, North Carolina 27834
(919) 757-6917

North Carolina Central University
D Institutional Management
Department of Home Economics
P.O. Box 19615
Durham, North Carolina 27707
(919) 683-6477

North Carolina Wesleyan College
Food Service & Hotel Management
Business Administration
Wesleyan College Station
Rocky Mount, North Carolina 27801
(919) 977-7171

University of North Carolina, Greensboro
D Food, Nutrition, Food Service Management
School of Home Economics
Greensboro, North Carolina 27412
(919) 379-5313

NORTH DAKOTA
North Dakota State University
Hotel, Motel, Restaurant Management
Food & Nutrition Department
Fargo, North Dakota 58105
(701) 237-7474

OHIO
Ashland College
Hotel/Restaurant Management
College Avenue
Ashland, Ohio 44805
(419) 289-5096

Bowling Green State University
Restaurant and Institutional Food Service
   Management
Department of Home Economics BGSU
Bowling Green, Ohio 43403
(419) 372-7833

Kent State University
Hospitality Foodservice Management
103 Nixson Hall
Kent, Ohio 44242
(216) 672-2075

Miami University
D Food Management, Home Economics
260 McGuffey Hall
Oxford, Ohio 45056
(513) 529-5915

The Ohio State University
Restaurant Management Program
1787 Neil Avenue
Columbus, Ohio 43210
(614) 422-5588

Youngstown State University
D Food & Nutrition
College of Applied Science & Technology
410 Wick Avenue
Youngstown, Ohio 44555
(216) 742-3344

OKLAHOMA
Oklahoma State University
Hotel & Restaurant Administration
HEW 424
Stillwater, Oklahoma 74078
(405) 624-6486

OREGON
Oregon State University
Hotel & Restaurant Management Program
Corvallis, Oregon 97331
(503) 754-3693

PENNSYLVANIA
Drexel University
Hotel, Restaurant, Institutional Management
32nd & Chestnut Street
Philadelphia, Pennsylvania 19104
(215) 895-2411

East Stroudsburg University
Hospitality Management
Prospect Street
East Stroudsburg, PA 18301
(717) 424-3511

Indiana University of Pennsylvania
Foodservice & Lodging Management
10 Ackerman Hall
Indiana, Pennsylvania 15705
(412) 357-4440

Mansfield State College
D Food Service/Dietetics
Home Economics Building
Mansfield, Pennsylvania 16933
(717) 662-4232

Mercyhurst College
Hotel & Restaurant Management
Glenwood Hills
Erie, Pennsylvania 16546
(814) 825-0333

The Pennsylvania State University
Hotel, Restaurant, & Institution Management
118 Henderson Building
University Park, Pennsylvania 16802
(814) 863-0009

RHODE ISLAND

Bryant College
Department of Hotel Restaurant &   D
Institutional Management
Smithfield, Rhode Island 02917
(401) 231-1200

Johnson & Wales College
Hospitality Management
Abbott Park Place
Providence, Rhode Island 02903
(401) 456-1000

SOUTH CAROLINA

University of South Carolina
Hotel, Restaurant and Tourism Administration
Columbia, South Carolina 29208
(803) 777-6665

SOUTH DAKOTA

Black Hills State College
Travel Industry Management
1200 University
Spearfish, South Dakota 57783
(605) 642-6867

South Dakota State University
Nutrition, Food Science & Restaurant
Management
College of Home Economics
P.O. Box 2275A, SDSU
Brookings, South Dakota 57007
(605) 688-5161

TENNESSEE

Belmont College
School of Hospitality Business   M
Belmont Blvd.
Nashville, Tennessee 37203
(615) 383-7001

University of Tennessee
M   Tourism, Food & Lodging Administration
220 CHE College of Human Ecology
Knoxville, Tennessee 37996
(615) 974-5445

TEXAS

Huston-Tillotson College
Hospitality Management
1820 East 8th Street
Austin, Texas 78702
(512) 476-7421

North Texas State University
Hotel Restaurant Management
Home Economics Department
P.O. Box 5248
Denton, Texas 76203
(817) 565-2436

Texas Tech University
Restaurant, Hotel and Institutional
Management
Box 4170, TTU
Lubbock, Texas 79409
(806) 742-3031

Texas Women's University
Coordinated Undergraduate Program
in Dietetics
P.O. Box 24134, TWU Station
Denton, Texas 76204
(817) 382-2158

University of Houston
Hilton Hotel & Restaurant Management
College
4800 Calhoun Drive
Houston, Texas 77004
(713) 749-2482

UTAH

Brigham Young University
M   Food Systems Administration
2218 SFLC
Provo, Utah 84602
(801) 378-6677

VIRGINIA

James Madison University
Hotel & Restaurant Management Program
Harrisonburg, Virginia 22807
(703) 568-6694

Radford University
Food Service Management
P.O. Box 5797
Radford, Virginia 24141
(703) 731-5386

**Virginia Polytechnic Institute
& State University**
M   Hotel, Restaurant, & Institutional
Management
18 Hillcrest Hall
Blacksburg, Virginia 24061
(703) 961-6783

Virginia State University
Hotel Restaurant Management
Box 427, VSU
Petersburg, Virginia 23803
(804) 520-6389

WASHINGTON

Washington State University
Hotel & Restaurant Administration
245 Todd Hall
Pullman, Washington 99164
(509) 335-5766

Washington State University
Hotel & Restaurant Administration
1108 East Columbia
Seattle, Washington 98122
(206) 464-6349

WEST VIRGINIA

Shepherd College
Hotel/Motel & Restaurant Management
Shepherdstown, West Virginia 25443
(304) 876-2511

D

WISCONSIN

University of Wisconsin-Madison
Foodservice Administration
Babcock Hall, 1605 Linden Drive
Madison, Wisconsin 53706
(608) 262-3046

University of Wisconsin-Stout
Hotel & Restaurant Management
Home Economics Building
Menomonie, Wisconsin 54751
(715) 232-2137

Originally produced for The National Institute for the Foodservice Industry and The National
Restaurant Association by HEINZ U.S.A., Division of the H. J. Heinz Company, Pittsburgh, Pa.

APPENDIX II

Some restaurateurs complain that they're so steeped in the business they no longer enjoy going to other restaurants. Their critical faculties are too sharp, and instead of relaxing they find themselves examining every detail of the place.

This is part of the price you pay. But, especially when you are thinking of opening your first restaurant, you have so much to learn that you would be extremely foolish to ignore what's happening in the restaurants available for your discreet inspection. The education is free—apart from what you spend in the place, of course. It can also be fun.

Being only human, your first and main focus will be on the food because that's the easiest thing to criticize. Your main interest here should be the scope of the menu, the flexibility of the kitchen, and interesting dishes—especially high-profit items, of which a good example is the delicious Moules marinieres (mussels in wine). Mussels, like squid, are practically a give-away item in the fish market, but will bring in gourmets by the score if they're done well. Some dishes are a bit fussy to do in a domestic kitchen, but easy to cope with in a restaurant kitchen, where the quantity sold justifies the effort.

If you are taking a properly professional approach, however, you will not wallow in criticism of the food. You should be noting the waiter's system, determining why some waitresses are better than others, and asking yourself what you might do to improve the service or in any way to make the restaurant more attractive.

Once you start looking you may be amazed by what you see. Has the boss noticed the dirty sneakers that waitress is wearing? (Oh, that's his wife.) Are two inch-square pats of butter really enough for two people, with six rolls in the bread basket?

Things you never thought about before will catch your eye, and ear: the hostess who says "Hi, folks, how ya doin'?" with the cheerfulness of a well-trained parrot every three minutes; the waitress who glances stagily at her watch to note the time she took your order, and writes it on the check, as though she were the nurse and you the patient; the waiter bellowing his description of a mysterious special for the eighth time, "It's more than a calf, less than a steer"; the bartender who listens as you interrupt his rehash of last night's game, and so on. You should ask yourself whether the restaurant is making maximum use of available space. Has space been carved out for just one more "deuce," while the kitchen is like a space capsule?

Naturally, you should also try to see the reasons for the restaurant's success. Location? Is it a landmark? Relentless advertising? Consistent high quality? Good value? Amusing gimmicks? An owner with personality? Appeal to a special area of the market? What's their rent? Does the restaurateur own the building? Is it just a flagship, not intended to make a profit? If there are any apparent disadvantages, how have they been overcome?

You should put yourself in the shoes of an insecure but determined social climber in the Victorian age who's been invited to a smart party, and who notices every nuance of pronunciation, phrase, and dress with a cold, Proustian eye.

There is no such thing as a "Good Food Guide to the United States." England has one, and France has its famous Michelin guide. Indeed, there are several to choose from. But America is so enormous that the subject is unwieldy, and a national guide would have to be the size of the *Encyclopaedia Britannica*. Most states have a Restaurant Association that will be happy to provide lists, and most major cities have various publications that list restaurants.

It's always wise to reconnoiter a restaurant you propose to visit, either by looking it up in the local guide or going to it, looking in on some pretext, and examining the menu. It's not unknown for people to ring up restaurants and say, "How much is dinner for two with a bottle of wine?" Most often the response is the true, but weak and not very constructive, reply, "It depends on what you have." A better reply is, "We have a varied menu—and our coq au vin is world-famous. If you had a couple of martinis, two shrimp cocktails, two coq au vin, two lemon tarts, two coffees, and a bottle of Beaujolais, your bill would be $_____, excluding gratuity." Or, perhaps better because quicker, "Our entrees average $12, and our wine list is from $12 to $50. The average bill for dinner for two here is $_____."

What you will find yourself noticing consciously is noticed by other customers *sub*consciously, and will implant a general impression in the mind, resulting in either a positive or negative impression. "Let's go to Cocky Leekie's," says one diner. "Yes—great idea. I like that place," says the friend. Or, with a frown, "Let's find some place else." "Why?" "Oh, I don't know."

Few people are sufficiently articulate to be able to say *why* they dislike or like anything. They'll often say they didn't enjoy the food when really they mean something quite different. But everybody knows what they themselves like.

The following is a list of successful restaurants in some of the major metropolitan areas. I hope that you will find visiting them interesting and enjoyable learning experiences!

New York
Lutece
The Four Seasons
Devon House
Le Cirque
Joe Allen's (also London, Paris, and Los Angeles
Elaine's
Oliver's
J.G. Melon (East and West)
P.J. Clarke's
The Russian Tea Room
Flutie's
North Star Pub

New Orleans
K-Paul's

Los Angeles (a notoriously under-restauranted, but quirky area)
Spago
Lingerie
Nucleus Nuance
Mickey Blairs
Jo's
The Authentic Cafe
Bistro Gardens

Saugus, Massachusetts
Hilltop Steak House

New Jersey
The Manor

Philadelphia

Morton's (also Chicago, Atlanta, Boston, Dallas, Denver, Washington, DC, and Los Angeles)

Miami

Joe's Stone Crab House

And any McDonald's, anywhere

Warning: Some of these restaurants are wildly expensive. You should check them out before reserving your table. If you really can't afford it, perhaps you can have a drink at the bar. If our fabled friend the haughty maitre d' asks if he can help, you can always say you're meeting Doctor Weinstein, or Henry Kissinger, but you're not sure whose name the reservation is under. Some of them are hateful places, in the author's view. Some are super. They all have one thing in common—they are, or appear to be, *successful*.

INDEX